BORO, L'ÎLE D'AMOUR

BORO, L'ÎLE D'AMOUR

THE FILMS OF WALERIAN BOROWCZYK

Edited by
Kamila Kuc, Kuba Mikurda, and Michał Oleszczyk

berghahn
NEW YORK • OXFORD
www.berghahnbooks.com

First published in 2015 by
Berghahn Books
www.berghahnbooks.com

© 2015, 2020 Kamila Kuc, Kuba Mikurda, and Michał Oleszczyk
First paperback edition published in 2020

All rights reserved. Except for the quotation of short passages
for the purposes of criticism and review, no part of this book
may be reproduced in any form or by any means, electronic or
mechanical, including photocopying, recording, or any information
storage and retrieval system now known or to be invented,
without written permission of the publisher.

Library of Congress Cataloging-in-Publication Data
Boro, l'île d'amour: the films of Walerian Borowczyk / edited by Kamila Kuc,
Kuba Mikurda, and Michal Oleszczyk.
    pages cm
    Includes filmography.
    Includes bibliographical references and index.
    ISBN 978-1-78238-701-5 (hardback: alk. paper) ISBN 978–1-78238-702-2 (ebook)
1. Borowczyk, Walerian--Criticism and interpretation. I. Kuc, Kamila, editor.
II. Mikurda, Kuba, editor. III. Oleszczyk, Michal, editor.
    PN1998.3.B673B68 2015
    791.4302'33092--dc23
                                                                    2015002024

British Library Cataloguing in Publication Data
A catalogue record for this book is available from the British Library

ISBN 978-1-78238-701-5 hardback
ISBN 978-1-78920-818-4 paperback
ISBN 978-1-78238-702-2 ebook

Contents

List of Illustrations	vii
Acknowledgments	viii

Introduction: A Private Universe Kamila Kuc, Kuba Mikurda, and Michał Oleszczyk	1
1. Boro: Escape Artist Kuba Mikurda	13
2. Borowczyk's Kunstkamera Marcin Giżycki	48
3. Animated Bodies: A Conversation between Kuba Mikurda and Jakub Woynarowski	54
4. Cruel Imagination: Borowczyk's Post-traumatic Surrealism Iwona Kurz	64
5. The Postcard Never Sent: Guy de Maupassant and Rosalie Prudent's Cinematic Confession Kamila Kuc	77
6. Boro: The Guide for the Perplexed Fernando F. Croce	89
7. Borowczyk's Serial Labyrinth: From *Goto, Isle of Love* (1968) to *Behind Convent Walls* (1977) James Snazell	93
8. Immoral Toys: On Borowczyk's *A Private Collection* (1973) Edwin Carels	103

9. The Beast with Two Backs: On Borowczyk's *The Beast* (1975)   111
   Phillip Warnell

10. Laugh in the Doll House: On Victorian Surrealism in the Films of
    Walerian Borowczyk   118
    Kamila Wielebska

11. Enjoying Excess: A Bataillean Interpretation of *Story of Sin* (1975) by
    Walerian Borowczyk and Stefan Żeromski   132
    Marta Rabikowska

12. The Beach, the Bubble, and the Boudoir: The Meeting Spaces of
    Walerian Borowczyk and André Pieyre de Mandiargues   148
    Jonathan Owen

13. Sex and the Sacred: The Obstacles to Desire Becoming its Objects   159
    Jakub Majmurek

14. Reflecting on *The Strange Case of Dr. Jekyll and Miss Osbourne* (1981)   166
    Budd Wilkins

15. The Perils of Emmanuelle: A Conversation between Odie Henderson,
    Simon Abrams, and Michał Oleszczyk   170

16. Revisiting *Love Rites* (1988)   183
    Kevin Lee

Walerian Borowczyk Filmography   189

Index   193

Illustrations

A. Still from *The Astronauts* (1959), copyright by Argos Films   x
B. Still from *Goto, Isle of Love* (1968), copyright by Argos Films   xi
C. Still from *Immoral Tales* (1974), copyright by Argos Films   186
D. Still from *The Beast* (1975), copyright by Argos Films   187
5.1 *Cher Maître* (2014), collage by Kamila Kuc   77

Acknowledgments

The editors would like to thank our writers for their commitment, enthusiasm, and patience. For the same reasons we would like to offer our gratitude to Berghahn Books, particularly Adam Capitanio and Molly Mosher. We would also like to thank the Polish Cultural Institute in London for their financial support. Finally, we offer our thanks to T-Mobile New Horizons International Film Festival, where the idea for this book originated.

Kuba Mikurda wishes to thank Daniel Bird, Olga Byrska, Danuta Gęgotek, Maria Herbich, Stanisław Jędryka, Irena Karel, Michael Levy, Joanna Łapińska, Izabela Łopuch, Jagoda Murczyńska, Michael O'Pray, Cherry Potter, Katarzyna Siniarska, Włodzimierz Śliwiński, Urszula Śniegowska, Noël Véry, and Zoé Zurstrassen.

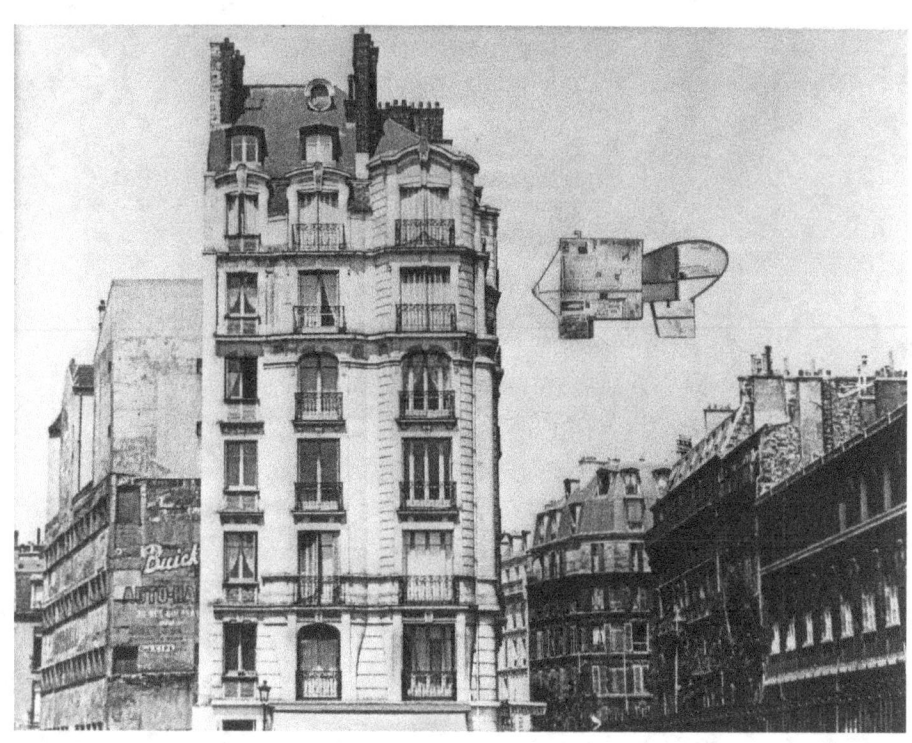

A. Still from *The Astronauts* (1959), copyright by Argos Films

B. Still from *Goto, Isle of Love* (1968), copyright by Argos Films

Introduction
A Private Universe

Kamila Kuc, Kuba Mikurda, and Michał Oleszczyk

In a seminal image from *Astronauts* (*Les Astronautes* [1959]), the first film Walerian Borowczyk made after immigrating to France, a DIY space shuttle traverses what looks like the most cluttered galaxy one could possibly travel to. All sense of proportion is gone: a vast landscape turns out to be someone's shoe, and tiny details acquire cosmic dimensions and surprising meanings. All this is fueled by a single man's curiosity: the titular astronaut, whose crazy quest seems to be to connect with and explore everything there is, from celestial bodies in the sky to a particularly heavenly body he sees in a lit window of an ordinary brownstone building … In one of the letters donated to Cinémathèque Française, Borowczyk writes of *Astronautes*:

> Man has always dreamt of making outer space into his home. But that's still impossible without a special garment. It would be a peculiar sight, indeed: a run-of-the-mill dreamer, traversing galaxies in his typical gray outfit. With a basket of tomatoes as provisions. That's exactly the guy I decided to make a film about.[1]

It is not very difficult to see this figure of an explorer and craftsman as a self-portrait of Borowczyk himself.

The usual story, which has become something of a film-historical cliché, goes that Walerian Borowczyk was an acclaimed filmmaker who went from art house stardom in the 1970s, to soft-core oblivion in the 1980s. Once hailed as one of the greatest visionaries of European cinema alongside Buñuel and Fellini, he ended his career as the director of late-night TV erotic series. As is often the case, the actual picture is much more nuanced and difficult to grasp. However it's certainly true that his films are equally cherished by fans of art house refinement as they are by fans of (s)exploitation flicks; the "rise and fall" or "artist turned pornographer" narrative simply cannot hold when confronted with the diversity and scope of Borowczyk's extremely prolific career.

Boro, L'Île D'Amour: The Films of Walerian Borowczyk is the first English-language edited volume exploring the work of this label-defying auteur — an "escape artist," if there ever was one, passionately countering people's attempts to pigeonhole his work. The book coincides with the revival of interest in Borowczyk's work (retrospectives, film restorations, new editions), which nonetheless remains marked by the lack of a comprehensive source on this maverick director. This collection serves as an introduction and a guide to the complex and ambiguous body of Borowczyk's work. Consisting of sixteen chapters, contributions range from panoramic views of the director's entire work and analytical takes on particular movies, to more personal, impressionistic pieces, thus offering a wide and diverse perspective on the filmmaker's work. This collection constitutes a platform for a wide array of writers (from the United Kingdom, United States, and Poland) to explore previously unnoticed aspects of Borowczyk's oeuvre.

"I conceived all my films in an instant"

It's fair to say that Walerian Borowczyk's body of work presents a significant challenge to any historian's attempt to classify it and ascribe it to a single narrative. For one thing, the sheer scope of the work, ranging from shorts and features to animation and vérité-like realism, suggests a sensibility so eclectic and voracious as to be positively unclassifiable. Borowczyk's multifaceted talents, which allowed him to excel in fields as diverse as drawing, poster art, advertisement, sculpture, animation, film, poetry, and prose, at first seem an ocean too wide and too deep to navigate, much less place firmly on a map and confine to a particular location.

Borowczyk famously claimed that he "conceived all [his] films in an instant, and only objective factors prevented [him] from making them in that instant" (Borowczyk 1973). He does not believe in artistic evolution; he's a creationist, pure and simple. And indeed, there is something instantaneous about his works—rather than present the development of a style, a sense of emerging mastery, a process of artistic self-recognition, they are defined and self-aware from the start. They are not a succession, but a constellation of works, where every element is as important as the next. Indeed, one is often puzzled when asked about "the best" piece in Borowczyk's oeuvre — his works are at their best when one approaches them all together, side by side.

Borowczyk's cinematic universe is a vast archive of multilayered collections of objects, texts, and images. These are interwoven in an audiovisual spectacle very precisely arranged by the eclectic stylist that Borowczyk was. Having studied painting techniques (particularly lithography), it is perhaps not surprising that his films explore, intentionally or not, the relationship between stillness and movement. The director's fascination with Étienne-Jules Marey's experiments further confirms this. Much has been written about Borowczyk's use of diverse imagery, but let's stress the most striking tendencies here.

Borowczyk's oeuvre can be characterized by a strong presence of more traditional art forms. These often constitute the very stuff of which his films are made: photography (*School* [1958]; *Rosalie* [1966]), collage (*Grandma's Encyclopedia* [1963]) and animated objects, watercolors and drawings (*House* [1958] made with Jan Lenica; *Angels' Games* [1964]; *Joachim's Dictionary* [1965]). More direct references to painting can be seen within the actual frames of his films, as in the case of *The Beast* (1975) in which Władysław Podkowiński's painting *Frenzy of Exultations* (*Szał uniesień*, 1894) decorates the wall. Not to mention Borowczyk's magnificent still life compositions (*Renaissance* [1963]). Moreover, a few of Borowczyk's works are composed of filmed paintings (the repollero technique) (*Rewarded Feelings* [1957] made with Lenica), and he also developed a new technique — pulverographie — "dustography" — which involves color photocopying. Borowczyk employed this method to illustrate his collection of short stories, *The Anatomy of the Devil* (1992). But his engagement with static art forms does not stop there. Borowczyk's fascination with the realm of painting is also visible in a calculated flatness that characterizes films such as *Blanche* (1971), where the impact of medieval iconography is particularly evident. Borowczyk frames the shots as if they were a painting, with the characters looking out of its frame. Though not medieval in its visual composition, a corresponding shallowness of picture can be found in *Goto, Isle of Love* (1968).

To the Moon and Back

One aspect that was often neglected by authors writing about Borowczyk was the adequate placement of him within cinematic trends that either coincide with his activity or precede and anticipate it in illuminating ways. More than any other auteur within a select group of international cinematic provocateurs (including such figures as Pier Paolo Pasolini, Oshima Nagisa, Andy Warhol, Dušan Makavejev, Russ Meyer, and Barbara Rubin), Borowczyk's sensibility is easily traceable to the influence of three major filmmakers that helped shape his own aesthetic: Georges Méliès, Sergei Eisenstein, and Luis Buñuel.

Each of the three represents a different aspect developed by Borowczyk: Méliès stands for the DIY film magic so often employed in Boro's animation (most notably in *The Astronauts*, which can be seen as a free-associative riff on *A Trip to the Moon* [1902]); Eisenstein for the ongoing fascination with montage; and Buñuel represents the methodical rebellion against bourgeois morality and religion, often enacted in terms of an absurd comedy of manners that surfaces even in the wildest of Borowczyk's features, such as *Theatre of Mr. and Mrs. Kabal* (1967).

Of the three, it is arguably Eisenstein that Borowczyk owes the most to: the entire Soviet school of montage seems to have had a profound effect on his sensibility (not a surprise in an artist taking his first significant steps amidst the heavy onslaught of propaganda in postwar communist Poland). In fact, one may be surprised by how many instances of inventive editing are to be found in Borowczyk's most famous sequences, including intensely erotic ones — climaxes in both "The Tide" and "Lucrezia Borgia," segments of *Immoral Tales* (1974), are dramatized less in terms of body movement or the actors straining to enact pleasure, but chiefly by inventive fragmentation of bodies, props, and costumes, which are then suggestively merged by the editing process. Screen sex in Borowczyk's films is more a matter of editorial splices than of physical thrusts: a strategy that echoes classic Soviet sequences, such as the thawing river in Vsevolod Pudovkin's *Mother* (1926), in which running torrents equal revolutionary fervor by means of rhythmic juxtaposition (see "The Tide" and witness the virtual repetition of that strategy in which the rising sea equals the oncoming ejaculation). In Borowczyk, the careful singling out of trembling limbs, furtive gazes, slightly parted lips and slowly hardening nipples all amount to an effect far more titillating than any conventional porn (focused on documenting intercourse, rather than on suggesting it) has to offer.

The work of Luis Buñuel, in some ways as eclectic and iconoclastic as Borowczyk's, is another strong influence — doubly appropriate, since *Immoral Tales* had in fact been awarded the L'Âge D'Or Award upon its initial release, thus displaying a link with Buñuel's notoriously explosive 1930 screen provocation. Borowczyk's interest in sex, surrealism, fetishism, as well as his biting critique of the Catholic Church all make him a direct heir to Buñuel, even if the latter's propensity for satire and elaborate dramatic structure was significantly stronger. Even allowing for all the differences, it has to be said that the sharp awareness of class divisions that Borowczyk so often brings forth in his work (most evidently in *Diptych* [1967]) seems very close to Buñuel's own take on society, consistently present in films as different as the documentary short *Land Without Bread* (1933) and *The Diary of a Chambermaid* (1964). Last but not least, sexual obsessions that Borowczyk habitually scrutinizes are explored with equal fervor by Buñuel, in such masterpieces as *Un Chien Anadalou* (1929) and *The Criminal Life of Archibaldo de la Cruz* (1955). It's not difficult to imagine the latter being paired with Boro's *A Private Collection* (1973) to form a perfect late-night double bill.

If Buñuel and Eisenstein represent the "revolutionary" strand in Borowczyk's influences, there is also a much more conservative framework one could apply to a reading of his work: that of strict, highly moralistic realism, represented by Roberto Rossellini and Eric Rohmer. While neither of the two seems an obvious influence at first, there are in fact close ties to be found between Borowczyk's approach and theirs. Rossellini's late work, in particular, provides a fascinating background for what arguably is Borowczyk's most accomplished feature film, *Blanche* (1971). The master of Italian neorealism, famous for such classics of postwar humanism as *Open City* (1945) and *Paisan* (1946), had shifted at the end of his career toward exploration of philosophical ideas rooted in the distant past, which allowed him to produce a number of works that remain absolutely original in their presentation of historical events and figures. It was in *The Taking of Power by Louis XIV* (1966) that Rossellini presented an entirely new way of staging history for the screen. Freed from the bombast of the standard Hollywood approach, which stressed visual opulence over meaning, Rossellini presented the everyday existence of the French royal court as matter-of-factly as possible, with its casual richness neither denied nor emphasized by the mise en scène. The result was uncanny: a documentary portrait of life two centuries ago, rich in detail and unburdened by trickery. It's difficult not to think of Rossellini's approach when one is watching *Blanche*: possibly the most successful depiction of the European

Middle Ages on screen (at least until Robert Bresson's *Lancelot du Lac* [1974], itself influenced by Borowczyk). Even though Borowczyk's film is slightly more stylized than Rossellini's (lighting and framing are often at odds with total transparency that Rossellini advocated so much), the basic impulse to liberate oneself from the established convention of staging the distant past in terms of a grandiose spectacle is identical.

The tie to Eric Rohmer is much subtler, as well as easier to define in terms of opposites that he and Borowczyk represent: while Rohmer gained international fame by producing *Six Moral Tales* (1962–72), Boro struck commercial gold by unleashing his *Immoral* ones (even though the first segment, "The Tide," starred Rohmer's regular, Fabrice Luchini). While Boro explored liberated sex rather freely, Rohmer applied a slightly secularized Christian ethic to matters of desire and fidelity — a chief difference between them. Both directors, however, shared a distinctive interest in minimalist expression by their actors, as well as attentiveness to landscapes, props, costumes and detail that make their work strikingly alike upon formal scrutiny. The frequent inserts of isolated objects and written text (notes, letters, signs) that is so plentiful in Borowczyk, also constitutes one of the stronger formal traits in Rohmer. Both artists were almost compulsively prolific and both were fascinated by highly formalized erotic behavior (courtship in Rohmer, seduction and coitus in Boro). What's more, both displayed great affection for historical costume, even though Rohmer ventured into that particular territory more rarely (*The Marquise of O* [1976] is probably the most famous example). Taken together, their bodies of work form two strikingly opposite artistic reactions of intellectually minded men variously shaped by Catholicism to the power of counterculture — all the more fascinating for sharing so many intellectual and aesthetic traits.

The greatest irony of Borowczyk's career is that he initiated so many movements and tendencies that thrived independently of his work that it's sometimes difficult to trace them back to their original source (one of the tasks of this book is to rectify that, of course). In fact, the entire montage-saturated decade of the 1980s, which saw the rise of the erotically charged music video, owes a lot to Borowczyk, who by that time had been relegated mostly to less personal projects, such as *Emmanuelle 5* (1987) and directing episodes of *Série Rose* (1989–91). Even such classics of commercialized erotica as Adrian Lyne's *9 ½ Weeks* (1986) or Zalman King's *Wild Orchid* (1989) seem to bear the influence of Borowczyk (as does Bob Fosse, whose famous "Airrotica" number from *All That Jazz* [1979] could have been influenced by Borowczyk's aforementioned use of fragmented bodies and isolated erotic gestures).

In a way, it's through Borowczyk's limitations that we can best place him within specific film traditions. For one thing, his art is not easily classifiable as progressive, since it's so completely isolated from any traces of queer sensibility — Boro's erotic utopia is almost exclusively heteronormative. Furthermore, his relationship to issues of race is also problematic and often verges on colonial smugness: from the silently submissive black servant in *The Beast* (1975) to the cartoonish, Daffy Duck-dubbing of the Japanese tourist in *Love Rites* (1988). What's most important, though, is that Borowczyk's definite lack of interest in individual personality may be the ultimate key connecting all of his work, as well as the feature that sets him eons apart from the other great Polish émigré director, Roman Polański.

With the exception of his sole Polish feature, *Story of Sin* (1975), which used the strong narrative arc provided by Stefan Żeromski's 1908 novel to present a character-driven story of *l'amour fou*, all of Borowczyk's films are premodern in their obliviousness to individual motivation and psychology. In one of the interviews included in the magnificent "Boro" box set, issued by Arrow Films just as this book neared completion, Borowczyk explains that his main theme is "the way we as people interact with the world around us," which is tantamount to saying that his interest is in epistemology, not psychology. In other words, just like Jean Painlevé, Jan Švankmajer, and the Quay Brothers (not to mention Wes Anderson), Borowczyk's universe is intensely focused on processes and objects that surround and envelop individuals, without ever truly penetrating them. His cinema is not that of immersion, but of analysis and fragmentation: even at its most erotic and illicit, it presents us with a collage of fragments — apparently incongruent at first — that achieve a synergy so complete, it occasionally reaches the intensity of a powerful climax.

Contributors' Chapters

This book offers a peek into Borowczyk's macrocosm, but in no way does it propose a fixed reading of it. If anything, it is hoped that in its experimental character, it will point toward areas of Borowczyk's work that still need further attention. We were extremely fortunate to have excellent writers and scholars sharing their expertise with us. Together, they form what the reader is about to experience in *Boro, L'Île D'Amour: The Films of Walerian Borowczyk*.

The volume opens with an extended biographical chapter by Kuba Mikurda. By means of researching his documentary film on Borowczyk, he has gained access to various archives in Poland, France, and the UK, including the Cinémathèque Française collection, donated by Borowczyk himself. He also met with many of Borowczyk's collaborators, as well as with people who corresponded with him. He then put the results of his research into a historical perspective, framing Borowczyk's work within the larger context of world cinema. The Borowczyk emerging from Mikurda's chapter is a true "escape artist": a filmmaker who defies all simple classification, crosses all possible borders and searches for new forms of expression and fresh challenges. He's a trickster, a provocateur, an eternal rebel, who replenishes his energy by entering into conflict with the critics, the audience and the film industry alike.

The distinguished historian of film and animation Marcin Giżycki argues in his chapter that three phenomena are key to Borowczyk: surrealism, Hy Hirsch, and Kunstkamera. He describes the way in which Borowczyk looks at animate and inanimate objects, and in the second part of the chapter addresses the influence of Borowczyk's background as an animator on his live-action films, in particular the construction of mise en scène and directing actors.

In an informed conversation, Kuba Mikurda and visual artist Jakub Woynarowski discuss various facets of Borowczyk's animated works, which defy easy definition and still inspire with their innovative mixture of playfulness, provocation, and formal audacity. Contrary to received opinions, they suggest there is a deep consistency between Borowczyk's animated and live-action films, which have largely been viewed as belonging to separate phases of the director's work.

In her pioneering chapter, "Cruel Imagination: Borowczyk's Post-Traumatic Surrealism," Iwona Kurz explores the influence of World War II traumas on Borowczyk. This theme is discussed relatively rarely in the context of his films, which at first glance can seem untouched by politics or ideology. As Kurz aptly shows, contrary to other distinguished Polish filmmakers of his generation — such as Andrzej Wajda or Stanisław Różewicz — Borowczyk never approached those issues head-on, choosing indirect strategies instead, such as the employment of surrealist imagery. Kurz closely analyzes two films by Borowczyk: *Angels' Games* and the "Erzsébet Báthory" segment of *Immoral Tales*.

Kamila Kuc's piece, the most unorthodox in this book, constitutes an exploration of Borowczyk's take on Guy de Maupassant's *Rosalie Prudent* (1886) through the lens of the original source. Kuc's text explores a fictional dialogue between a number of cultural icons, which are brought together in this scenario because of the subjects and themes that dominate their work. The players here, apart from de Maupassant and Borowczyk themselves, are Nietzsche and Tolstoy, while Ligia Branice makes an appearance as Rosalie Prudent. The aim of this fictional piece was mainly to draw attention to Borowczyk's use of camera and sound, as well as his employment of rigorously minimal mise en scène. Kuc also wished to highlight certain themes that underpin many of Borowczyk's films, namely his take on motherhood.

Fernando C. Croce, known in the cinephiliac universe as the master of the short critical form, turns his eye to four of Borowczyk's films, only to discover a disquieting richness of textures indicative of the films' power to seduce.

James Snazell's piece investigates the importance of Borowczyk's visual background (particularly his preference for lithography) to the later development of his visual sensibility, from *Goto, Isle of Love* to *Behind Convent Walls*. The emphasis here is on Borowczyk's use of still imagery in his films, as seen in his employment of photography, collage and painting techniques. As Snazell aptly puts it: the attachment of Borowczyk's films to such tags as surrealism and eroticism fall apart, as "Borowczyk's work slips and slides when you attempt to shoehorn his work into neat categories."

A Private Collection is the subject of Edwin Carels' chapter, in which he argues that the film announces Borowczyk's aesthetic strategy, centered on attacking the hypocrisy surrounding pornography and sex. Carels proposes that Borowczyk's "insistence on the evasion of the eye of the law," turns *A Private Collection* into more "than a straightforward documentation." Carels also draws the reader's attention to Borowczyk's engagement with sculpture.

Never before have Borowczyk's films been written about in regard to any connection with Shakespeare. In his gripping and original chapter "The Beast with Two Backs," Phillip Warnell draws parallels between *The Beast*, "a tale of tails," and *Othello*, via Jean Cocteau's *Beauty and the Beast* (1946). Warnell argues that in Borowczyk's film the beast and the monarch are treated as a palimpsest, "a duo of refinement and perversion." Using Derrida's understanding of the sovereign, Warnell argues that the figure of the beast in Borowczyk's film is treated as one beneath the law, thus beauty and the beast eventually becomes beauty as the beast.

As its title suggests, Marta Rabikowska's chapter "Enjoying Excess: A Batailleanne Interpretation of *Story of Sin* (1975) by Walerian Borowczyk and Stefan Żeromski," uses Bataille's writings to investigate the relationship between Żeromski's 1908 novel and Borowczyk's 1975 adaptation of it. Rabikowska provocatively argues that there is not one film made by Borowczyk in which "love does not smell like death." Her chapter addresses a significant gap in Borowczyk scholarship, as she not only discusses contemporary responses to both Żeromski's novel and Borowczyk's film but offers new translations of Żeromski's complex novel in an attempt assess its impact on the film.

Kamila Wielebska introduces an original notion of "victorian surrealism," which she recognizes in Borowczyk's films, particularly in *Immoral Tales*, *The Beast*, and *The Strange Case of Dr. Jekyll and Miss Osbourne*. Her investigation into these films is strengthened by a wide literary and philosophical perspective. She also asks an uncomfortable question in trying to establish whether Borowczyk's films are chauvinist or pro-feminist in their approach.

Jonathan Owen focuses mainly on *A Private Collection* and *Immoral Tales* in his discussion of the meeting spaces of Borowczyk and his friend and fellow traveler through the erotic, André Pieyre de Mandiargues. Owen argues that the latter's affair with the cinema was at its best when collaborating with Borowczyk. Both men were, as Owen points out, united by their sympathy for surrealism and fascination for objects.

In his erudite chapter entitled "Sex and the Sacred: The Obstacles to Desire Becoming its Objects," Jakub Majmurek shows how Borowczyk's films often feature religion and religious imaginary, or to be exact — symbols, images and rituals associated with the Roman Catholic Church. Majmurek explores the dialectics of desire and law/prohibition, which fuels Borowczyk films with an ever-present erotic tension. Addressing Borowczyk's fascination with objects, Majmurek suggests that it may have been triggered by his Catholic background and this religion's relation toward sacred artifacts.

The Strange Case of Dr. Jekyll and Miss Osbourne gets a close reading in a sparkling chapter by Budd Wilkins (of *Slant Magazine*, amongst other publications), who connects it both to surrealist tradition and exploitation cinema.

Simon Abrams, Odie Henderson and Michał Oleszczyk engage in a vivid dialogue about what is perhaps the least loved of all Borowczyk films, *Emmanuelle 5* — widely seen as Borowczyk's ultimate act of succumbing to mainstream commercial erotica. They try to identify the film's redeeming features, as well as discern differences between the European and American cuts.

One of Borowczyk's final efforts (his last finished feature), *Love Rites*, gets a reading by the supreme director of visual essays, Kevin B. Lee, who starts by singling out a particular image and uses it to fuse the film's complicated relationship to touch, sex, and speech.

Note

1. A typescript, dated 28 August 1961, found in the collection of the Cinémathèque Française.

Bibliography

Borowczyk, W. 1973. "Wszystkie Moje Filmy Wymyśliłem Jednocześnie." *Film* 9.

Kamila Kuc, Ph.D. is a multimedia artist, curator, and writer. Her films have screened in venues and at film festivals nationally and internationally, including: Whitechapel Gallery, British Film Institute, Institute of Contemporary Arts London, Anthology Film Archives New York, and Ann Arbor Film Festival. She is the author and editor of numerous books and articles on experimental media, including *Visions of Avant-Garde Film* (Indiana University Press, 2016) and the first study of Polish avant-garde film, *The Struggle for Form: Perspectives on Polish Avant-Garde Film 1916–1989*, co-edited with Michael O'Pray (Columbia University Press, 2014). She is also the co-founder, with Sam Jury, of *Disasters of Peace* — a creative initiative that encompasses research, writing, making, and curating.

Kuba Mikurda, Ph.D. is a filmmaker and film scholar, and "Linia Filmowa" book series editor (Korporacja Ha!art Press). He has edited and co-edited books about contemporary filmmakers (Terry Gilliam, Brothers Quay, Guy Maddin, Tsai Ming-liang) and surrealism in Polish cinema (with Kamila Wielebska). He teaches at the Film School in Łódź. In 2013 he published *Corpus Delicti*, a visual essay about Borowczyk's objects (designed in collaboration with Jakub Woynarowski), and he has directed a feature documentary, *Love Express. The Disappearance of Walerian Borowczyk* (2018), for HBO Europe.

Michał Oleszczyk, Ph.D. is a film critic, script consultant, and translator based in Warsaw. He teaches film studies in the "Artes Liberales" Department at the University of Warsaw, as well as script development at Warsaw Film School. He is a regular contributor to *RogerEbert.com, Slant Magazine,* and numerous Polish media outlets. His work has also appeared in *Cineaste, Sight & Sound,* and *IndieWire.* He published the first Polish book on the work of Terence Davies, and has co-authored (with Kuba Mikurda) three books on the work of Guy Maddin, Brothers Quay, and Terry Gilliam. His Polish translation of J. Hoberman and Jonathan Rosebaum's *Midnight Movies* was published in 2011.

CHAPTER 1
Boro
Escape Artist

Kuba Mikurda

Walerian Borowczyk was born 21 October 1923 in the village of Kwilicz near the city of Poznań.[1] The village has a church, a palace and a landed gentry-owned farm. His father's first name is Wawrzyniec; the mother is Maria (née Banaszkiewicz). In his later years, Walerian Borowczyk (WB) alters the given date of his birth. He claims to have been born on 2 September 1932 — nine years later — and not in Kwilicz but in Wojnowice (Borowczyk 1993: 131).

In the same year, 1923, George Méliès burns all his films and throws them to the torrents of the Seine, while Walt Disney and his brother establish The Walt Disney Company. WB will refer to both throughout his lifetime — he adores Méliès and hates Disney with a passion. WB often speaks and writes of his father, only occasionally mentioning his mother. Wawrzyniec Borowczyk worked at the railway and was an amateur painter. Many years later, when asked about his painterly influences, WB answers: "My own father's painting, the fourteenth-century Italian painter Tomaso Capelli, too, and Henri Lecourbe" (Borowczyk 2004: n.p.). The last two have never existed. "He was a perfect painter for me, I grew up inside his colorful world," he writes (Borowczyk 2007: 32).

> Looking at his watercolors, one is tempted to name him one of great French impressionists of nineteenth century. He's unknown; he painted solely for a circle of his friends and for his son. He never exhibited his work … I chose my own path because of him. (Borowczyk 2007: 27)

WB's father dies in May 1975 — the news reaches Borowczyk in Cannes, where he is showing his *Story of Sin* (*Dzieje grzechu*) in the main competition (Borowczyk and Clarens 1976: 46).

Not much is known of WB's childhood — from 1939, he attended Ignacy Jan Paderewski High School in Poznań. He says he was fourteen when he saw a 16mm camera in a shop window display: "It was open, revealing all the internal mechanisms. I was spellbound" (Borowczyk and Adler 1985: 23). The period of German occupation of Poland was spent by him in Luboń, "doing the labor [Germans] forced us to do, digging holes used to build foundations for bridges" (Borowczyk 2007: 29). One night, young WB sneaked to the train station and covered an entire locomotive in colorful patterns. He came back in the morning to watch it as it started to traverse the barren landscape.[2] This was his first movie: made without a camera, shown without a projector.

In 1943, in the neighboring Żabikowo, a former brick factory had been turned by the Germans into a Nazi penal-investigative camp. Since WB's father worked as a railway man, WB must have heard often of the transport of prisoners, and possibly passed the gate of the camp quite frequently. It wasn't until twenty years later, in his animated short *Angels' Games* (*Les Jeux des Anges*) that he dared to show what was happening behind those gates (or perhaps what he was projecting onto them …?). After many years, he recollected that in 1945, just after the camp was liberated (on 26 January), he was there to see it and witnessed the charred dead bodies of the prisoners who the Germans deemed unfit for transportation; they forced them inside a barrack before setting it on fire. He describes a dramatic scene:

> *Just as many locals did, I arrived at the place of the atrocity, but it was too late: all we could do was look at the cinders and the smoking wood of the barrack walls. No one, obviously, had a camera on them to capture this tragic sight. [...] I used my drawing skills and I pictured the charred bodies of the martyrs with my pencil on a piece of paper.* (Borowczyk 2007: 29)

WB's drawing, signed "The evidence of German crime," is printed two months later on 8 April by the local newspaper, *Głos Wielkopolski* (*The Voice of Greater Poland*); WB calls it "my first published drawing" (Borowczyk 2007: 29).

After the end of the war, the 22-year-old WB does his final exams and moves to Kraków to study at the Fine Arts Academy (Akademia Sztuk Pięknych, or ASP) — "My childhood dream was to travel to Kraków, a city I equaled with art itself. To study at ASP was my main goal: it was there, I believed, that I could become a painter" (Borowczyk 2007: 32). The school quickly disappoints him.

As he wrote: "You become a painter despite the Academy, not because of it; you succeed despite your professors, not thanks to them" (Borowczyk 2007: 32). He further wrote:

> School can serve as a forum, a meeting place for young people – or people in general – who have the same passion. More often than not, the stairways and corridors of schools are the true classrooms and lecture halls, and it is often there that the future of the art form is determined. (Borowczyk and Adler 1985: 23)

For five years, he shares his dormitory room with Jan Tarasin and Jerzy Tchórzewski. He meets Andrzej Wajda, who after completing the first year transfers to Film School in Łódź (WB: "It was easier, quasi-artistic" [Borowczyk 2007: 33]). While in school, he purchases a 16mm camera and makes his very first films (*August* [*Sierpień*], *Magician* [*Magik*], *Crowd* [*Tłum*]). After many years, he will admit: "I had bought my camera because I was fascinated by its mechanism, not to use it for professional purposes" (Borowczyk and Adler 1985: 23).

In 1947 he meets Ligia Brokowska, the great love of his life; his future wife and muse. He is a 24-year-old artist. She is 15 and just graduating from Hoene-Wroński High School. On 25 May 1950, they are married in a secular ceremony. Ligia is not yet 18 (her birthday is in December). WB presents her with a volume of poetry, *The Red Glove* (*Czerwona Rękawiczka*) by Tadeusz Różewicz ("Wife's lips are moist / Salty and sad / White skin of winter's sleep / Vulnerable and readily apparent" [Różewicz 1948: 4]). Soon afterwards they leave for Warsaw where Ligia starts attending acting classes at the PWST (National School of Theatre).

1953–59

At first, WB creates artwork and satirical drawings with a clear anti-imperial, anti-American, anticapitalist and/or anticlerical message. He publishes mainly in *Pins* (*Szpilki*), a cult satirical periodical. After many years he declares that he "had criticized capitalism voluntarily, which I continue to do till this day" (Borowczyk 2007: 58). For his cycle of lithographs depicting the construction of the Nowa Huta district, he receives the 1953 award from the communist authorities. The jurors don't seem to mind that the Nowa Huta of WB's vision is a bleak desert, populated by just a few enigmatic construction machines. After many years, WB will not be harsh on the Polish 1950s: "Artists had liberty, but it was liberty under surveillance. For painters, there was almost total liberty within the framework of socialism. In spite of everything, we were free. For the generation of painters after the war, the style was post-expressionist, abstract and sometimes surrealist" (Borowczyk and Adler 1985: 23).

In 1954, the 31-year-old Borowczyk travels to Paris for the first time (in fact, it may be his first ever trip abroad). He makes, among other films, *Living Photographs* (*Żywe fotografie*) and a film shot in the studio of Fernand Léger at Gif-sur-Yvette. This is how he recounts that time:

> I was traveling through France as a painter would. I had this 16mm camera and I shot footage. At [Léger's] studio, everything was static, of course, save for a black cat which I didn't fail to film. ... Also in Paris, I made a 20-minute documentary, which I called Living Photographs, since it consisted of non-related shots, each of which had its own story and its own dramaturgy. It was an animated photo album. (Borowczyk et al. 1969: 38)

At the same time, he makes *Autumn* (*Jesień*), which will be remembered after many years by the influential film critic Aleksander Jackiewicz in the following manner:

> I remember [Borowczyk's] beginnings – an amateur film made in one of the Warsaw clubs devoted to narrow film stock. It was some sort of a melancholy walk in an empty park, set in an autumnal landscape, until you could see the colors lit up, the flowers bloom and the long-gone summer come back for a few fleeting moments. (Jackiewicz 1964: 11)

WB starts designing film posters—some of them reveal elements that will return later in his films (the roses from the poster for Jerzy Kawalerowicz's *The Real End of the Great War* [1957] show up in *Diptych* [1967], and the table filled with evidence from Erich Engel's *Blum Affair* [1948] is seen in *Rosalie* [1966]). He meets the graphic designer Jan Lenica with whom he teams up to produce animated inserts for the national newsreel cycle (*Strip-Tease* and *Education Days* [*Dni oświaty*]; both 1957), as well as the jazzy commercial of the state-owned youth periodical, *Banner of Youth* (*Sztandar młodych* [1958]). Together, they also sign *Once Upon a Time* (*Był sobie raz* [1957]), a collage animation considered by WB to be his first "real" film, which they follow by *Rewarded Feelings* (*Nagrodzone uczucia* [1957]). The very first film signed solely with WB's name is *School* (*Szkoła* [1958]).

At the same time, Ligia starts her acting career in film. In 1956, she makes her debut in *Winter Twilight* (*Zimowy zmierzch*) by Stanisław Lenartowicz. Pleased with the outcome, Lenartowicz casts Ligia in his following feature, *Encounters* (*Spotkania* [1957]). The ecstatic audience members send letter upon letter (WB later donated some of them to the Cinémathèque Française archive). That second role costs Ligia her place at PWST — a law takes effect, prohibiting students to act in films and television for fear of them suffering "demoralization." Ligia transfers to the National Film and Television School (PWSFiT) in Łódź.

WB and Lenica plan to make an adaptation of Franz Kafka's *Penal Colony*, "a colorful two-act film made with the intent of showing it at the festival in Brussels" (Borowczyk, Lenica, and Kowalski 1958: 8). The casting process is complete when film units "Kadr" ("Frame") and "Po Prostu" ("Just So") withdraw their backing — the official reason is that the production would be too expensive (although, considering Kafka's anti-totalitarian stance, there might just as well have been some unofficial reasons as well). Tadeusz Kowalski of *Film* magazine does an awkward interview with Borowczyk and Lenica in the famed Warsaw café "Nowy Świat" ("New World"); once the conversation turns toward the trouble with film units, the journalist suggests: "Let's talk about something cheerier, now!" In the interview, WB and Lenica speak as if in a single voice; they proclaim their artistic creed, completely at odds with the Polish Film School aesthetics of Andrzej Wajda, Andrzej Munk, and their kind:

> We believe the cinema has been killed together with the death of French avant-garde. What we would love most, would be to go back to Méliès. To go back to a place where the image reigns supreme and movement itself dominates ... We don't wish to confine ourselves to just one stylistic direction, but to use everything that spurs the imagination, moves one and makes one laugh, gives the eye something to enjoy ... We would like to create graphic arts in movement, in color, enhanced with sound. (Borowczyk, Lenica and Kowalski 1958: 9)

They also declare they will form their own film unit very soon.

In the end, instead of *Penal Colony*, WB and Lenica make *House* (*Dom* [1958]). The film, just like *Once Upon a Time,* is made within the "Kadr" film unit, headed by Lenica's brother-in-law, Tadeusz Konwicki (an accomplished writer and soon-to-be filmmaker himself). It is in *House* that WB casts Ligia for the first time.

At roughly the same time, Ligia plays the leading part in Stanisław Jędryka's short film *The Stadium* (*Stadion* [1958]). She spends most of her time in Wrocław, with WB visiting her regularly. Jędryka asks WB to work as a "visual consultant" on the film — WB agrees, and it is thanks to him that Alina Szapocznikow's sculptures are featured in the film.

House is one of Poland's official submissions for the experimental film competition, taking place as part of Expo '58 in Brussels. It is the first World Expo after the war. It is an immense event: logistically, artistically and architecturally — the first official celebration of the postwar "New Europe." More than 40 million visitors will see it in the end. There are some incidents — the Russians accuse the Americans of stealing the Sputnik design from their stand, and someone tears a page off the manuscript of Mozart's "Requiem" (reportedly the one containing the composer's very last words). The competition includes the crème de la crème of international film avant-garde, including Kenneth Anger, Stan Brakhage, Maya Deren, Ken Russell, Agnès Varda, Peter Kubelka, Abel Gance, Georges Franju, and Roman Polański. *House* wins the main award (Polański's *Two Men and a Wardrobe* [*Dwaj ludzie z szafą*, 1958] receives an honorable mention). WB and Lenica's victory is extremely prestigious — it brings them a $10,000 check (an astronomical amount for Polish citizens of the time) and allows them to personally meet key filmmakers from all over Europe and the United States (it is most likely there that WB meets Chris Marker for the first time). For both artists, this is the turning point of their respective careers.

1959–69

WB receives several offers of work in Western countries. He meets Anatole Dauman, a French producer of Polish origins. He is the founder of Argos Films and a legend of French filmmaking (in the upcoming years, Dauman will produce films by Alain Resnais, Jean-Luc Godard, Robert Bresson, Oshima Nagisa, and Wim Wenders). It is for Argos Films that WB makes *The Astronauts* (*Les Astronautes*

[1959]), co-signed by Chris Marker, who also works with Dauman. Marker wasn't, however, the actual co-director of the film — his name was needed to make it possible for non-resident WB to work legally in France. Marker's input is allegedly confined to a single decision: that of changing a canary featured in the narrative to an owl.[3] Featured in the film is Dauman himself along with the other owner of Argos Films (Philippe Lifchitz) and Ligia Borowczyk, starring as a girl being spied upon by the main character, an amateur astronaut. *The Astronauts* receives a string of awards and strengthens WB's position. At the same time, Dauman produces Alain Resnais' *Hiroshima Mon Amour* (1959).

WB signs a five-year exclusive contract with Jacques Forgeot, the owner of Les Cinéastes Associés film studio located in Saint Maurice, near Paris. WB and Ligia leave Poland and stay in Saint Maurice. After many years, WB states: "I didn't leave Poland because of censorship. I signed a contract ... and my job was to make feature films and shorts in complete freedom, based on my own screenplays" (Borowczyk 2007: 43).

"In complete freedom" and "based on my own screenplays" — this is what seems to matter most to WB. He throws himself into work, making one film after another: shorts, advertisements, etc. It is not uncommon of him to cut away the name of the advertised product and include the remaining short in his "official" filmography. The French have the hardest time remembering his name ("Borowicz," "Borowski"), which is why he shortens it to "Boro."

Chris Marker is enchanted by Ligia; he takes numerous pictures of her. The photos appear in the cycle "Starting Back" and make it to the cover of an official guidebook to Poland, published by Éditions du Seuil. Marker shoots Ligia strolling around Paris in a leather bodysuit. He casts her as one of the "women of the future" in his own science-fiction short, *La Jetée* (1962).

In 1962 WB stops communicating with Lenica. First, he writes to him:

The real author is the one who came up with the ideas for those films. Which of those films did you invent yourself? Should I remind you what the facts were? None of them were conceived in your head or soul. Even your hands weren't too busy as the films were being born. They were much busier counting the money rolling in. You usually nodded off during filmmaking. ... We may fool some obtuse film reviewers, but let's not fool each other! ... In Poland, back in 1957, I teamed up with you because that allowed me to realize my ideas on 35mm ... in "Kadr," ran by your brother-in-law. ... As for the films, authorship of which I so generously shared with you, let me give you a piece of advice: stop posing as their maker.[4]

Their paths split for good — in the following years Lenica will develop an impressive career of his own.

Subsequent shorts by WB — *Renaissance* (1963), *Grandma's Encyclopedia* (*Encyclopédie de grand-maman*, 1963), *Angels' Games* (1964), *Joachim's Dictionary* (*Le Dictionnaire de Joachim* [1965]) — literally overflow with ideas, each is different from the next; each represents a style all its own. WB combines various techniques of animation, trick photography and live-action. He outdoes himself with each finished film. It's the most dynamic period of his career — he makes as many as several films a year. He's awarded at festivals. His films are shown globally and are eagerly bought by distributors and television stations. WB's stature is growing, even though the wider audience is barely aware of him; he's appreciated by a small group of opinionated connoisseurs.

In January 1965, WB opens the exhibition "Camera Obscura" at the Paris cinema Le Ranelagh with a special program of his shorts, "Two Hours with Walerian Borowczyk." Many important people from the film and art world arrive, among them André Breton, François Truffaut, Agnès Varda, Alain Robbe-Grillet, and Lotte Eisner (WB kept their RVSP cards, with Truffaut's one stating: "Unfortunately not" in the "Accompanying person" box[5]). WB remembers that André Breton, the "Pope of Surrealism," was generous in his praise: he put his arm around him and said: "Walerian Borowczyk: dazzling imagination!" thus officially anointing WB as a surrealist (Borowczyk 2007: 51). Invited to take part in a survey on film surrealism by *Etudes Cinématographiques*, no. 41/42 (1965), WB expresses some reservations about the movement; he fully agrees on only one point: "Surrealism is a program of absolute non-conformism, both in life and in poetry, which is fully applicable to cinema. I'm all for it" (Borowczyk 1965: 155).

WB makes *Rosalie*, his first short that's almost exclusively live-action. For nearly the entire running time of 15 minutes the camera shows Ligia's face, as the actress speaks the monologue of Maupassant's alleged perpetrator of infanticide. *Rosalie* wins the Silver Bear at the Berlin Film Festival. Next year, *Theatre of Mr. and Mrs. Kabal* (1967) opens — it's his first fully animated feature (every WB film from that period was a "first" in some respect). At the beginning of *Theatre of Mr. and Mrs. Kabal*, WB shows up onscreen, talks to Mrs. Kabal and introduces himself: "My name is Boro." After a while, he is replaced by Mr. Kabal: a small, fidgety figure whose main passion is for peeping at half-naked women. Several critics, including Daniel Bird, maintain that *Theatre of Mr. and Mrs. Kabal* is the most autobiographical of all WB's films, with Mr. and Mrs. Kabal representing Boro and Ligia, and their house in the middle of nowhere portraying the place at Saint Maurice, where they lived in isolation from the outside world.

WB is approached by the Museum of Modern Art (MoMA), which expresses interest in doing a reprise exhibition of "Camera Obscura." The curator Willard Van Dyke addresses him in the letter: "I consider you to be the most important modern animator."[6] WB corresponds with MoMA for two years (1966–67); plans for an exhibition are drawn, which include a film installation and a list of titles to be screened. In December 1967, MoMA suddenly pulls out; the official reason being copyright issues (several of the films could only be shown as a part of a set).

After *Theatre of Mr. and Mrs. Kabal*, the 44-year-old WB receives the Max Ernst Award for his contribution to the field of animation. After Breton, Ernst's award is yet another gesture associating WB with "classic" surrealism. European critics react enthusiastically to *Theatre of Mr. and Mrs. Kabal* with Robert Benayoun of *Positif* equaling WB to Beckett and Ionesco. One of the film's fans is John Ford — WB writes down his words, spoken at a Montreal dinner: "You cracked the secret we are all fighting to crack: you made a commercial movie without surrendering your personality" (Borowczyk 2007: 54). WB calls *Theatre of Mr. and Mrs. Kabal* an "anti-Disney film." After the Cannes screening of the film, WB receives a letter from Antoni Bohdziewicz, a key figure in postwar film production in Poland, who becomes the head of the newly founded "Tor" ("Track") film unit in 1968. They begin corresponding about a feature length adaptation of Juliusz Słowacki's Romantic poem "Mazepa," which WB would make in Poland. *Mazepa* would be "Tor's" first film, as well as WB's first live-action feature. Stanisław Różewicz, an acclaimed film director as well as the brother of Tadeusz (who authored *The Red Glove*, the wedding gift of WB to Ligia), remembers it:

> Boro sent me the script, he said he'd like to make this movie in Poland. The script was good and he was a "quality" director. The people in charge of Polish nationalized film business were suspicious of the idea, though. An émigré director one could never be sure of ... Some colleagues were also hostile: "We don't need competition from France." We failed to make it happen. (Różewicz 2012: 12)

WB's live-action feature debut is *Goto, Isle of Love* (*Goto, L'Isle d'amour* [1968]), which most probably evolved from an earlier project based on *Gulliver's Travels*. The film takes place in a bleak, claustrophobic world; a crossover of a military stronghold and a concentration camp (with the echoes of the aborted *Penal Colony* project quite apparent). In the film, the world seems to have stopped at the end of the nineteenth century when an earthquake tore the titular island from the solid ground. At the center of the film we find the island's dictator, Goto III, and his beautiful wife, Glossia. WB creates this world in an abandoned factory once belonging to Pierre and Marie Curie. He sees to every detail; he paints the sets, he crafts props himself. He's directing the actors during a shot; he shouts directions at them, treating them as if they were paper cutouts ("lift your arm, lift your head, move right").[7] The distinguished French actor Pierre Brasseur has enough of this: he stops the scene mid action and yells at Borowczyk, ordering him to shut up. This is an isolated incident, though — on the set of *Goto* it's WB who is the real dictator; it's him who decides everything. He's in his own world — an isolated world, in which time has stopped around 1887.

May 1968 — students and workers hit the streets, Paris is ablaze, riots abound, crowds clash with police; enthusiasm and anxiety are palpable. Only WB stays within the four walls of his own private world, making *Goto*. The unions forbid the crew to continue their work — Pierre Brasseur receives threats and has to stop working for a while. A vote is held among WB's crew: only one person wishes to stop, so the work continues.

"Yes, he was a dictator," remembers cameraman Noël Véry, "but only till Ligia walked on the set. Once Ligia entered, WB was a little doggie at her feet." WB used special lighting for Ligia to make her complexion as bright as possible. No amount of light was sufficient when it came to Ligia, so WB kept nagging the Director of Photography (DoP), Guy Durban: "More, stronger, brighter!"[8] Ligia's heroines always bear names evoking light, purity and beauty: Rosalie, Glossia, Blanche, Clara.

WB's friends — Dauman and Marker — look with sympathy at *Goto*, but nobody really knows what to expect. The film proves to be an immense success: the critics speak in unison, the reviews are enthusiastic. In 1969 WB receives an award from the guru of French film criticism himself, Georges Sadoul. He gives interviews to press, radio and television. He makes the cover of *Cahiers du Cinéma* together with Sergei Eisenstein (the title: "Eisenstein, Borowczyk –The

Problem of Direction"). The issue features commentaries and an interview with the director; it runs for several pages and is conducted among others by the editor-in-chief, Jacques Rivette. WB voices his "dictatorial" view of film art:

> *I do not see film as collective art. Contrary to what everyone says, cinema is not a collaborative art at all … [My] actors are all immensely talented, but for me they serve as paper cut-outs, capable of playing anything. (Borowczyk 1969: 33)*

In answer to a question about whether he "generally likes what Godard does," he covers the microphone with his hand and says: "Not particularly." He criticizes the events of May 1968 in France:

> *You can rebel against the uniforms all you like, it won't change a thing. Every single one of those long-haired boys has an ID and doesn't throw it away. … One committee is easily replaced by another. (Borowczyk 1969: 44)*

Franco's Spain deems *Goto* an anti-fascist picture and prevents it from being distributed. In Poland, most of the censorship committee votes in favor of the movie, but it is still disliked by the secretary of the Central Committee, Stefan Olszowski, who vetoes it (according to WB, the problematic scenes included the ones with the flytrap device, which were seen as a satire on the rationalization movement[9]). At the beginning of 1969, *Film* magazine describes *Goto* and quotes favorable reviews from the French press. In one of the issues, there's news about the plans to make *Mazepa* and the acclaimed critic Aleksander Jackiewicz speculates on what the finished film might be like ("Maybe Borowczyk will try to show what happened with [*Mazepa*] after the end [of Słowacki's drama]?" [Jackiewicz 1969a: 2]). In April, Jackiewicz writes about *Goto* — he saw the film abroad and calls it a failure; he says that WB may be a great animator, but his storytelling skills are lacking. He writes:

> *A feature film requires a writer, a teller of tall tales. Feature film tells a story with images. Borowczyk, on the other hand, is just a craftsman of images. He's a graphic designer, a painter. His fingertips possess wisdom. Why is it that people always wish to be what they are not? (Jackiewicz 1969b: 10)*

WB pens an answer and sends it to *Film* magazine, requesting it to be published. He calls Jackiewicz's review a "literary attempts of a failed novelist;" he criticizes him for presenting a "stunningly naïve" reading of *Mazepa* and ends up by quoting Pierre Brasseur's opinion of him, calling him a "con" ["prick"] (permitting the magazine to replace the word with three dots). *Film* refuses to print the letter, saying that WB has used "decidedly abusive" language and that the letter "violates the civility we closely follow in Polish national press." In response, WB sends yet another, much longer letter, in which he attacks Jackiewicz with panache worthy of a baroque scribe ("vacuous prose, bristling with painted feathers of pure pretense," "tragi-comical, provincial mystification"), threatening that if *Film* doesn't publish his letter, the matter will be "widely publicized by serious film magazines with international readership."[10] *Film* does not publish the letter, and Jackiewicz writes positively of *Theatre of Mr. and Mrs. Kabal*, even though he criticizes WB's interview for *Cahiers du Cinéma* (— for failing to mention Lenica, for detaching himself from the Polish Film School and for being "unpleasant, ... narcissistic ... playing a fool"). He finishes his piece thus: "Borowczyk: an unpleasant man and a talented artist; a small man on one hand, a significant work on the other" (Jackiewicz 1969c: 10). WB is furious: he writes an open letter, which he sends to all major periodicals in Poland (he even kept the postage receipts, including ones for *Life of Warsaw* [Życie Warszawy], *Politics* [Polityka], and *The People's Tribune* [Trybuna Ludu]), as well as to the secretary of the Central Committee of the Communist Party, the head of the National Committee of Cinema and to "Tor" film unit. He writes: "The systematic publishing of Alekander Jackiewicz's slanderous and personally insulting pieces by *Film* is detrimental to the entire Polish press."[11]

He also announces that, because of the situation, he is forced to abandon the plans of making *Mazepa* in Poland. Not a single magazine publishes the letter. The head of "Tor," Antoni Bohdziewicz, tries to change WB's mind; he writes that "there is a discrepancy between a mere press incident, represented by the Jackiewicz piece, and the artistic chance"[12] that making *Mazepa* could effect. Still, WB is adamant: he maintains that the negative pieces by Jackiewicz were purposefully synchronized with the rejection of *Goto* by the Central Committee, and that prior to this *Film* had referred to the film in positive terms. "I despise snitches of this sort; those folk ruffians made an enemy of the people out of me"[13] — he writes, and adds that he will make *Mazepa* in France.

From now, writing baroque polemics will become the order of the day throughout WB's career. He reacts in this fashion to all negative comments in the Polish press — he quotes foreign magazines, he points out inaccuracies, he questions the competence of a writer (the autobiographical book he wrote toward the end of his life, *What Do I Think When I Look at a Polish Woman In the Nude* [*Co Myślę Patrząc na Rozebraną Polkę*], is a veritable collection of pieces like that, with an entire slew of critics being called frauds). He is meticulous; it happens often that he picks at one particular sentence and proves at length just how wrong it is.

1969-76

After the success of *Goto*, WB is developing several projects at once. He wants to make *Love Is Not a Sin*, a contemporary story starring Jean-Pierre Léaud and Ligia; he's making plans for his own version of *Snow White*, which includes a cast of people with dwarfism (he hates the Disney version, calling it "the most immoral film ever made, as well as the most perfidious piece of pornography, veiled evil ..., [a film] cloaking its sexual perversion in its anecdote" [Borowczyk 2007: 76]). Neither project gets made; instead, WB makes the French version of *Mazepa*, with a trace of Snow White (*Blanche Neige*) preserved: WB changes the name of the main female character from Amelia to Blanche.

Blanche (1971) is yet another artistic success — WB may be the first director to present a naturalistic vision of the Middle Ages, later elaborated on in such works as Robert Bresson's *Lancelot du Lac* (1974) and Terry Gilliam's *Jabberwocky* (1977). There's a conflict on the filmset: George Wilson demands that Ligia Borowczyk (billed as Ligia Branice) is replaced by Catherine Deneuve. Shooting is put on hold, but WB is adamant about keeping Ligia; at last, Wilson agrees to finish the film with Ligia as the lead.[14] As with *Goto*, many of the props and the set design are prepared by WB himself. *Blanche* is awarded the Grand Prix at Berlin and receives a string of other honors. The film also draws a larger audience, both in France and abroad: in the United Kingdom, the film stays on screen for more than a year.

Right after *Blanche*, Ligia accepts the leading part in Stanisław Jędryka's *The Vest* (*Kamizelka* [1971]), based on a short story by Bolesław Prus (she's joined on screen by veteran actor Tadeusz Fijewski and a young Jerzy Zelnik, who in a couple of years will star in WB's own *Story of Sin* [1975]).

WB is 49 years old — he is an established artist and it seems there's a great career ahead of him. First he won all there was to win in the field of animation, and now he's conquering the world of live-action film. He's preparing many projects at once; he wishes to try every genre there is. In an interview for *Film* magazine in 1973, he says:

> *An artist's development exists solely in the mind of the historian who prepares the chronology of his work. Words such as "individuality" and "variety" are more precise than "artist" or "development". I conceived all my films in an instant, and only objective factors prevented me from making them in that instant. (Borowczyk 1973: 2)*

WB's to-do list includes: *Perfect Love* (an adaptation of *Siberian Lady Macbeth* by Leskov), *Ordeal in the Olive Garden* ("I wish to present Jesus simply as a man sentenced to death, with no religious overtones"), *Jo&CO* (a comedy about a gangster and a 6-year-old boy), *The Siege* (adaptation of a symbolist novel by Maurice Chappaz, starring Michel Simon and Charlie Chaplin), *Strangers from the Basement* (based on Jean Cassou's novel), *Unperfect Love* (based on a screenplay by Gerard Kemmet, starring Malcolm McDowell), and *College Temple* ("a comedy showcasing various types of physical pleasure").[15] He also resumes talks with "Tor" film unit — he plans to adapt the 1908 novel *Story of Sin* (*Dzieje grzechu*) by Stefan Żeromski. Apart from the latter, none of these projects ever get made.

In 1972, Anatole Dauman hires WB to shoot a new, wilder ending for Alain Fleischer's *Les rendez-vous en foret*, an adult fairy tale that proved to be too literary and too self-conscious for Dauman's taste. For that purpose, WB prepares a costume of a hairy beast, but it is never used — Fleischer goes to court to prevent the new version from being made. A few months later, WB remembers the legend of a beast, which had allegedly roamed Gévaudan and its vicinity in the eighteenth century (Tohill and Tombs 1995: 229). WB includes the history of the beast in a project he starts developing with Dauman — a portmanteau film called *Immoral Tales* (a purposeful reference to Eric Rohmer's *Moral Tales* cycle).

In spring 1973, WB comes to Oberhausen Film Festival to preside over the jury. He also plans to present a rough cut of his new short film, *A Private Collection* (*Une Collection particulière*) — a film presentation of some nineteenth-century erotic toys (it will later be revealed that WB had devised and made all the devices himself). There's controversy over a short fragment of the film: archival footage featuring a woman having intercourse with a dog. "A museum piece, shall we say," said WB after many years. "That was also a problem. They made a terrible fuss about it in Oberhausen, Germany, where I belonged to the festival jury. But finally they showed it, in all its glory, to a full house" (Borowczyk and Kessler 1994: 98). The shock is all the greater for the fact that WB's films, as charged as they were, had never until this point shown actual sex. A similar situation happens in the fall of the same year in London, where Borowczyk presents a working version of *Immoral Tales* (*Contes Immoraux*), featuring the *Beast of Gévaudan* segment, removed from the final version. The London audience, familiar with Borowczyk only from his animations, *Goto* and *Blanche*, is taken by surprise at the very least. The reporter for the *New Statesman* writes: "What on earth does the British Film Institute think it is up to? [WB's film] sent even the National Film Theatre's normally unshockable audience shuffling out shamefaced" (Tohill and Tombs 1995: 221).

A shorter, four-segment version of *Immoral Tales* is released in French cinemas in 1974. It has a mighty competitor: millions of viewers of both genders flock in to see *Emmanuelle*, one of the biggest box office successes in the history of French cinema. Still, *Immoral Tales* triumphs with the audiences, as well, it is the second most profitable erotic film of the year. However, the critic for *Playboy* magazine stresses that artistically *Emmanuelle* is no match for *Immoral Tales*.[16] Other critics are divided, and confused as to how to approach the film. Some say that WB merely provokes — and not in the most tasteful of manners. Just as they collectively proclaimed WB's greatness — just as they put him on magazine covers alongside Fellini and Eisenstein — he suddenly behaves like an ungrateful schoolboy, eager to mock their praise. WB's sympathizers point to the stylistic consistency of *Immoral Tales* with WB's surrealist background, as well as stress the visual beauty of the film. In interviews, WB defends his film with the fervor of a French moralist, a libertine and a proponent of sexual revolution — "Sex and eroticism is one of the most moral aspects of life. Eroticism does not kill, does not annihilate, does not lead one to evil, does not enable crime. To the contrary – it brings peace and fulfillment, as well as honest pleasure. ... Our modern sexual taboos are mostly the invention of the nineteenth century. It's more and more often that we reject those canons. Many countries eschew censorship in those matters entirely. ... I never hear of anyone who would be brought to a life of crime by *Immoral Tales*" (Borowczyk and Markowski 1975: 17–18). In WB's view, *Immoral Tales* realizes the ideal of "absolute non-conformism," which he had tied to surrealism back in 1965 — "non-conformism of life, of poetry and of cinema."

At Locarno, *Immoral Tales* is shown on an enormous screen in the main market square. The projection is disturbed by a violent thunderstorm, but the audience stays firmly in their seats. After the projection, WB walks into a bar where he meets Rainer Werner Fassbinder. They strike up a dialogue. Fassbinder: "Borowczyk, why didn't you show an erect penis in your movie?" WB: "There were plenty of these in the audience, despite the storm raging on" (Borowczyk 2007: 68).

From the early 1970s onwards, world cinema takes an active part in sexual revolution. At about the time of the premiere of *Blanche*, several films open, each of which challenge the audience with explicit sexual content: Ken Russell's *The Devils* (1971), Bernardo Bertolucci's *Last Tango in Paris* (1972), Pier Paolo Pasolini's *The Canterbury Tales* (1972), Gerard Damiano's *Deep Throat* (1972). There's a veritable festival of naked bodies going on in French cinemas. It starts timidly, only to gain rapid momentum. At first, soft-core prevails. The same year *Immoral Tales* opens, the government of Giscard d'Estaing gets rid of censorship altogether. In April 1975, there's the first official premiere of a hard-core film: *History of the Blue Movie*. More than 200 thousand viewers see it. The next one, *Exhibition* (1975), reaches a half-million audience. Pornographic films are shown in big theaters on the Champs-Élysées and in small provincial cinemas. More and more "pornographic" films by acclaimed filmmakers are made, such as *Glissements progressifs du plaisir* (1974) by Alain Robbe-Grillet and *Salò, or the 120 Days of Sodom* (1975) by Pier Paolo Pasolini.

At the same time, in Poland, the new head of "Tor" film unit, Stanisław Różewicz, fights for *Story of Sin* to happen. The notoriety of *Immoral Tales* doesn't help things — besides the accusation against Borowczyk as "an émigré artist," he's now fearful of making "pornography for the money of the state." Różewicz:

The entire unit had to play an elaborate game to enable Borowczyk to make this film. Everyone was against it: the film community, the authorities, as well as the clergy, with no permit given to shoot inside real churches. (Różewicz 2012)

WB plays it tactically. Upon his visit to the ministry, he says: "Mister Minister, I already talked to the bishop, the church is very opposed to making this film" (Różewicz 2012). Just to spite the ideologically adverse church, the authorities agree to have the film made.

On his way to Poland, WB has an accident — his car drives off the road just past the Polish border and falls on its roof. WB describes the accident in almost filmic terms:

I drove non-stop, throughout the night, so that I crossed the Polish border in the morning. I played the radio, listening to Chopin on full volume and getting drunk on Poland. After I left the highway, I found myself on a narrow, winding local road with the surface tilted in the wrong direction. As I speeded, the car drove off the road into the field, razed a lone fruit tree and after doing several flips it fell down, crushed, on the ground. I was alone; luckily I managed to crawl out from it, covered in blood. The motor was silent, but Chopin's Mazurkas were still playing in the Sunday quietness. (Borowczyk 2007: 70)

WB spends the next two weeks in a Radziejowice hospital, seeing actors, accepting costume design, etc.

Story of Sin is made in a record amount of days. All collaborators stress Borowczyk's discipline and professionalism: 70 shooting locations in 60 days. WB becomes fast friends with DoP Zygmunt Samosiuk — both appear in a casino scene, with Samosiuk in full drag as WB's nagging wife. *Story of Sin* is shot in a fresh visual style unlike that of previous projects — the camera is very active, mostly handheld. There's a lot of tension on the set between WB and the main actress, Grażyna Długołęcka.

The ministry is flooded with informant notes from local party offices, as well as reports from the screenings of the dailies. Różewicz gets a call from the minister himself: "What kind of pornography are you making there?!" (Różewicz 2012). In the end, however, the authorities don't tamper much with the film. Helena Nowicka:

During the official test screening, the film production officials objected to some explicit close-ups, as well as to the inclusion of several erotically themed lithographs. We had to cut out several shots. In fact, the entire scandalous atmosphere served as a terrific promotional campaign. (Hollender and Turowska 2000: 61)

Story of Sin is seen by 8 million viewers in Poland alone and makes a record 84 million zlotys (a typical film cost about 9–12 million at the time). Compared to *Immoral Tales*, or *The Beast* (*La Bête*), *Story of Sin* seems very tame, but remains highly controversial in 1970s Poland. Długołęcka claims that her starring role in *Story of Sin* destroyed her career:

The movie was too daring for its time. Ever since I made it, I was invited to act in nude shower scenes. ... My parents were especially affected by all this. Still, I believed that since I embarked on an acting career, I should have the courage it takes. (Hollender and Turowska 2000: 61)

During a press screening, WB attacks Jerzy Płażewski, arguably the most influential Polish film critic of the time, famous for using a flashlight-enhanced pen to jot down his notes in screenings. WB is furious that Płażewski dares to look away from the screen in order to take notes — he's missing precious frames WB put in their given places for a reason. *Story of Sin* is the Polish entry for Cannes' Main Competition in 1975. The Palme d'Or goes to *The Chronicle of Smoldering Years*, an epic tale of twentieth-century Algerian history. Later the same year, a feature-length version of *The Beast* opens in France. Just like *Immoral Tales*, it was produced by Anatole Dauman's Argos Films — the truncated segment from *Tales* is now positioned as the heroine's dream in a contemporary story. *The Beast* attracts less viewers than *Immoral Tales*, but it follows the pattern set by midnight movies of that era shown in New York City (such as *Pink Flamingos* [1972] and *El Topo* [1970]), and becomes a cult hit. It's not accepted to A-class film festivals, but it is screened at a Horror and Science Fiction Festival in Avoriaz. Many critics ignore *The Beast* altogether, with a few of them putting Borowczyk on their personal black list. WB himself quotes Freud and claims that *The Beast* is in fact a film about the work of the dream and it merely reveals a fantasy present in European culture from ancient times to, among others, *The Beauty and the Beast*. One year after *The Beast*, Christmas 1976, the new version of *King Kong* opens, which includes almost identical scenes of half-naked beauty being chased by the beast, save for the final copulation. *King Kong* becomes a hit and earns half a billion dollars.

Immoral Tales and *The Beast* meet censorship problems in most countries they open in. In Germany, *Immoral Tales* remains banned until 2010. In Italy, the censorship office variously agrees and withholds the distribution permit. Finally, a version shortened by 13 minutes is shown, with the chapters rearranged and with fragments of *A Private Collection* used for punctuation, together with an ironic commentary by Giuseppe Berto, designed to take the edge off the film. In Poland, *The Beast* and *Immoral Tales* are not shown in cinemas till 1992. In the UK, *The Beast* provokes a lengthy discussion at the British Board of Censors and is finally distributed in selected London cinemas as a redacted version with an "X" certificate in 1978. According to David Thompson, the final scenes of that version were so severely cut that watching them made one think of an avant-garde film using stroboscopic effect.[17]

1976–84

WB is planning an adaptation of *Iron Temple,* an installment in the adventure cycle by Jean Ray, focusing on Harry Dickson ("an American Sherlock Holmes") in a story of aliens from outer space, Aztecs, monsters, tigers and the titular temple near London, which routinely sees human sacrifice. WB would like to shoot it for Argos Films, so Dauman is checking the rights issues. At the same time, WB gets in touch with the Hakim brothers, the legendary French film producers (involved with Buñuel's *Belle de Jour* [1967] and Antonioni's *Eclipse* [1962]). At first they talk about a project of *Belle du seigneur* based on the 1968 novel by Albert Cohen, but WB proposes a Prix Goncourt-winning novel by André Pierre de Mandiargues, *The Margin* (WB already adapted Mandiargues' short story "The Tide" as the first segment of *Immoral Tales*). He convinces them that Sylvia Kristel (of *Emmanuelle* fame) would be perfect for *The Margin*.[18]

The Hakims agree to produce *The Margin*. The project is very promising — WB comes fresh off the commercial success of *Immoral Tales*, the book has just won a prize, the actors are popular (besides Sylvia Kristel, Joe Dallessandro of the Warhol Factory is to make his European debut in the film). However, a big commercial production leaves much less space for WB's creative freedom. What's worse, Spanish authorities do not want the shooting to take place in Spain (the action of the novel takes place in 1920s Barcelona), explaining that they are concerned with the good name of their country. In a later interview, WB will say:

> *The local press wrote some furious articles against the project. Back then, Generalissimo Franco still ruled the country, and the fascist didn't like the idea of this hive of prostitution being publicized. They said, "foreigners come to Spain to make a movie, and what do they use to represent Spain? Brothels and whores!" (Borowczyk and Kessler 1994: 98)*

The Hakims convince WB to move the action to contemporary Paris. WB:

> *The French producer chickened out; he came to me with newspaper clippings, saying that no insurance agency would work with us under these circumstances. So we made the film in Paris, where the trouble continued immediately! (Borowczyk and Kessler 1994: 98)*

For WB, it's the very first feature film of his to take place in the contemporary era. He deals with it by confining most of the action to hotel interiors, which look pretty much as if time had stopped there in the 1920s. There are further alterations, though: the Hakims want the main character to drive a classier car ("A big, majestic Citroen! That's the kind of car the public likes to see!" [Borowczyk and Kessler 1994: 98]), they want more contemporary music in the film (Pink Floyd, Elton John, etc.). WB tries to navigate the tricky situation. The movie he ultimately makes is a compromise, which pleases neither him nor Mandiargues. WB: "The movie has a very cold surface, I find it a bit too chic. There are some good sequences in it, however" (Borowczyk and Kessler 1994: 98). *The Margin* is a fond memory for Kristel, though:

> It's a strong part, perhaps my favorite one. Walerian seems haunted by his erotic fantasies and by his propensity for fetishism ... The movie wasn't successful and the distribution was confined to, as it is politely called, the experimental art house circuit. Not many people saw me in the picture, which is a shame. (Kristel 2010: 110)

Because of Sylvia Kristel's presence, some countries distribute the film as *Emmanuelle 77*.

After *The Margin*, WB makes a short but poignant film entitled *Letter from Paris* (*Brief von Paris*), a bleak vision of a Moloch-like city, overwhelming and attacking the senses from all directions, impossible to contain. In *Letter from Paris*, the camera movements are feverish and chaotic, as in the most dramatic sequences of *Story of Sin*. It's Paris as a nightmare, Paris by Kafka, Paris as a claustrophobic trap.

WB arrives in Italy, where he makes *Behind Convent Walls* (*Interno di un convento* [1977]). The film is made near Castel Gandolfo. Despite the relative freedom he had on the production, WB ultimately claims he set out to make a different film.

> It was meant to be a different film entirely, but two of the actors I wanted – Michele Placido and Monica Vitti – were not available, so we had to do something else. The producer needed a film, it was already pitched to the distributor. (Borowczyk and Kessler 1994: 99)

WB adds that the masturbation scene was added upon the producer's wish: "The producer wanted me to do a very explicit scene, and he got it. ... We used a body double for those inserts. ... However, the sequence was filmed by me and Tovoli" (Borowczyk and Kessler 1994: 99).

During the casting process for *Behind Convent Walls*, WB meets a 17-year-old Marina Pierro. Pierro becomes WB's new muse and fellow traveler; he ends up making five movies with her. *Behind Convent Walls* marks the final appearance by Ligia — it's as if two of WB's muses are passing each other on the screen. Under Pierro's influence, female characters in WB's films change — the ethereal, luminous, passive women played by Ligia become the strong, carnal and active ones played by Marina.

Marina appears in the longest segment of a new film called *Heroines of Evil* (*Les héroïnes du mal*) — in 1978, WB shoots scenes at Forum Romanum. WB remembers:

You can only make documentaries there. We had to sneak in like thieves, with our cameras hidden beneath out cloaks. All of us bought tickets, all six of us, and then we just waited for all the visitors to be gone. [It was there] that we shot the ablution scene. The guard spotted us, but we convinced him that we are making a documentary. (Borowczyk and Kessler 1994: 99)

In 1980, WB makes *Lulu* based on Wedekind's play — he takes the project over from Liliana Cavani. For the first time, he casts Udo Kier, who also stars in his next film, based on Robert Louis Stevenson's *The Strange Case of Dr. Jekyll and Mr. Hyde*. WB claims that he has discovered the previous version of the novel, which — according to rumor — was burned by Stevenson himself after his fiancé asked him to destroy it. He admits later that it was a hoax. He wants the movie to be titled *Dr. Jekyll and Miss Osbourne*, so as to stress the equal narrative status between the characters of Fanny and Jekyll. The producers insist on a more suggestive (more "erotic") title *Dr. Jekyll and His Women*. Jekyll is one of very few male leads in WB's cinema — perhaps even his porte-parole; Jekyll's praise of transgression at one point seems to be the creed of WB himself.

WB makes yet another Italian film: *The Art of Love* (*L'Art D'Aimer* [1983]), based on Ovid's work. Despite an intriguing cast (Marina Pierro, Michel Piccoli, Laura Betti), the film is a flop. Rumor has it that the producers demanded more daring scenes from Borowczyk, and when they failed, they forged his signature and edited in some hard-core bits. WB tries suing them in an attempt to regain control over his film.

In the meantime, distributors all over Europe change the titles of WB's films, so that they bring to mind the clout of *Immoral Tales*. In Italy and in the UK, *Heroines of Evil* becomes *Immoral Women* or *Immoral Angels*; in Germany, *Behind Convent Walls* is changed to *Immoral Novices*. The directors of sexploitation films capitalize on *The Beast*'s fame — both *Beauty and the Beast* (1977) and *Beast in Space* (1980) use actresses from Borowczyk's film.

WB is working on new projects: *Ancestral Mansion* and *Nefertiti*. He visits London in order to talk to the screenwriter of *Ancestral Mansion*, Cherry Potter. His English is not strong enough, but he brings her a picture of a chastity belt made of pearl — it would be one of the main props in the film. More than talking about the script, he's interested in visiting the Natural History Museum, the London Dungeon and a store specializing in elaborate door knobs.[19] The stars of the film are supposed to be Terence Stamp and Kate Bush.

WB travels to Tunisia where he scouts for locations and objects for *Nefertiti*. He meets the agreement with Argos Films and finishes the script for *The Iron Temple*; he is developing new ideas: *Grigia*, based on Robert Musil's work; *Maria* (based on *The Dead* by Georges Bataille), *Madness/Lucia* (based on Tommaso Landolfi), and *Little Criminals* (based on Nadine Monfils). None of these projects ever get made into a film.

1984–89

The producers back out of *Nefertiti* and *Ancestral Mansion* at the very last moment.

WB returns to animation; he makes *Scherzo Infernal* (1984), which is part of a project called *L'infernal amant*. He establishes a production company, Allegro (which means "quickly").

WB meets Alain Siritzky, producer of the *Emmanuelle* series. Siritzky looks for ways to revive the cycle, which has a significantly smaller audience after four installments (the screenplay for the next film is being written by yet another 1970s scandalist, Jean Rollin). Siritzky sees Borowczyk's name as a brand that can rejuvenate the series. He describes WB as someone [who] "can do everything: write, lighting, set design, edit and even do the poster" (Tohill and Tombs 1995: 227). As the new wave of cheap pornography is crushing the old guard, the two former rivals of 1974 decide to join forces. The film is advertised with the slogan: "The names of Borowczyk and Emmanuelle are finally joined together!"

The film is shot on Reunion Island, a French colony in the Indian Ocean. A conflict ensues on the set between WB and the main actress, Monique Gabrielle, known from *Bachelor Party* with Tom Hanks. WB abandons his work and returns to Paris. After many years, he recollects:

> *The leading lady, Monique Gabrielle, was American and totally inexperienced. She didn't want to accept any directions. ... The actress had a portfolio, including layouts from "Penthouse" that looked pretty rough to me. But as we were filming, she suddenly refused to go on. I have the feeling she thought I wanted to do a hardcore film with her, but this wasn't the case. Maybe our translator failed us, I don't know. She wanted more money. I said goodbye and took the next plane to Paris. I was involved in the editing of the final cut, but I didn't direct it. It's not my movie.* (Borowczyk and Kessler 1994: 99)

Photographs remain of WB at Cinemation studios, working on special effects for *Emmanuelle 5*. One can see him obsessively fixing the papier-mâché model of the Grand Canyon, as well as the model plane inspired by Howard Hughes' Spruce Goose. Later on, WB will say: "The movie has only one sequence directed by me, the film-within-a-film at the beginning. My assistant did the rest. Sititzky, the producer, used my name to gather the funds" (Borowczyk 2007: 67). In his autobiographical book, WB admits authorship of one more fragment: the areal footage of the island and the plane crash. He claims to have carved his initials on the film negative with those fragments. The conflict with Siritzky is described in more dramatic terms, with the producer as the foe: "He cried and moaned, begging me to agree, so I said I will do two shots for him. The double paycheck bought me a house in Rome" (Borowczyk 2007: 68).

Still, there are several allusions to WB's earlier work in *Emmanuelle 5*: a hat from *Astronauts*, the erotic toy from *A Private Collection*, a close-up of a part of the motorboat that looks like the flytrap from *Goto*, a woman imprisoned on an island by an exotic dictator, etc. The entire Cannes sequence, together with "Love Express" (the film-within-a-film starring Emmanuelle and having its premiere at the festival), is especially self-reflexive, with the voice-over narration describing "Love Express" in terms critics normally used for WB's pictures, comparing it to Disney, Méliès, and Mandiargues. The entire sequence is WB's satire of artistic erotica: of festivals that show it and the audience who wants to watch it.

Emmanuelle speaks in formulas that WB himself would probably agree with ("Is your film pornographic?" — "It's provocative, but not pornographic"; "What do you think of censorship?" — "Censorship violates the right of men and women to experience pleasure"). She says those things not as a rebel, though, but as the star of the festival and as one very much expected to say that. In Cannes, as portrayed by WB, Emmanuelle is safe and her film is a hit — the modern bourgeoisie doesn't avert their eyes in shock, but rather lines up for the screening (the voice-over informs us that the film is played 24 hours a day). It's true that Emmanuelle has to escape the crowds, but it's a crowd of admirers, not of "moral majority" crazies. This way, as it seems, WB is ironically commenting upon the market value of a scandal and suggests that artistic provocation became part of the free market game.

Alain Siritzky produces a new version of *Emmanuelle 5* for the American market. Extra footage is shot by Steve Bartnett, who the opening credits identify as the co-director. The studio space is rented out by Roger Corman, whose New Horizons is the film's distributor. In its new incarnation, *Emmanuelle 5* becomes an action comedy flick — Emmanuelle is wielding a machine gun and shooting up an army of guys in cork helmets. What's left out is all the interracial sex sequences and several signature erotic touches by Borowczyk.

In the mid 1980s, WB meets Alain Sarde, who by that time had produced such films as Roman Polański's *The Tenant* and Jean-Luc Godard's *First Name: Carmen* (in later years, he will produce such films as *Mullholland Drive* [2001] and subsequent features by Polański: *Bitter Moon* [1992], *The Pianist* [2002], *Venus in Fur* [2013]). Sarde gives WB a small budget and a carte blanche. WB decides upon an adaptation of *Tout Disparaitra (Everything Must Go)* by Mandiargues, starring Marina Pierro. He is not aware he is making his last feature film. The movie opens in 1988. It's barely noticed in France — WB writes a long letter to Sarde, accusing him of not caring about the film's distribution and promotion. He demands the unpaid part of his fee and is livid at the changes Sarde tried to enforce (interestingly enough, he claims he's always willing to recut his film, providing there are important reasons to do it, such as meeting the demands of an audience in a specific country), he further denies that the film is "not erotic enough" (quoting French censorship's assessment of the film as "strong"), he criticizes the change of title to *Love Rites (Cérémonie D'Amour)*. At the end of his angry letter, he criticizes Sarde's taste in lingerie.[20] Sarde's reply is curt: he attaches the check and finishes with: "Sending you no regards."[21] In a 1994 interview, WB says of *Love Rites*:

It got rave reviews in Italy. Unfortunately, in France it wasn't marketed well. The producer [Alain Sarde] thought he would get a juicy porno, and when he saw the film I had made, he avenged himself by refusing to promote it. (Borowczyk and Kessler 1994: 100)

When interviewer suggests that "there are rumors of a hard-core version," WB replies:

I wouldn't stand a chance in competition with that. I don't have the ambition. That's a different kind of audience, I think. No, Love Rites *was deliberately soft. (Borowczyk and Kessler 1994: 100)*

1989–94

The last film projects WB finishes are the episodes of a French-German series called *Série rose* (aka *Softly from Paris*), a cycle of 25–30 minute erotic period films, adapted from libertine classics (Mirabeau, de Sade, Retif de la Bretonne, but also Maupassant and la Fontaine). Between 1989 and 1991, WB directs four episodes: an adaptation of a guide (perhaps fictional) to Parisian brothels from 1791 (two years after the French Revolution) (1989); the story of Golden Lotus, a prostitute from ancient China (1990); an adaptation of "The Story of Kamara z-Zaman and His Beloved" from *Arabian Nights* (1991); and one story from Boccaccio's *Decameron* (1991). The latter — which is effectively WB's last film — is a *Blanche*-like variation, starring Marina Pierro. The main character has the same name (which is different from the one in Boccaccio) and an older, jealous husband, who imprisons her in her room, as well as a lover who breaks through the wall to get to her. In sharp contrast to *Blanche*, though, everything ends well — Blanche reaches a climax in the arms of her lover. Again, the comparisons of the two Blanches best capture the difference between WB's two muses, as well as between the two types of characters they played in his films.

Each episode takes place in a different time and space, as well as in a different world: Paris right after the revolution, ancient China, legendary Middle East, and medieval France. As he did before in *Immoral Tales, Behind Convent Walls, Heroines of Evil, Lulu,* and *Dr. Jekyll*, WB is adding new eras and places to his catalog. He is not laissez-faire about his TV work — he prepares himself for the

Arabian Nights episode with the same care he's displayed throughout his career (notes, sketches, storyboards).

In the first half of the 1990s, WB mobilizes himself one last time — he publishes a collection of short stories, and he tries to get financing for new projects. In interviews, he gives a new birth date: 1932, which is nine years later than his actual one. In the Afterword to the Polish edition of *Anatomy of the Devil* ("purposefully egocentric and necessarily autobiographical"), he writes:

> *I was born in Wojnowice, Greater Poland region, in 1932 and not in 1923, as many dictionaries and magazines mistakenly claim. Had I been born in the times of [sixteenth-century Polish poet] Mikołaj Rej, I would be called Walerian Borowczyk of Wojnowice. It's interesting to mention that it was in the same 1932 that Andre Malreaux wrote in his Preface to* Lady Chatterley's Lover: *"Our task is to destroy our sexual myth, to make a value out of the erotic."* (Borowczyk 1993: 131)

The same date is repeated by Christian Kessler, the author of the essay and the interview published by *Video Watchdog* in 1992: "Born in Kwilicz, Poland, in 1932, and not as is usually claimed, in 1923." Furthermore: "When we got together for this interview in the summer of 1992, Walerian Borowczyk appeared to me to be a very friendly, gray-haired man of about 60, not unlike a younger, friendlier version of Samuel Beckett" (Borowczyk and Kessler 1994: 98).

In 1990 WB sends a letter to the makers of *Série rose* (Hamster, FR3, with the name of the series' literary director, Jacques Salles, mentioned). He pitches a project for a contemporary series "Uncommon Loves," attaching descriptions of seven episodes: the first one is "Poverina," which will later be the opening segment of *Anatomy of the Devil*.[22] The same year, he corresponds with Anatole Dauman. He begins cordially: "Dear Friend!" He informs him that "the beautiful country of France" has granted him citizenship, and that from now on he's "France's child (or perhaps its lover?)." He asks Dauman for the permission to change the title of his project *Maternity* to *The Beast 2* (since Argos holds the rights to *The Beast*). He writes: "It will be a nod to the time when I was a free artist, and Anatole Dauman was my producer."[23] Making a reference to the cult title is supposed to prompt funding for the production.

A copy of the script for *Maternity* remains, with WB's handwritten notes; he changes all the names to ones appearing in *The Beast*, making the main female character a member of the l'Esperance family.[24] *The Beast 2* is supposed to be a Polish-French-German coproduction. In an interview for *Gazeta Wyborcza* in 1992, WB says: "It should be popular in Poland. The working title may be *Uncommon Zoophilia*, but its real subject is maternity" (Borowczyk and Bielas 1992: 9). The film is never made.

In 1992, WB publishes a collection of his short stories under the title *Anatomy of the Devil*. He describes them thus: "I want to make the reader feel like he has just left the cinema, with the movie still reverberating in his head. I would also like to adapt some of those stories for the screen" (Borowczyk and Kessler 1994: 101). Mandiargues writes the recommendation. The collection doesn't get many reviews, but the reception is rather positive. The same year, WB sends a letter to the director of the Rome-based company Imp. Ex. Multimedia (using a special letterhead, which mentions all his most important films and affiliations). Again, he pitches the "Uncommon Loves" series, but this time he uses a different formula, closer to *Série rose* — he proposes twenty-one episodes (even though, as he claims, he "could have proposed a hundred as easily"), each taking place in a different place and time. He marks each title with a date when the film is taking place, and the range is considerable, from "Milesiak" based on Aristide de Milet (second century BC), through to Thais (400), Wanda (600), Bocaccio's *Decameron* (1350), right up to Rasputin (1916) and contemporary tales, including stories from *Anatomy of the Devil* ("Blessed Poverina, Patron of Wicked Little Girls," "The Ear, Signed Vincent," and "The Gold Washers"). The list includes several projects he had been developing earlier as feature films: *Love Is Not a Sin* (1960s), *Madness Named Lucia* (1945, based on a Landolfi book), and *Dear Daddy* (Marquis de Sade at Bastille) (1789). Each title is marked by a note, indicating how advanced the work is — six projects are marked as "ready for shooting," three as "résumé prepared," twelve as "needs to be written." He suggests he would like to make *Infamous Dialogues* and *Love Is Not a Sin* first. Just like *Série rose*, the project for "Uncommon Loves" is a catalog of erotic tales.[25] None of them is ever produced.

In 1992 *Immoral Tales* and *The Beast* finally open in Poland. The audience and the critics are rather cool in their reaction. Jacek Szczerba writes in *Gazeta Wyborcza* that:

> Immoral Tales *have lost their edge over the years. It's good that it's paired with Borowczyk's short* A Private Collection, *which brings together some fin*

de siècle erotic toys. Both films should be regarded with the same amused, condescending eye. (Szczerba 1992: 9)

When asked what he thinks of his films opening 20 years after their international premiere, WB says:

It's an interesting experiment. Those films are watched in art houses in the West. They're part of history of film. They get mentioned in encyclopedias. In Poland, someone unprepared may not even notice they were made years ago. I see them as films that are very much contemporary and agreeable to the religious audience. They are erotic, but there is no contraception or abortion in them. Healthy babies are being born. I believe in my educated and cultural viewer. (Borowczyk and Bielas 1992: 9)

Jacek Szczerba will get his just desserts after some years in *What Do I Think When I See a Polish Woman in the Nude*. It will be there, as well, that WB quotes a rumor that some Silesians gave a donation for a special Holy Mass in exchange for the film producer's soul (in a different place, Polish critic Zygmunt Kałużyński claims that the story in fact dealt with Oshima Nagisa's *In the Realm of the Senses* [1976]).

Poland witnesses a significant loosening up of sexual mores — the first issue of *Playboy* magazine is published (TV film critic Tomasz Raczek is the editor-in-chief), Polish television (despite some protests from the Christian party, ZChN) shows the first part of *Emmanuelle*. WB corresponds with Raczek about possible publication of one of his *Anatomy of the Devil* stories in *Playboy*. In an interview WB claims he is still working on the Nefertiti story, this time approaching it as a novel. He says that pornography does not exist objectively; it is created by the eye of the beholder. Question: "It is said that Pasolini, Ferreri, Bertolucci and you had effected a sexual revolution in cinema in 1970s. What kind of a revolution does the cinema need now? What should we drag out to the light of day?" Answer: "We were making movies. Revolution happened afterwards. You should always, without moment's rest, administer blows to stupidity that's spreading around the world" (Borowczyk and Bielas 1992: 9). He praises John Paul II and admits that, because of the pope's poor health, he was considering removing the "Lucrezia Borgia" segment from the Polish version of *Immoral Tales*:

> *I feared being accused of purposeful provocation. ... The Pope just went through surgery. Poles have immense respect of John Paul II. I didn't want to inadvertently hurt someone's feelings or to be accused of referencing the current Pope. (Borowczyk and Bielas 1992: 9)*

He adds that a solution like that wouldn't form a precedent:

> *It was once shown in a truncated version, and I agreed to it. It was in 1981, St. John Night, and* Immoral Tales *were opening a night marathon on French TV. It was right after the attempt on [John Paul II's] life. TV asked my permission to show the film without the final segment. I agreed. (Borowczyk and Bielas 1992: 9)*

He points to the fact that John Paul II is filling painful gaps in the history of the Church and ends by saying: "I believe in Wojtyła the Pope" (Borowczyk and Bielas 1992: 9). (He says similar things of John Paul II in *What Do I Think When I See a Polish Woman in the Nude.*)

After some tribulations with publishing houses (two of them wanted to publish it), *Anatomy of the Devil* is published in Poland (the translation is by Jerzy Lisowski and by Ligia Borowczyk). WB does not come to Poland to promote it, but he sends in a tape with the recorded afterword. In it, he announces he will write *What Do I Think When I See a Polish Woman in the Nude*. In a nod to Boccaccio, whom he quotes at the very beginning, he says:

> *I will cause a cry of wild fury with my book. I will turn into a hissing serpent, but I will bite only the untalented, undistinguished authors. The talented and distinguished ones will be left by me in peace. Zygmunt Kałużyński will comment: "you should read it till the end, and then give some money for the Mass." (Borowczyk 1993: 132)*

The cover of the polish edition is a massive accumulation of enthusiastic words from the reviews of WB's work — a hefty chunk of text, complete with the titles of magazines the reviews come from.

In 1993, WB corresponds with the Polish poet and journalist Artur "Cezar" Krasicki, who requests WB to read his "masturbatory manifesto" (*Wal pókiś młody* [*Beat While You're Young*], 1994). WB responds when the book is already being printed: "Your manifesto is a mature, final blow dealt to the twitching carrion of hypocrisy."²⁶ He has some reservations, though:

> *The expression "to beat the meat", as masculine as it is cruel, has been widely used by the Poles for centuries, but nevertheless we should all avoid torturing our meat, even verbally. Isn't meat healthier when you handle it gently? ... In my film* Immoral Tales, *Therese the Philosopher, as she is slowly reaching climax, discards the cucumber she has been using and opens her prayer book, to find the picture of a man. ... Autoeroticism is not that different from eroticism. It's not self-abuse or aberration, but love of oneself. Autoerotism is a normal and full erotic act, in which orgasm is possible only in contact with another being – usually an imaginary one.*²⁷

He adds that, for him, true masturbatory cinema is the work of Stan Brakhage:

> *As the head of the jury created by the King of Belgium (sic!) to award the best experimental films, I proposed giving the award to a seven-hour film by an American called Stan Brakhage. It was nothing but seven hours of masturbating in front of a mirror! ... A real art house film. It was given the royal honor unanimously.*²⁸

In 1994, WB answers a letter from a Cinémathèque in Grenoble, which is giving him a carte blanche. WB quotes fragments from *Encyclopedia of Film*, namely the entries devoted to pioneers of cinema (Émile Cohl, Emile Reynaud, Georges Méliès), heavily underlining the words "died in poverty," "grave unknown." He asks to honor them with a minute of silence. He's furious at the indifference of various institutions he proposes retrospectives of his short films to. He finishes by saying: "I decided to destroy my films" and quotes Ovid: "We don't know what lies beneath, and you cannot want something you don't know the nature of. Would anyone know of Homer, had *The Illiad*, that immortal work, never seen the light of day?"²⁹

1994–2006

After 1994, WB stops attempting to make new films. In *What Do I Think When I See a Polish Woman in the Nude*, he writes that he "forced himself into retirement." However, several pages later, he praises the video camera and says he shot footage of Natalia Borkowska, Ligia's mother, as she sang (Borowczyk 2007: 65).

Paradoxically, it is at this time that a new generation expresses interest in WB's work. Bertrand Mandico makes a short film inspired by WB in the mid1990s. Hearing of this, WB wants to meet him. The encounter never takes place.

In 1997 WB oversees the preparation of an exhibition of his drawings, sculptures and photos, entitled "Walerian Borowczyk – l'imagination fulgurante" at the Museum of Annecy (the exhibit is curated by Maurice Corbet). The sleeve note in the catalog informs that WB was born "in the first half of the 20th century."

In 1999 the Etiuda & Anima festival in Kraków organizes a retrospective of Borowczyk's films — Borowczyk doesn't want to come; he questions the quality of the prints. The same year, Grażyna Długołęcka, who played Ewa in *Story of Sin*, gives an interview to *Przegląd*, accusing Borowczyk of sexual harassment. WB's reaction is very strong: in 2001, he publishes a book *My Polish Years* (*Moje polskie lata*; Polish edition 2002) in which he defies Długołęcka's charges. A few years later Długołęcka would say that her words were purposely manipulated to make the interview sound more scandalous.[30]

Around the year 2000, WB donates his archive to Cinémathèque Française. More and more often he refuses to attend screenings of his films, saying that the quality of the prints is too low.

In 2001, there's a retrospective of WB's films at LUX in London, curated by Daniel Bird. WB does not attend, even though in his book he will claim to have shown up at the screening of *The Beast* (shown in an uncut version for the first time in the UK) (Borowczyk 2007: 78). The same year, the British channel Film 4 shows *The Beast* in its "Cinema Extreme" series (it is introduced by Mark Kermode), while Terry Gilliam mentions *Angels' Games* as one of his 10 favorite animations of all time. In France, Bertrand Bonello directs *The Pornographer* (2001): according to many, the film is largely inspired by WB's life. In Poland, during the work on a feature film *Island R.O.* (2001), Jan Lenica dies. Lenica's *Island R.O.* apparently had evolved from a project Lenica and WB had once developed in the 1950s. (The first scene of the film is identical to the abandoned Gulliver project.)[31]

In 2003 *Encyclopedia of Cinema*, edited by Tadeusz Lubelski of Jagiellonian University, is published. WB is furious with the entry describing his career; in *What Do I Think When I See a Polish Woman in the Nude* he speaks in vile terms of both Lubelski and his son Julian, who wrote the entry (Borowczyk 2007: 88).

At the same time WB receives a congratulatory letter from the Polish Minister of Culture, Waldemar Dąbrowski — he replies that he greatly appreciates it, but he'd rather see *Blanche* being shown by Polish television (he gave the tape to Zygmunt Kałużyński) (Borowczyk 2007: 90).

Due to the upcoming DVD release of *The Beast* by Cult Classics, Florence Dauman asks Borowczyk to record a short introduction — WB sends her the requested video shot with a digital camera.

In 2004, Rafał Księżyk interviews Borowczyk for *Playboy*. When Księżyk requests some edits, WB withdraws the print permission altogether, then includes his answer in *What Do I Think When I See a Polish Woman in the Nude*.

On 2 February 2006, WB dies in a hospital near Paris; the cause of death is cardiovascular complications due to a heart condition.

In 2007, *What Do I Think When I See a Polish Woman in the Nude* finally appears. There's a quotation from the Polish poet Julian Tuwim on the cover, which serves as a declaration of WB's love for Ligia:

> *And I think, and I recollect, and I remind myself, / And I pray, and I cry, and I shake people's hands, / And I laugh to myself, and I don't know what I'm doing, / And I'm moved as I say: me and my wife, my wife, to my wife ...* (Borowczyk 2007)

Since then, every year there are new exhibitions, publications and retrospectives devoted to WB "b. boro" Borowczyk (1923–2006) — an exhibition in Warsaw's Centre of Modern Art (CSW, 2008); the books: Jeremy Mark Robinson, *Walerian Borowczyk: Cinema of Erotic Dreams* (2008); Pascal Vimenet (ed.), *Walerian Borowczyk* (2009); Alberto Pezzotta (ed.), *Associazioni imprevedibili: Il cinema di Walerian Borowczyk* (2009); Jeremy Mark Robinson, *The Beast: An Erotic Fairy Tale* (2013); Kuba Mikurda and Kuba Woynarowski, *Corpus Delicti* (2013); the films — *Boro in the Box*, directed by Bertrand Mandico (2011); *Himorogi*, directed by Marina and Alessio Pierro (2012); *Obscure Pleasures*, directed by Daniel Bird (2014); retrospectives — T-Mobile New Horizons in Wrocław (2013); and PCI/BFI in London (2014). In 2013, a Kickstarter campaign is introduced with the purpose of digitally restoring *Goto, Isle of Love*. In 2014 Arrow Films releases a unique double format Blu-ray/DVD box set "Camera Obscura" produced by Daniel Bird and Michael Brooke. A restored version of *Dr Jekyll* (with an original WB title — *Dr Jekyll and Miss Osbourne*) follows soon after. In 2015, a book of essays on WB, *Boro, L'Isle D'Amour*, edited by Kamila Kuc, Kuba Mikurda and Michał Oleszczyk is published by Berghahn Books.

Translated by Michał Oleszczyk

Notes

1. Based on Borowczyk's passport application dated 01.09.1980.
2. Based on a conversation with Filip Bajon.
3. Based on a conversation with Daniel Bird.
4. A letter to Lenica in Borowczyk's files at Cinémathèque Française.
5. Borowczyk's files at Cinémathèque Française.
6. Willard van Dyke's letter to Borowczyk in Borowczyk's files at Cinémathèque Française.
7. Based on a conversation with Noël Véry and Daniel Bird's interview with Noël Véry, Dominique Duvergé-Ségrétin and André Heinrich produced for the DVD edition of *Goto, Isle of Love* (Nouveaux Pictures, 2009).
8. A conversation with Noël Véry and Daniel Bird's interview with Noël Véry, Dominique Duvergé-Ségrétin and André Heinrich produced for the DVD edition of *Goto, Isle of Love* (Nouveaux Pictures, 2009).
9. Borowczyk's files at Cinémathèque Française.
10. Borowczyk's files at Cinémathèque Française.
11. Borowczyk's files at Cinémathèque Française.
12. Bohdziewicz's letter to Borowczyk in Borowczyk's files at Cinémathèque Française.
13. Borowczyk's letter to Bohdziewicz in Borowczyk's files at Cinémathèque Française.
14. Based on Daniel Bird's interview with André Heinrich produced for "Camera Obscura" (Arrow Films, 2014).
15. Borowczyk's files at Cinémathèque Française.
16. As quoted on the American poster for *Immoral Tales*.
17. Based on a conversation with David Thompson.
18. Borowczyk's letter to the Hakim brothers in Borowczyk's files at Cinémathèque Française.
19. Based on a conversation with Cherry Potter.
20. Borowczyk's letter to Sarde in Borowczyk's files at Cinémathèque Française.
21. Sarde's letter to Borowczyk in Borowczyk's files at Cinémathèque Française.
22. Borowczyk's files at Cinémathèque Française.
23. Borowczyk's letter to Dauman in Borowczyk's files at Cinémathèque Française.
24. Borowczyk's files at Cinémathèque Française.
25. Borowczyk's files at Cinémathèque Française.
26. Borowczyk's letter to Krasicki, Artur Krasicki's archive.
27. Borowczyk's letter to Krasicki, Artur Krasicki's archive.

28. Borowczyk's letter to Krasicki, Artur Krasicki's archive.
29. Borowczyk's files at Cinémathèque Française.
30. Based on a conversation with Grażyna Długołęcka.
31. Borowczyk's files at Cinémathèque Française.

Bibliography

Borowczyk, W. 1965. "Témoignages: W. Borowczyk." *Etudes Cinématographiques* 20.
Borowczyk, W. 1973. "Wszystkie Moje Filmy Wymyśliłem Jednocześnie – Mówi Walerian Borowczyk." *Film* 9.
Borowczyk, W. 1993. *Anatomia Diabła*. Warszawa: Polski Dom Wydawniczy.
Borowczyk, W. 2000. *Moje Polskie Lata: Dzieje Grzechu*, trans. L. Brokowska. Paris: Hypnos média.
Borowczyk, W. 2007. *Co Myślę Patrząc na Rozebraną Polkę*. Warszawa: Oficyna Wydawnicza Rytm.
Borowczyk, Walerian, Jan Lenica, and Tadeusz Kowalski. 1958. "Ludzie, Którzy Chcą Wrócić do Meliesa." *Film* 51.
Borowczyk, Walerian, Jacques Rivette, Michel Delahaye, and Pierre Sylvie. 1969. "Entretien avec Walerian Borowczyk." In *Cahiers du Cinema*, no 209.
Borowczyk, Walerian. 1973. "Wszystkie Moje Filmy Wymyśliłem Jednocześnie – Mówi Walerian Borowczyk." *Film* 9.
Borowczyk, Walerian and Andrzej Markowski. 1975. "Erotyka Łagodzi Obyczaje." *Film* 4.
Borowczyk, Walerian and Susan Adler. 1985. "Enticements to Voyeurism." *Cinema Papers* 50.
Borowczyk, Walerian and Katarzyna Bielas. 1992. "Anatomia Diabła." *Gazeta Wyborcza* 262.
Borowczyk, Walerian and Christian Kessler. 1994. "The Borowczyk Inquistion." *Video Watchdog Special Edition* 1.
Borowczyk, Walerian, Jean-Paul Sarré and Anatole Dauman. 2004. "Jean-Paul Sarré and Anatole Dauman interview Walerian Borowczyk." In *Beast Bis: The Work of Walerian Borowczyk. A DVD booklet for Cult Epics: The Beast. Special Edition*.
Borowczyk, Walerian and Rafał Księżyk. 2006. "Piękno i Bestie: Rafał Księżyk Talks to Walerian Borowczyk." *Film* 4.
Hollender, Barbara and Zofia Turowska. 2000. *Zespół Tor*. Warszawa: Prószyński i S-ka.
Jackiewicz, A. 1964. "Zapiski Krytyczne: Borowczyk." *Film* 27.
Jackiewicz, A. 1969a. "Aktualności." *Film* 10.
Jackiewicz, A. 1969b. "Zapiski Krytyczne: Debiut Fabularny Borowczyka." *Film* 19.
Jackiewicz, A. 1969c. "Zapiski Krytyczne: Boro." *Film* 25.
Kristel, S. 2010. *Undressing Emmanuelle: A Life Stripped Bare*. New York: Harper Perennial.
Różewicz, S. 2012. "Reżyser to Chirurg i Psycholog." *Przegląd* 48.

Różewicz, T. 1948. *Czerwona Rękawiczka*. Warszawa: Spółdzielnia Wydawnicza "Książka."
Szczerba, J. 1992. "Zwietrzały Libertynizm." *Gazeta Wyborcza* 198.
Tohill, Cathal and Pete Tombs. 1995. *Immoral Tales: European Sex & Horror Movies, 1956–1984*. New York: St. Martin's Griffin.

Filmography

Archival TV and radio interviews from *Institut national de l'audiovisuel*.
Borowczyk self-interview for *The Beast* (Cult Epics, 2004).
Boro in the Box (2011), directed by Bertrand Mandico.
Himorogi (2012), directed by Marina and Alessio Pierro (2012).
Obscure Pleasures (2014), directed by Daniel Bird (Borowczyk interviewed by Keith Griffiths).
Interviews with Borowczyk's collaborators directed and produced by Daniel Bird for "Camera Obscura" (Arrow Films 2014), *The Story of Sin* (Nouveaux Pictures, 2004), *Goto, Isle of Love* (Nouveaux Pictures, 2009).

Kuba Mikurda is a filmmaker and film scholar, and "Linia Filmowa" book series editor (Korporacja Ha!art Press). He has edited and co-edited books about contemporary filmmakers (Terry Gilliam, Brothers Quay, Guy Maddin, Tsai Ming-liang) and surrealism in Polish cinema (with Kamila Wielebska). He teaches at the Film School in Łódź. In 2013 he published *Corpus Delicti*, a visual essay about Borowczyk's objects (designed in collaboration with Jakub Woynarowski), and he has directed a feature documentary, *Love Express. The Disappearance of Walerian Borowczyk* (2018), for HBO Europe.

CHAPTER 2
Borowczyk's Kunstkamera
Marcin Giżycki

Walerian Borowczyk or Boro, once upon a time, was a darling of French film critics, praised by the likes of Terry Gilliam and idolized by Brothers Quay. Had he only completed two feature films — *Goto, Isle of Love* (1968) and *Blanche* (1971) — his place in the history of cinema would still be secure. Fortunately, he did make many more films besides these two — and many of them are in fact crucial for understanding his more famous works.

In almost every article published in Poland after his death in 2006, one could read that he was an artist almost completely unknown in his own country. In recent years, though, there have been exhibitions held in Warsaw and Poznań, combined with a film retrospective and an international academic conference. Serious scholarship has been devoted to his work. He has been analyzed (and rightfully so) from the perspective of gender studies. Collections of his own writings have been published, including literary pieces, journalism, autobiography, and polemics. The latter reveal, incidentally, that there have been a significant number of texts written on Borowczyk in Poland already — if not in the spirit the director himself would approve of.

Upon his death, the Polish media was filled with obituaries, most of which painted a portrait of a pornographer (if not a sex addict, plain and simple). Stories of Boro's own sins became public knowledge. Suddenly one could read a lot about him, as well as track down his work online: most of it ripped in horrific low resolution, sometimes carved into pieces, with the wrong soundtrack added — but still, giving at least some idea of his artistic choices and sensibilities.

The Polish problem when it comes to Boro is not exactly oblivion, then, but rather the monotonous way in which he is usually portrayed. This book, devoted entirely to the enfant terrible of world cinema, should provide a good opportunity to appraise his work anew, so that the obvious erotic traits of it don't overshadow its other, noteworthy aspects. It can also serve as a reminder that, prior to his career as a scandal-maker, Borowczyk was widely regarded as an innovative, highly original animator. Even if that reputation became somewhat tarnished in his later years — not always through Borowczyk's fault — one should pay close attention to his animated work in order to understand his later, live-action films. As it happens, there are four keys to Boro's sensibility: surrealism, Hy Hirsch, kunstkamera, and automata.

Surrealism

Borowczyk and his early collaborator, Jan Lenica, represent that rare breed of Polish filmmakers who openly claimed their spiritual affinity to surrealism. Boro also repeatedly expressed his fascination with curious gadgets, including erotic ones of course, as well as with assorted rubbish of the type one could find in a forgotten attic. His passion for collecting is more than obvious in *A Private Collection* (1973), in which he presents some of the pieces he had acquired (as well as crafted, although that is not admitted within the film). It is not necessary, however, to be acquainted with that short film in order to recognize that Borowczyk, just like Max Ernst and André Breton before him, was an uncommon connoisseur of old-fashioned illustrations and trinkets. This is immediately apparent in films such as *Once Upon a Time* (1957) and *House* (1958), both made with Lenica. In the former, pieces of old drawings come to life, and in the latter, not only old lithographs, photos and postcards have lives of their own, but also objects get animated — such as a mannequin's head and an all-devouring wig.

The surrealists, and Dadaists before them, showed great devotion to ordinary objects. By juxtaposing them in paradoxical ways, they freed unexpected meanings contained within them. "Beautiful as the accidental encounter, on a dissecting table, of a sewing machine and an umbrella" — one of the works by Man Ray (*L'Enigme d'Isidore Ducasse*) was inspired by that very phrase. Marcel Duchamp went as far as exhibiting a urinal as a work of art (a banal gesture nowadays, not so in 1917).

For Borowczyk, practically any object can become a fetish. He salutes them; he looks at them with great attention. In *Renaissance* (1963), a group of objects locked inside a fin-de-siècle room (a table, a wicker basket, a family photograph, a porcelain-headed doll, a trumpet, some books, a religious picture, an alarm clock, etc.) are literally reborn from the ashes left by an explosion — together with a hand grenade, which will explode as soon as the rebirth is complete (and thus start the cycle all over again). What we witness is a paradoxically reversed circle of life: annihilated objects materialize anew and rejuvenate before our eyes, only to turn into nothingness again and so on into infinity. Can one imagine a more forceful statement of faith in the everlasting power of objects? In their magical force? In their hidden life? Witness the ostentatious manner in which the rebirth happens. It's not achieved by the mere act of "reversing the tape", as many incorrectly believed. It's a veritable spectacle of matter in movement. The props don't just reconstruct themselves, as if a magic wand has just touched them. They flaunt their proprieties; they dance and present themselves — they are enjoying their regained existence prior to returning to their proper positions where a new, inevitable destruction will await them in the wings. Ka-boom!

Hy Hirsch

Speaking of explosions; at the very beginning of *Renaissance*, on the panel preceding the story itself, Borowczyk provides us with one more hint that could help us unlock the origins of his own art. He dedicates the film to Hy Hirsch. I may be wrong, but I don't recall any scholarship that has tried to unravel the meaning of that gesture. Hirsch (1911–61), though quite forgotten nowadays, is definitely one of the true spiritual fathers of Borowczyk's oeuvre. Older than the Polish artist by some twelve years, Hirsch worked as a cameraman and film editor in Hollywood, but he gained true recognition as a photographer. He worked in advertising. In the 1930s and 1940s, he did help several young filmmakers on the West Coast (the likes of Harry Smith, Jordan Belson, and Larry Jordan), who then went on to become pioneering artists of American film avant-garde. Later on, Hirsch himself followed in their footsteps and made his own abstract films of considerable beauty. In 1955, he moved to Paris (where Boro would soon become his neighbor) and started to photograph dug-out streets, houses falling apart, pale remnants of advertisements, and walls full of old, torn posters. The latter photos — spontaneous urban collages — particularly interested the future *nouveaux réalistes*, who (just like their contemporaries in the pop art movement in the United States and England, and, prior to them, the surrealists themselves), developed a veritable cult of ordinary objects and popular art. Hirsch died suddenly of a heart attack, just as nouveau réalisme started to emerge. He would forever remain the incomparable poet of the rubbish heap. You can recognize Hirsch's world in the scorched room of *Renaissance*; in its peeling wallpaper, sooty photographs, remnants of furniture, and pieces of objects scattered around.

Kunstkamera

Objects themselves, as well as collections of them, play an important role in Borowczyk's oeuvre, which leads us to the concept of kunstkamera — of the filmmaker as a collector and connoisseur of things. As was stated before, Boro loved gadgets and curios. It is with equal fondness that he gazes upon the (quite revolting) flytrap in *Goto, Isle of Love* and the antique spring-powered fan in *Story of Sin* (1975). In *Angels' Games* (1964), an entire arsenal of objects is gathered and presented — most of them are machines of torture. In *Rosalie* (1966), pieces of evidence gathered in a courtroom seem to interest the filmmaker more than the main character herself. These are seemingly ordinary objects — a belt, manicure tools, bed sheets, a shovel — but as soon as exhibit labels are attached to them, they cease to be ordinary. In *Goto*, a classroom is full of glass cases filled with scientific paraphernalia of unknown purpose. The entire film is, in fact, filled with objects like that. In the short documentary portrait of the painter Ljuba Popović (*The Greatest Love of All Time* [1977]), the camera pays as close attention to the brushes, paint tubes, palettes, and hammers as it does to the paintings by the Serbian artist themselves. The spectacle of married life of the Kabals (in *The Concert of Mr. and Mrs. Kabal* [1962] and *Theatre of Mr. and Mrs. Kabal* [1967]) is in fact an illusionist's seance, in which the props — instruments, trunks, "severed" limbs — become the actors proper. This list of Borowczykian objects could be extended forever. The conclusion, however, remains consistent: people in Boro's films, as consumed by passion as they are, are subservient to the objects, not the other way around.

Automata

Or perhaps the people are mere objects, as well …? Human characters in Borowczyk's films often seem like robots. B-o-r-o: four out of five letters necessary to spell "robot." A coincidence? In his early animated shorts, such as *School* (1958), the artist has literally animated his actors. First, he took pictures of them with a still camera, and then he photographed the photographs, shaping movement upon the editing table. Still, the mechanical — perhaps even soulless — quality that ensued in the characters' appearance on the screen had perhaps originated from the director's interest in yet another category of peculiar objects: namely, automata.

In *A Private Collection*, we see a few simple automata: erotic toys, such as a copulating couple, masturbating doll, etc. It is not difficult to imagine an actual automaton being included in the collection. An automaton is not just a robot — rather, it is a mechanical mannequin, a humanoid, or (in its modern incarnation, as it were) an android. It is a human-made, human-like object, designed to perform specific tasks. Literature knows both intelligent and unintelligent automata. The height of automata popularity (the first examples of which date back to ancient times) is to be found in the eighteenth and nineteenth century. Automata were constructed most often by watchmakers, including Pierre Jacquet-Droz (1721–90) and his son Henri Louis Jacquet-Droz (1752–91), whose reincarnation can be found in *The Piano Tuner of Earthquakes* (2005), a feature film by avowed Borowczyk admirers, Brothers Quay.

Automata were also designed by Jean Eugène Robert-Houdin (1805–71), a famous illusionist and watchmaker by trade. It was soon after the famed magician's death that his theater, located in Montmartre, was bought by none other than the greatest magician of the silver screen Georges Méliès (1861–1938), with many of Robert-Houdin's handmade props still stored inside. Most likely, it is due to this fact that Brian Selznick, the author of the book that became the basis for Martin Scorsese's *Hugo* (2011), included an automaton made by the maker of *A Trip to the Moon* (1902) in his story. I believe that for Borowczyk, the mere idea that the Méliès he loved so much could have also manufactured automata, had to be truly inspiring.

With no true automata at his disposal, Borowczyk did his best to turn his actors into ones. Not so much by means of making their movements seem mechanical (even though some purposeful artifice is easily discernible in Borowczyk's direction of actors), but by means of psychology. Characters in Boro's films act as if they are programmed; fixated upon a single idea — whether we discuss the corporal from *Goto*, the baron from *Blanche* or the Count Bodzanta and the bandit Pochroń from *Story of Sin*. The longing for a living automaton is to be found also in one of Borowczyk's short stories collected in the volume *Anatomy of the Devil*. A little girl lures the male character to a run-down palace in Venice, where her sister is performing sex acts for money. After she removes her clothes, though, the sister appears to be a robot from the waist down: "A surrealist creation, a siren; half incarnation of divine beauty, half the work of a master craftsman" (Borowczyk 2014: 20).

Borowczyk's films are kunstkameras: curiosity shops, the owner of which is meticulously arranging his trophies, cataloging and dusting them, and describing them. He then removes these trophies from their cases and drawers, so that for a brief moment they live a film life of their own — until the great "ka-boom" happens yet again.

Translated by Michał Oleszczyk

Bibliography

Borowczyk, W. 2014. *Anatomy of a Devil: Short Stories*, trans. M. Levy. London: Arrow Films.

Marcin Giżycki is an Associate Professor at the Katowice School of Technology, Poland. He is an Artistic Director of the International Animated Film Festival *Animator* in Poland and a Senior Lecturer at the Rhode Island School of Design in Providence. He is the author of seven books and a number of documentary, experimental and animated films.

CHAPTER 3
Animated Bodies
A Conversation between
Kuba Mikurda and Jakub Woynarowski

Kuba Mikurda: Borowczyk many times swore that there were no "periods" within his work and that "all of his films [were] conceived in an instant," with only technical factors determining the actual order he made them in (Borowczyk 1973: 2). Still, scholars of Boro usually divide his filmography according to technical and generic criteria. This results in a division between animated and live-action films (as well as, perhaps, his short and feature-length work), and his artistic and erotic work. These classifications seem obvious at first, since we've become accustomed to these criteria. Still, as we watch Boro's films we quickly become aware of just how arbitrary and disputable they are. Boro himself had vocally protested all descriptions of himself as a "specialist" in anything (be it animation, erotica, or anything else) and it seems it wasn't pure contrarianism on his part; rather, an artistic consequence.

Jakub Woynarowski: I believe that Boro's intermedia thinking — blurring distinctions between particular media — is somewhat characteristic of many visual artists making a crossover into filmmaking. Besides Borowczyk, one could also mention such people as Peter Greenaway, David Lynch, Terry Gilliam, or Jan Švankmajer. Modern art is necessarily interdisciplinary in its nature — it's predominantly conceptual, not technological. It happens more often than not that the choice of a particular medium results from particular ideas. Even if the starting point is provided by a particular medium or a specific technique, the finished work is often self-reflexive. Borowczyk himself, in his work, concentrated on a variety of "missteps" (and stressed it in various interviews and texts); moments in which the tension between the idea and the medium becomes clearer than it usually is. This approach is quite typical of many artists working in the period following the great avant-garde, of which Borowczyk was also an heir (chiefly through his deliberate allusions to surrealist traits). It is not particularly surprising, then, that Borowczyk puts his live-action and his animated efforts into a single category — for him, every film is about animating static images. It is through statements like that that he points our attention to the category of montage — animation in the classic sense of the word is really a film in which the dynamics of the image is a consequence of a particularly dense accumulation of spliced edits.

KM: Do you have the impression that there is something in his multimedia approach that can be branded as vivacious, spontaneous, or perhaps even naïve (as in naïve art, so valued by Borowczyk)? Don't you think that his art is motivated by a kind of child-like curiosity, making him try this and that (and that ... and that, too!) ...? In some of his interviews, he says that in order to realize all of his ideas he would need around 300 years. In others, he frequently states that only form matters; that only form provides one with room for inventiveness and originality. His shorts all top one another in terms of the sheer amount of ideas — every single one has something new and fresh to offer. Anyone who ever worked with Boro stresses that he worked very quickly; that it was difficult to keep up with him–he would start a new project as soon as he finished the previous one. It is not without reason that he named his production company "Allegro!"

JW: This rush and being incapable of keeping up with all of his ideas is often mentioned by Peter Greenaway. He also doesn't see film as a "synthesis of other arts," but considers the medium to belong to a yet bigger group, which also includes literature, multimedia installations, and even computer games. Greenaway likes to rub filmmakers up the wrong way by saying how imitative of painting film really is. Terry Gilliam also comments on the curiosity one can witness in the works by many a creative filmmaker-artist: "Most artists would agree that the main goal is to open our eyes to the world. Sometimes all you need to do is deconstruct something, turn a thing upside down, in order to look at it in an entirely different way" (Gilliam cited in Mikurda and Woynarowski 2011).

KM: There's also David Lynch, who you mentioned before. Asked about the reason he makes films, Boro said that there's something "in his hands." There's a similar thing going on with Lynch: just like Boro, he also makes props and set decoration himself, and when he is not shooting a movie he "busies his hands" with something else, such as sculpture, installations, or furniture. Boro also made furniture, and closed himself off within a deserted factory in order to make *Goto, Isle of Love* (1968) — just like Lynch did when he was making *Eraserhead* (1977). One more thing: I think that neither Boro nor Lynch treat feature films as the primary, most prestigious form of expression available. And that's often the unspoken assumption, providing a career model still perceived as "obvious" — a filmmaker's development should proceed toward making a feature film. Everything she or he is making beforehand — be it commercials, music videos, installations, shorts — count only as exercises and dry runs. It is the feature that provides the actual test and serves as a rite of passage, making or breaking a "real" filmmaker. Boro always stated something to the contrary: to him, a feature film is a form like any other; the advantage of which is that the way the distribution business is set up it reaches the largest number of viewers.

JW: Besides, someone who is accustomed to relative freedom in the art world will have trouble succumbing to the professional logic that defines so much of the film world (as well as to the hierarchical mode of thinking that pervades it quite strongly). An artist like that will always feel a bit like a play-loving kid forced into a classroom. For a true intermedia artist, film is only one of many tools at her or his disposal: it can easily be discarded once it's drained of further potential. It is similar with Borowczyk, who didn't eschew his art-world habits once he made the crossover into the world of feature filmmaking. What's more, he continued to explore new territories, as his late "sound sculptures" testify.

KM: Yes, one could say that for Boro a feature film itself is an exhibition space of sorts: one which he uses to display his objects, installations, illustrations, calligraphy, or animations. In a way, his every film is a "private collection," only with proportion reversed: while in *A Private Collection* (1973) objects dominate the story completely, in Boro's feature films they succumb to it, albeit not fully. Animation never disappears completely from Boro's films — and I do not only mean animated inserts, like the motif of a painting that opens and closes its eyes (present in the short commercial *The Museum* [1964] and then repeated in *Emmanuelle 5* [1987]), or animating photographs and drawings by rapid camera movement. I mean mostly the situations in which characters themselves become animators, by using their own hands or various contraptions that make images move. Lucrezia Borgia does it in *Immoral Tales* (1975), when she flips separate images of a horse's penis, so that it hardens and becomes limp again. Or scenes in which a character leafs through a book of illustrations, handles paintings, or even destroys them — like Lucy in *The Beast* (1975), Thérese the Philosopher in the second segment of *Immoral Tales*, or Fanny in *The Strange Case of Dr. Jekyll and Miss Osbourne* (1982). Not to mention *The Greatest Love of All Time* (1976), which is entirely focused on the painter's hand transforming his canvass, or *A Private Collection*, in which images are "triggered" into movement in a variety of ways — including by making gestures, releasing springs, pressing levers, and light exposure, etc.

JW: This sort of "animation" can also be defined as supplying widely known paintings from the history of art with backstories. You have just mentioned *The Museum*, in which paintings live a life of their own after the opening hours are over. In several other of Boro's films, paintings also "descend from the walls:" the beast in an animated version of Józef Podkowiński's *Frenzy of Exultations (Szał uniesień)* which actually hangs on one of the walls inside the l'Esperance mansion; the three main characters of *Heroines of Evil* (1979) are a bit like Raphael's *Three Graces*– a painting left on show under the opening credits. The first segment of that film tells the story of Margherita, who poses for Raphael's *La Fornarina*. In *The Art of Love* (1983), we see tableaux vivants adapted from Roman frescoes. Each of those images is known to us from their respective museum context, which takes away all possibility of movement from them — it is Borowczyk's work that sets them in motion anew; it serves almost as a Dionysian supplement to those Apollonian images.

KM: There is yet another way of "animating" images and objects, which is by presenting them in reaction shots. The grammar of film editing has accustomed us to the situation in which a narratively important moment is punctuated by a reaction shot of a character. In Boro's films, that reaction shot space is often occupied by close-ups of objects, as if such objects were observing the scene and reacting to it. Thanks to this device, the film projects emotions on objects. Just as Brothers Quay, who have openly admitted they were influenced by him, Boro shoots objects as if they were people and people as if they were objects. As he said in an interview for *Cahiers du Cinéma,* actors are like paper cutouts for him. An anecdote from the set of *Goto, Isle of Love* has it that it was in this very way that Boro was directing the distinguished French actor Pierre Brasseur. He shouted at him during the making of the shot: "The actor enters! The actor goes left! The actor raises his hand!" Brasseur, aghast, ordered him to shut up: he was not accustomed to such "manual control."

JW: One could also say that in Borowczyk's cinema, human figures either resemble dolls (as when they are presented in wider shots against a flat, box-like space), or they simply become groups of separate objects ("cut out" of a bigger whole with the framing eye of the camera). In Borowczyk, the defragmented body is an animated still life, just like in Arcimboldo's paintings and with Jan Švankmajer (influenced by Arcimboldo), who films people in a manner strikingly similar to that of Boro, to mention only the fetishist close-ups of bodies in *Conspirators of Pleasure* (1996). Incidentally, a lot connects Boro and Švankmajer: their concentration on objects, blurring the lines between live-action and animation, fascination with crime and erotic excess, surrealist inspirations, variations on literary classics, combining film and art practices, as well as conflict with communist censorship.

KM: And their disdain for Disney! For Boro, Disney is public enemy number one. He accuses him of three things: slavish realism, turning animation into industry, and sexual hypocrisy. First of all, the realist drawings in Disney films meant, to Boro, a true betrayal of imagination and animation alike. Of all the possibilities offered by animation, Disney chose the simple recreation of reality, sometimes with a layer of visual effects on top. That was unforgivable in Boro's view. Second of all, Disney's practice of dividing the work between teams of designers and animators took away the personal and craftsman-like dimension from animation, and it was that dimension that was particularly valued by Boro. Cinema, as he strongly believed, ceased to be an art once industry had replaced the artisan, eschewing individual craft in favor of an army of "specialists." To Robert Benayoun's opinion that "all animators are alchemists," he replied that indeed he does feel like an alchemist, for alchemy contains an element of risk — an alchemist never knows what the result of her or his experiment will be.[1] Disney, to the contrary, was a mere chemist for him — someone who had worked out a formula and stuck to it. The formula proved to be so potent that Disney's films are in fact being made long after Disney's death. Third of all, Boro detected hypocrisy in Disney — his toying with sexual fantasies, accompanied by a strong denial of all elements that could be deemed unpalatable by the widest possible audience. All you have to do is compare Boro's *The Beast* with Disney's *Beauty and the Beast* (1991) — two films exploring the very same fantasy — to see just what he meant.

JW: What we are looking at here are, in fact, two lines of animation's historical development: one commercial, one experimental. In the case of the former, the frame of reference is provided by conventional film production, in the case of the latter we are dealing with widely defined intermedia art. One provides the viewer with a programmed message, the other with an open structure susceptible to a variety of interpretations. It is useful to remember in this context that film's prehistory is identical to the history of animation. Until the "moving photograph" actually arrived, cinema belonged to a different order altogether — one that could be defined (following Julian Antonisz, the Polish apologist of non-camera animation) as a "visual-locksmith-mechanical-entertainment-illusionist-optical experiment" (Antonisz and Fejkiel 1980: 21). Before the Lumière Brothers' invention became popularized, one could actually argue that there existed a veritable universe of non-camera intermedia animation, actively co-created by the viewer. As Antonisz so aptly observed: "It is this very branch of cinema in which thousands of ideas became obsolete. It is by unearthing those matters and by connecting them to new techniques that one can achieve a wondrously new quality" (Antonisz and Fejkiel 1980: 21). Ewa Borysiewicz analyzed this aspect extensively in her book on his work, *Kinetic Rush* (*Rausz kinetyczny*). According to her diagnosis, non-camera filmmaking should be perceived as a political project, as defined by Jacques Rancière: one that frees the author from the bounds of institutionalized rules and one that activates the viewer by means of recreating the intimate, carnal bond between the work itself and its viewing public (Borysiewicz 2013: 74). Pre-cinematographic machines, which used elementary forms of animation, were often — especially in a fairground context — closely connected to the sphere of the body. It's not irrelevant to remind ourselves of the etymology of a term like "peep show," which denotes a spectacle looked upon through the symbolic keyhole, associated equally with pre-cinematographic animation and with forbidden eroticism. This, in fact, provides also the meeting point for experimental animation and pornography. It's undoubtedly the point at which key traits of Borowczyk's sensibility all intertwine — he was, in fact, an apologist for cinema of the senses, cinema freed from institutionalized restrictions. The full realization of that goal was, according to his own statements, to make films without using the camera. He also asked the next logical question: if there is cinema without the camera, is there cinema without the projector?

KM: Well, is there?

JW: The answer to that question is to be found in cinema's pungent prehistory, full of technological solutions that are very far from the formatted definition of cinema that dominated the twentieth century. That forgotten world is filled with erotic machinery not unlike the contraptions presented by Borowczyk in *A Private Collection,* as well as with kinetic objects similar to those populating Boro's exhibitions of "sound sculptures." It is also, most definitely, the area of cinema in which — apart from visual and aural substance — the tactile dimension comes in with full force. In non-camera cinema the film image is irrevocably joined with the director's physical body, which serves quite literally as the originating point of screen illusion. In Antonisz's case, the tactile dimension was closely connected to the "seismographic" apparatus, which transferred the movements of the animator's hand onto the film stock. In Andrzej Pawłowski's work, the spontaneously created "kineforms" were brought into existence by means of improvised operations within the projection machine itself. In Stan Brakhage's oeuvre, tactility was connected to physical found objects, attached and pasted onto film stock, of which fragments of plants or moth's wings are only two of the most popular examples. In the contemporary context, interesting examples of tactile cinema are provided by the Lebanese artist Rabih Mroué, who did the exhibition dOCUMENTA (13) in 2012, which included a series of flipbooks based on YouTube videos, all documenting the deaths of civilians during the recent war in Syria (Mroué and Lambert 2012). In order to watch the few seconds of film, the viewer had to flip through a booklet containing an incredibly drastic succession of images. This is a perfect example of non-projector cinema serving as a political work. The artist himself said that he wanted to get people more engaged in what they were watching. The brutal realism of those records stands in sharp contrast with the mode of presentation, typical of devices much more "entertaining" in their character, which has been known from time immemorial. It is also important to remember that the old pre-cinematographic machines also could have fulfilled a cathartic function. A good example is the screenings organized with the use of a fantascope in eighteenth-century Paris, the function of which was to relieve the trauma of revolutionary terror. In the end, the screenings were banned by the authorities as a form of political activity. Incidentally, the classic "magic lantern" has much in common technically with modern animation. The direct heirs of that tradition were not the Lumières, but the artists inspired by the Georges Méliès tradition; George himself was often avidly invoked by Borowczyk.

KM: The "back to Méliès" approach can be looked at in a wider context, as coming back to the "cinema of attractions." Tom Gunning used this term to describe films from the early silent cinema period, which "showed" more than they "told" — special effects and visual attractions were more important than the plot itself. Boro's films stem from this very tradition (Gunning 1986). Both in his animations and in his "erotic" films, Boro doesn't really tell stories, nor does he develop characters — he multiplies strong visual elements, which Sergei Eisenstein termed "attractions," understanding the term as a concrete measure of analyzing a film. The attraction is designed to animate the viewer's body; it's the exact meeting point of animation and eroticism. In *Joachim's Dictionary* (1965), the word "animation" is visually explained in precisely this way: we see an animated body, namely a finger stretching and flexing in a variety of ways. Boro admits that this is his goal: first to move the viewer and only then invite reflection on the viewer's part: "Film should be perceived in the most basic way, *physically*. It is through the eye and the ear that the centers of thinking get moved."[2] Interestingly enough, film scholar and found footage artist Peter Tscherkassky tried to prove in his film *Coming Attractions* (2010) that it is within advertising that cinema of attractions is best preserved as an influence. Some examples of that are provided by Borowczyk's own commercials, including *The Museum*, *Tom Thumb* (1966), and *Holy Smoke* (1963) — one of his most overtly political films!

JW: It's true that what we are dealing with here is not so much animated cinema as cinema that animates the viewer, who remains corporally involved in the production of cinematic illusion. This participation becomes even stronger due to the employment of sound, which can also be instrumental in the construction of film space. In such animations as *Theatre of Mr. and Mrs. Kabal* (1967), *The Astronauts* (1959), or *Angels' Games* (1964), their elaborate soundtracks become the substitute for the tactile dimension mentioned before. By means of gaining specific acoustics, the depicted world becomes all the more tangible, and what follows is more real. Sound for Borowczyk is often hyper-expressive, though, bordering on traumatic; in his films a living organism is either an automaton undergoing elaborate torture or annihilating itself in a self-destructive drive. *Angels' Games* provides us with an especially apt illustration of that, since the film is focused on the degradation of the human form, which becomes a piece of meat digested by an elaborate, mechanical system. The acoustic "concert" transports the viewer outside the boundaries of make-believe, which is usually associated with animation. I think that those experiences with sonic material in film have then influenced Borowczyk's "sound sculptures." Just like with pre-cinematographic toys, the illusion was triggered only under the condition of a viewer's participation. The sonic "interaction" was supposed to be enhanced by a specifically designed color code.

KM: All this is very consistent. For example, elements of the sculptures connected with movement are usually red. Similar things happens on the storyboards: Boro draws them with a single color, then marks in red the elements that are supposed to be moving and thus attract the viewer's attention. In certain animations, like *Scherzo Infernal* (1984), the color red marks erotic zones. Red is used selectively in both *Theatre of Mr. and Mrs. Kabal* and in *Goto* as the color of blood, which appears only briefly in *Goto*, thus announcing the epic bath of blood in *Immoral Tales*. As Boro said himself, his strategy is to turn color into a stimulus; he wants the viewer (accustomed to colors in the everyday world and in run-of-the-mill cinema) to witness and feel the color anew.

JW: I think that these are the instances when Borowczyk's "artistic" temperament finds its fulfillment. One of the main goals of avant-garde and post avant-garde art, especially if it's rooted in the strategy of subversion, is to attempt to make the viewer reconsider her or his ready-made beliefs in well-known reality. It's not about facile relativism, but about a truly political fight with the oppression of propaganda, hiding itself underneath common wisdom. Instead of absorbing the ready-made interpretational clichés and allowing one to "comprehend" reality quickly and painlessly, one should chiefly (and this is what Boro seems to be attempting) try to experience it once again, this time with full awareness, using the sensual instruments that our body provides us with.

Notes

1. In an interview from *Obscure Pleasures* (2014) directed by Daniel Bird, featured on Arrow Films' *Camera Obscura* (2014).
2. In a letter from 26 August 1961, found in Borowczyk's archive at Cinémathèque Française.

Bibliography

Antonisz, Julian and Jan Fejkiel. 1980. "Film Skończył Się z Nadejściem Braci Lumière ... Rozmowa z Julianem Antoniszem." *Kultura* 27.
Borowczyk, W. 1973. "Wszystkie Moje Filmy Wymyśliłem Jednocześnie – Mówi Walerian Borowczyk." *Film* 9.
Borysiewicz, E. 2013. *Rausz Kinetyczny: Animacja Bezkamerowa Antonisza Jako Projekt Polityczny*. Warszawa: Stowarzyszenie 40 000 Malarzy and Zachęta Narodowa Galeria Sztuki.
Gunning, T. 1986. "The Cinema of Attractions." *White Angle* (8)3–4.
Mikurda, Kuba, Jakub Woynarowski, et al. 2011. "Wezmę to, to i to: Z Terrym Gilliamem Rozmawiają Autorzy Książki." In K. Mikurda (ed.), *Wunderkamera: Kino Terry'ego Gilliama*. Warszawa and Kraków: MFF Nowe Horyzonty/ Korporacja Ha!art.
Mroué, Rabih and U. G. Lambert. 2012. "Interview with dOCUMENTA (13) Artist Rabih Mroué." Retrieved 10 December 2015 from http://premierartscene.com/magazine/rabih-mroue-interview.

Jakub Woynarowski graduated from the Academy of Fine Arts in Kraków where he teaches institutional criticism, the archeology of avant-garde and post-humanist philosophy. He is an interdisciplinary artist, designer and independent curator and has created many projects located between theory and practice of visual arts. He is co-editor of the books *Wunderkamera* (2011) and *Corpus Delicti* (2013), a member of the editorial board of Korporacja Ha!art, and the author of the artistic project exhibited at the Polish Pavilion at the 14th Architectural Biennale in Venice. He was awarded the prestigious "Polityka Passport" as the Artist of the Year 2014.

CHAPTER 4
Cruel Imagination
Borowczyk's Post-traumatic Surrealism

Iwona Kurz

> *There are numerous historical precedents or analogies in* Erzsébet Báthory *– of inquisitions and pogroms and invasions. Borowczyk has evoked a violent invasion in the village scene that wouldn't be out of place in many a historical epic movie. There are further layers to this episode in* Immoral Tales, *though – and that is the concentration camps. It didn't strike me the first couple of times I watched the film, but the images of women being rounded up and taken away and then prepared in showers in order to be killed for some tyrant evokes the ovens [...] [It] is about a mass murderer, after all, even though it seduces the viewer with beautiful imagery and plenty of nudity.*
> —Jeremy Mark Robinson, *Walerian Borowczyk: Cinema of Erotic Dreams* (2008)

Those words were written by Jeremy M. Robinson in the first (and for a long time the only) monograph of Walerian Borowczyk. The book is both devotional and enthusiastic in tone, with all the strengths and weaknesses implied by such an approach. The author does not, in fact, offer a uniform and cohesive interpretation of the work by the artist who gave us *Story of Sin* (1975), but instead presents a long catalog of issues that one can and should consider in relation to the work in question. The perspective Robinson assumes is one of a seemingly naïve viewer: specific film images speak to him only in relation to other film images. The images are similar to each other and connected to one another — together, they create a configuration of sorts.

Within that configuration are pictures depicting various forms of violence, especially the violence that dominated the twentieth-century; how we imagine the Holocaust is a very special case. Those images are shrouded in taboo; the

Holocaust is revealed to be the last stand in which the rule of appropriateness can be applied by many viewers and executed (as well as internalized) by many artists. This is why it seems even more unsettling to correlate those images with a body of work as erotic as that of Borowczyk's.

Robinson is by no means the only critic who has compared the mass extermination in the third novella of *Immoral Tales* (1974) to the Holocaust, and the film is not the only one within the director's oeuvre to bring to mind such an association. Reminiscences of the catastrophe of the war are mostly discernible in Borowczyk's animated shorts, such as *House* (1958, co-directed with Jan Lenica), *Renaissance* (1963), and especially *Angels' Games* (1964). Most festival catalogs describe *Angels' Games* as being influenced by the experience of Nazi and Stalinist totalitarianism; the association of its content with concentration camps is almost habitual by now.[1] What we are dealing with here is, in fact, an artistic and generic alibi. The abstract form of film animation easily allows for a traumatic reading, while a metaphorical approach protects the artist from the accusation of violating a taboo. At the same time, *Angels' Games* (awarded both by the main jury and by the critics' jury at the Tour Film Festival in 1964[2]) mark the pinnacle of acclaim for Borowczyk's skills as an animator, positioning him squarely as a "serious" artist.

However, this very artist had abandoned the world of animation (at least as far as strict definitions are concerned, since he undoubtedly continued to animate his actors). *Immoral Tales* is often seen as the fatal misstep of his career, marking a move toward cinema classified as either erotic or downright pornographic. The realistic narrative of four separate tales would look even more confusing if one was to look at them through a lens other than that of a costume drama vision of the past.

The association with the Holocaust refuses to disappear, though. One justification for it can be found in the director's personal history. During the Second World War, Borowczyk was a forced laborer in a small village of Luboń. He couldn't yet realize the full scope and nature of the Nazi system of extermination; and yet at the same time, just like most Poles under German occupation, he himself was subjected to institutionalized violence and thus was functioning within a culture in which the public was aware of the presence of terror — both through official announcements by German authorities and through the hushed voices of hearsay, gossip, and underground publishing. This artistically inclined teenager was thus subjected to knowledge of the Fort VII camp in Poznań, as well as its subsection in Żabikowo, near Luboń. On 8 April 1945 *Głos Wielkopolski* (*The Voice of Greater Poland*) published a short note, written in a style characteristic with the period, informing its readership of yet another German crime. As the overseers of Żabikowo camp flew from the approaching forces of the Soviet Red Army, they tried to cover up their crimes by massively executing the prisoners and then setting their corpses on fire. The charred bodies remained as evidence. This macabre news item was accompanied by a drawing, signed: "Fragment of the burnt prison camp in Żabikowo," underneath the headline: "Evidence of German Crime" (Borowczyk 2007: 60–61, 309). According to Borowczyk, it was his very first artistic drawing to be published — his perspective was that of a witness to the uncovering of the corpses. No one around had a camera, so Borowczyk used his pencil as a device to record the ghastly sight.

He learned how to draw from his father, a railway man and an amateur painter. It wasn't until later that he had received formal artistic education, by which time his was a mind already partly shaped by many distressing experiences and their memory traces. This is the very trait that connects many of the representatives of the so-called Polish "1920 Generation," or "The Generation of Columbuses" ("*pokolenie Kolumbów*"), who entered their adult life (often prematurely) amidst the Second World War. Borowczyk, born in 1923, is a peer of the likes of Andrzej Wajda (with whom he studied at the Fine Arts Academy [ASP] in Kraków), Andrzej Munk, Andrzej Wróblewski, Tadeusz Różewicz, and Tadeusz Borowski — to name only the artists for whom the "Polish experience" was the starting point, or even the chief force behind their artistic activity (Bird 2010: 83). Wartime experiences marked all of their identities with pronounced historical fatalism. In the cases of Borowski and Różewicz, this marked identity was not merely national, but could be defined as connected to the fundaments of Western civilization; for them, the war had revealed the dark heart beating at the center of it.

Borowczyk's response to war experience is different. The Żabikowo incident I have described was included by Borowczyk in a memoir (in many ways an inflammatory one), entitled *What Do I Think When I See a Polish Woman in The Nude* (*Co myślę patrząc na rozebraną Polkę*, 2007). That alone indicates the weight the event carried for him. At the same time, Borowczyk never did speak of his wartime experiences in absolute terms, nor did he say much about his experience of totalitarianism — stressing, for example, that he had left Poland because of professional, contractual reasons, not political ones. This and similar evasions could of course testify to the artist's reluctance toward what he saw as facile interpretation, branding his works with a set of easy labels. In one of the interviews for *Film* magazine, for example, he reacts to a suggestion that *Angels' Games* originated from the horrors of war he had experienced with the following words: "Not only war brings horror with it. The horrors of peace are often even more difficult to survive" (Borowczyk and Księżyk 2006: 70).

Still, it seems that something else is at stake here, something redolent of Roman Polański's (b. 1933) strategy, which did transform his own wartime experience (incomparable to Borowczyk's, since Polański lived through the war as both a child and a Jew) into an aesthetic and ethical prism, used by him to describe any reality he focused on. With Polański, the horrors of war are not merely a part of the historical period one describes, but they do not mark the end of a given civilization or its slipping into animalistic behavior; they are simply the eternal facts of human life. It is in this view that Borowczyk, similar to Polański — besides all other aesthetic choices that set them apart — is not, in fact, a historian or a post-apocalyptic prophet, but someone who diagnoses permanent structures of human thinking and feeling.

It is easy to see the images of decapitated bodies that are so plentiful in *Angels' Games* (together with the images of numerous formless bodies, suggestive of Baconian human knots) as echoes of deformed, charred corpses seen by the 12-year-old Borowczyk, or — more generally — all bodies that had met their end in the flames of the camps. An association with the Second World War is forced upon the viewer in an indirect, ironic fashion: the film opens with a statement, written in French, English, and Russian, stating that any resemblance of the film to actual people and events is "purely coincidental." This simple, extra-diegetic element clearly points at his intention to build an allegoric construction — not historical, but universal; representing not a single event (the Holocaust), but rather using an association with it to create its own symphony of gleeful cruelty (the eerie melody, written by Bernard Parmegiani, only reinforces that feeling). Time is drained away — what remains is timeless, which is a mode Borowczyk often employs in his feature films. The "costume drama" aspect of his feature films usually redeems them from the burden of history itself, turning mere anecdotes and stories into resounding tales for the ages.

Thus, Borowczyk eradicates "the past" and "memory," making the duration of a single image all the stronger. The film itself — an exploration of a bleak concrete maze of a dystopian city — is enclosed within a single train ride. In the opening shots, much longer than the final ones, the camera is looking out from the train carriage at fleeting patches of dark landscape, with an occasional object zipping past the screen with violent force. The whole dynamics of the movement, joined to the spinning of the wheels, suggestively evokes the experience of being on a train: not being able to perceive things precisely, succumbing to the rhythm of the motion and the sound of the train, being inside an object larger than ourselves — one headed to an unknown destination, perhaps. Strange objects popping up before our eyes suggest gun barrels, but they are gone so quickly we cannot really tell. The destination of the journey proves to be a city of cruel angels — or rather of angels that are not so much cruel by nature, as deeply involved in cruel games and play, morphing shapelessly into heaps of flesh and bleeding blue ooze all over the concrete chambers they inhabit. As the Borowczyk scholar Kuba Mikurda noted in a private conversation I had with him, the color of the ooze is in fact "Prussian blue" — the same color as the trace left on walls by hydrogen cyanide, which was used in German gas chambers to murder the prisoners. What we see on screen is an all-devouring machine in the midst of an inexorable process. The typical childish play of fitting variously shaped bricks into similarly shaped holes is taken to its macabre, realistic extreme: here, everything will be pushed against the hole so hard till it has no other alternative but to fit, even at the cost of mutilation. The tubes resembling the pipes of an organ turn out to be multi-barreled guns (but they may also indicate pipes filled with lethal gas). All this is projected onto the smooth, cold walls of concrete: as if the gas chamber itself was the actual projection room of the imagination.

The precision and vividness of this construction are the best illustration of the words spoken by Borowczyk many years later:

> *Film as such is the most reliable art of movement there is, for it is art of perpetual movement. When we look at a moving object, the eye stops; when the object stops, the eye begins to move, striving to peruse the static image – thus, film provides us with movement that is eternal.* (Borowczyk 2007: 115)

The movement of images, their orchestration, and the inclusion of other images with them (from images of the Holocaust to the reimaging of surrealist paintings) enhances Borowczyk's animation, and *Angels' Games* is the most brilliant example of it with an exceptional quality that is both kinetic as well as purely filmic.[3]

The memory of the Holocaust becomes disarmed, as it were, by becoming part of a chain of other images, all serving the primary goal of recreating the universal mechanism of cruelty. The surrealist principle of marrying opposites, based on the constant exchange between the wondrous and the automatic, is displayed particularly clearly here. The structure of the film and the relationship between the characters and objects are all subject to the rule of mechanization with the railway and totalitarian associations powerfully "extracted" from the viewers' minds. At the same time, none of those associations are consequently realized or utilized — one image is immediately followed by the next, provoking elation at an animator's art amidst the horror of what is depicted.

In *Angels' Games* — just as in *Renaissance* (1963), *House* (1958), or *School* (1957) — Borowczyk serves as Aristotle's prime mover. I do not know if he ever spoke of himself in these terms, but as an artist he was definitely interested in wielding complete power over matter. It is confirmed by both his own words and the numerous opinions on his style of work — as well as indirectly by the sheer perfection of his work, be it animated or live-action in nature. This is the reason why the step toward shooting live-action films became logical — it meant accepting the particular challenge that total control over animated objects presented: the challenge to wield a demigod's control over a set filled with living people.

At the same time, Borowczyk actively shares surrealists' interest in cruelty. This interest originated from surrealism's societal rhetoric, and was instrumental in its function. The stated purpose of the surrealists — deconstruction of bourgeois structures of imagination — required a clean, decisive cut. Only shock and trauma could force the viewer out from traditional forms of thought and action. The emblematic representation of that very "cut" is the visual motif found in Luis Buñuel's *Un chien andalou* (1929), in which a razor is literally cutting through an eyeball. This was, in turn, closely related to another issue: that of surrealists' interest in the irrational, instinctive, as well as in the borderline — which is to say their interest in the exploration of aggression, violence and rape as forms of radical transgression of the inherited definition of culture. All this was often tied to eroticism, itself yet another "borderline form."

It is here that Borowczyk is likely to be seen as following the thought of Georges Bataille. In the latter's writings, eroticism is understood as an epistemological challenge and a cerebral transgression of sexuality as it has been given to us. This very challenge is closely tied to other forms of transgressing cultural taboos, namely those based on violence. The common denominator here is the organized, deliberate mode of action:

> Violence, not cruel in itself, is essentially something organised in the transgression of taboos. Cruelty is one of its forms; it is not necessarily erotic but it may veer towards other forms of violence organised by transgression. Eroticism, like cruelty, is premeditated. Cruelty and eroticism are conscious intentions in a mind, which has resolved to trespass into a forbidden field of behaviour. (Bataille 1962: 79–80)

Bataille opens his book with a strong statement: "Eroticism, it may be said, is assenting to life up to the point of death" (Bataille 1962: 11). It seems that this dialectic is very much present in Borowczyk's erotic philosophy as well (Vimenet 2008: 8).

This very theme is also explored in *Immoral Tales*, a film famously received with rather mixed feelings by the critics. It seems that for many, the film was too explicit: both in its presentation of sex ("too little is left to the imagination" [Richardson 2006]) and in its accusation that Catholicism is the driving force behind repressed sexuality. The film contains four segments, each set in a different historical era. The narratives are ordered from the most historically recent to the oldest. It has to be said, though, that even the "modern" story looks like a costume drama in its choice of props, set design, and garments. The stories are filled with images that are evocatively naturalistic, such as those of somebody tenderizing a cabbage or milking the cows.

The erotic encounters in the film are shown with various amounts of intensity, but the overall strategy of Borowczyk is to spread the image field. On the whole, mainstream cinema escapes eroticism, and pornography focuses on nothing but eroticism (reducing it to mere sexuality). Borowczyk treats eroticism as a subject for reflection, thus putting it right at the center, but also embroidering it with a multitude of neighboring elements. It is through this strategy that both the act of looking and the act of seeing becomes a theme. It is very clear in the first segment of the film ("The Tide") that the boy riding a bike (played by Fabrice Luchini) is trying to tear his eyes away from his cousin's (Lise Danvers) buttocks — presumably because the thoughts they provoke in him are too formidable to be fulfilled in that instant, which is why he chooses to look at the seaside landscape instead. The landscape is beautiful, but the beauty of it is not that of a postcard; we see some cows grazing (cows appear in three segments of the film) and barbed wire surrounding the pastures, and only then, somewhere in the background, do we see the sea. This landscape later proves to be quite forbidding, since the young couple have to fight muck and sharp stones. The impression of realism is further reinforced by the soundtrack: the film is light on words, but the sounds are very elaborate, not only providing ambience for the action, but practically encasing it with palpable sonic substance. Eroticism is thus presented directly and seen as merely part of a wider reality of the material dimension of the world and of everyday human practices.

All four segments, quite strongly, are connected more or less by a clear indictment of Catholicism as a structure of repression and limitation. All four are also concerned with power, which is executed upon "naturalness," binding it but also introducing it to the secret of "proper" eroticism. This power is wielded most brutally in the third segment, which focuses on the character of the "Bloody Countess," Elizabeth Báthory. The segment is an adaptation, as suggested by Michael Richardson (Richardson 2006: 114), of Valentine Penrose's novel *Erzsébet Báthory: La Comtesse sanglante* (Penrose 2006 [1962]), which provides yet another link between Borowczyk and not only surrealist imagination as such, but the actual surrealist circle (Bird 2010: 80).

It is in this story that the intimations of the Holocaust appear — intangible at first, but nevertheless persistent; suggestive of a feeling one cannot exactly put one's finger on. These associations are all intertwined and – taken together – form a chain of sorts. First, there is the tranquility of the village, filled with everyday labor and quotidian pleasures — that tranquility is destroyed by the arrival of the members of the court, luring young girls with a vision of a better life up in the castle. They select them for transportation quite literally, as we see in the shots of babies being inspected to determine their sex. Then there is the bathhouse, in which the girls experience intimate, non-sexual closeness, but also some violence. The latter explodes with full force when the girls, closed in the vast room, succumb to hysteria as they all fight one another to get a scrap of the Countess' lace garment. The fight is terminated by the swish of a sword by Istvan (Pascale Christophe), a guard of the Countess, who will later be revealed as a girl in boys' clothing and betray Elizabeth for a heterosexual romance. We only see the effect of violence: the bloodied blade and (in full accordance with the gruesome legend) Elizabeth Báthory's bath of blood; the character of Elizabeth is performed by Paloma Picasso in a truly vérité style (the bathtub was filled with actual animal blood).

On the level of mere anecdote, it's hard not to notice the typical surrealist, anti-feminism of the story: the scenes of heterosexual love and the ultimate choice of Istvan all stand in sharp contradiction to the Countess' lesbian lust, which requires a bloody substitute of closeness in order to be fulfilled. (The conservative nature of erotic delineation between genders may, in fact, be one of the reasons for Borowczyk's growing alienation from his audience in the years to come.)

The visual structure of the tale, though, is another matter, and the fact remains that it simultaneously provokes associations with the Holocaust while clearly operating within the category of the gaze, which is stressed by multiple close-ups of eyes, as well as of places and devices designed to be looked at. One is tempted to say that the entire film is a sequence of exchanged looks, had it not been for the fact that many of them are merely gazes being thrown, as vacuous as they are unrequited. There's a separate tale unraveling parallel to the action: it is para-narration built of images — a *para-pictura*, so to speak.

A little girl peeks at a couple making love. The peasants look silently at the selection of the girls. The group departs from the village thus leaving the place deprived of sexual and reproductive power. All that is left behind is a barn — there are two gaping holes in the door, and even though no one is looking through them, the camera lingers on there. Istvan is then overseeing the girls by means of a mirror, which allows him to watch them as they shower; he also sees the sudden outburst of violence, which at first glance can be mistaken for an act of lovemaking. The naked girls crowd the window space, all trying to steal a peek outside, most likely still unaware of their own imprisonment. The Countess looks at them from above as they all stand in the room, which will ultimately provide the location for their ruthless slaughter.

It is useful to evoke a wider film context at this stage. The first half of the 1970s marked only the beginning of a wider discussion on the practice of aestheticization of Nazism. Some allusions, linking Nazism and sexuality, appeared as early as the immediate postwar — in the films of Roberto Rossellini, but the overt linking of Nazi politics with aesthetics and sex only became a theme in Luchino Visconti's *The Damned* (*La caduta degli dei* [1969]) and Liliana Cavani's *The Night Porter* (*Il portiere di notte* [1974]). These dates seem significant, in that they point to a shift in reflection and imagination regarding Nazi violence — *Immoral Tales*, also made in 1974, can be seen as partaking in that very shift. In the same year Susan Sontag wrote her famous essay "Fascinating

Fascism,"[4] in which she expressed criticism of Leni Riefenstahl's awe at the beauty of Nubian people and of an American fascination with everything branded with the SS signature. There was also the sexploitation background, which was pertinent to Sontag's argument, but most likely unknown to her at that time. *Ilsa, She-Wolf of SS* premiered in October 1975, as if to validate the author's intuition, and Lee Frost's *Love Camp 7* (1969) paved the way even earlier as perhaps the first sexploitation film ever set within a concentration camp. It was after this film opened that Nazi porn and Nazi sexploitation came of age as a genre in its own right.

Nothing could be further from Borowczyk's aesthetics than Nazi porn — and it is not only the matter of a lack of historically specific settings. The third segment of *Immoral Tales* creates a multilayered exposition. The look of the film is defined by pastel colors, which are violently interrupted by outbursts of red — especially in the image of the room filled with young girls. At the same time, this form is striking when compared with the actual content of the imagery (Robinson calls the character of Elizabeth "the calmest Bluebeard in cinema" [Robinson 2008: 73]). Borowczyk's imagination as connected to violence identifiable with Nazism is constructed in a completely different manner from the imagination one can observe in the works that use props and settings invoking the Second World War and the Holocaust, where he often chooses open obscenity or merely utilizes a fig leaf of an artistic alibi in order to exploit. Borowczyk both reveals the special status of images associated with the Holocaust and opposes it. Here, too, we can speak of the process of spreading images mentioned before — the director doesn't allow one to avert one's eyes from those images, but neither does he force one to focus on them, choosing instead to embed them in a consistent and multilayered visual narration. With his treatment of pornographic imagery, he once again eschews a literal approach and rejects a situation in which he could focus solely on the violence (or sex), without showing how it is entangled in a cultural (and narrative) whole — a whole that transcends the limits of a single historical event. Several years later, Jean-Luc Godard will call for a new form of editing in *Histoire(s) du cinéma* (1988–1998): one that reveals the Holocaust's cruelty without actually depicting it.

Borowczyk's intentions are clearly set not for the remembrance of past events, but for the very act of looking at images that are being presented. The reference to concentration camps in *Immoral Tales* is not pointed to directly (or even indirectly, as in the case of the triple disclaimer opening *Angels' Games*), but the analogy is still overwhelmingly clear. There is no doubt that the question is not merely located in the eye of the viewer (especially since the film opened well before popular culture became suffused with such imagery). This visual layer functions as a painterly support or sub-image — an element of the projection that's fully present at every stage; one that constantly demonstrates the analogical and structural endurance of violence. The director reaches such a point in the image's functioning when it ceases to function in two separate ways, but truly becomes a double image (the rabbit-duck illusion): one that triggers two registers of seeing at once, not as an alternative, but as a conjunction based on analogy. (Just like a series of failed logotypes,[5] which — once they become associated with sexual acts — can never again escape that unwanted meaning.)

One could evoke one more film here that occupies the middle ground between cinema and visual arts; namely Artur Żmijewski's *Berek* (1999), in which the artist staged two groups of naked people chasing each other in a basement space and in a former crematory. The work remains controversial. The artist himself commented on it in the following manner:

> *The work is filled with cruel play, sadism, nudity and child-like carelessness at the same time. It's full of naïveté, laughter, kid's joy. My goal was to recreate a situation. It happened that way: a bunch of naked people in a gas chamber. But instead of horror, we get giggles, toys, erotic play – innocent diversion. – What a relief! What a vulgar slaughter! But please, tell me: the slaughter didn't take place? I beg you, tell me: it didn't happen, right? – Of course it didn't, it was just an illusion. (Żmijewski 2002: 52)*

The mere movement and play of naked adults sets imagination to work, inexorably forcing it toward images of gas chambers. Still, what could those images mean in themselves nowadays? The images created by Borowczyk can also be called an illusion; an illusion that is simultaneously courted and wished away. At one point, Elizabeth Báthory personally starts to wipe away images made by the girls under the showers. The black chalk markings at first look perfectly innocent — is there a little sun, perhaps? — but then reveal themselves as quite graphic depictions of erect penises. We have seen them in numerous public toilets of the world. Those images, made by the young girls, and inadvertently directed against the Countess, undermine the seeming luxury of a castle's walls; its opulence becomes eradicated and profanely violated, but then that subversive gesture itself suffers from invalidation, and doubly so: the drawings themselves are wiped away, as are the girls who made them.

In *Angels' Games*, the director revealed the mechanical, automatic structure of violence; in Elizabeth Báthory's tale, he shows its quiet, persistent and forever veiled presence.

Translated by Michał Oleszczyk

Notes

1. See for example the BFI website listing the five most important works by Borowczyk at: http://www.bfi.org.uk/news-opinion/news-bfi/lists/walerian-borowczyk-five-essential-films.
2. See for example opinions expressed by Cathal Tohill and Pete Tombs, who described it as "a strange and unforgettable film" (Tohill and Tombs 1995: 221) or the famous judgment made by Terry Gilliam, who singled out Borowczyk's film among the ten best animated films ever made — "*Les Jeux des Anges* was just extraordinary: that sense that you are on a train with walls of the city going past, and then the sound of angels' wings – incredible" (Gilliam 2001).
3. As noted by, for example, Mieczysław Porębski, who highlighted the filmic (and not painterly or graphic) quality of Borowczyk's work (Porębski 1964).
4. Published for the first time in *The New York Review of Books* on 6 February 1975. See Sontag 1975.
5. See for example *Top 15 Worst Logo FAILS Ever*, "Bored Panda" at http://www.boredpanda.com/worst-logo-fails-ever/.

Bibliography

Bataille, G. 1962. *Death and Sensuality: A Study of Eroticism and the Taboo*. New York: Walker and Co.

Bird, D. 2010. "Devils' Games: Surrealism in Polish Emigre Cinema." In K. Wielebska and K. Mikurda (eds.), *A Story of Sin: Surrealism in Polish Cinema*. Warszawa and Kraków: Era Nowe Horyzonty and korporacja Ha!art.

Borowczyk, Walerian and Rafał Księżyk. 2006. "Piękno i Bestie: Rafał Księżyk talks to Walerian Borowczyk." *Film* 4.

Borowczyk, W. 2007. *Co Myślę Patrząc na Rozebraną Polkę*. Warszawa: Oficyna Wydawnicza Rytm.

Gilliam, T. 2001. "The 10 Best Animated Films of All Time." *The Guardian*, 27 April 2001. Retrieved on 1 March 2015 from http://www.theguardian.com/film/2001/apr/27/culture.features1

Penrose, V. 2006 [1962]. *The Bloody Countess: Atrocities of Erzsébet Báthory*, trans. A. Trocchi. Washington D.C: Solar Books.

Porębski, M. 1964. "Uwagi o Genezie Twórczości Filmowej Borowczyka i Lenicy." *Kwartalnik Filmowy* 4.

Richardson, M. 2006. *Surrealism and Cinema*. Oxford and New York: Berg.

Robinson, J. M. 2008. *Walerian Borowczyk: Cinema of Erotic Dreams*. Maidstone: Crescent Moon Publishing.

Sontag, S. 1975. "Fascinating Fascism." *The New York Review of Books*, 6 February 1975. Retrieved on 1 March 2015 from http://www.nybooks.com/articles/archives/1975/feb/06/fascinating-fascism/

Tohill, Cathal and Pete Tombs. 1995. *Immoral Tales: European Sex and Horror Movies 1956-1984*. New York: St. Martin's Griffin.

Vimenet, P. 2008. "Filozofia Erotyczna." In U. Śniegowska and P. Vimenet (eds.), *b. Boro. Borowczyk. Walerian Borowczyk (1923-2006)*. Warszawa: Centrum Sztuki Współczesnej Zamek Ujazdowski.

Żmijewski, A. 2002. "Spisek Słabych." In I. Kowalczyk (ed.), *Niebezpieczne Związki Sztuki z Ciałem*. Poznań: Galeria Miejska Arsenał.

Iwona Kurz is a lecturer and Deputy Director of the Institute of Polish Culture at The University of Warsaw. Her main fields of interests are the history of Polish culture of the nineteenth and twentieth century from a visual studies perspective; the visual memory of the Shoah, the anthropology of body and gender, and the anthropology of visual culture. She is the author of *Twarze w tłumie* (*Faces in the Crowd: Views of the Heroes of Collective Imagination in Polish Culture 1955-1969* [2005]), which received the Bolesław Michałek Award for the best film studies book in 2005. She is the co-author of *Obyczaje polskie: Wiek XX w krótkich hasłach* (*Polish Everyday Culture: 20th Century in Short Entries* [2008]), editor of *Film i historia: Antologia* (*Film and History: Anthology* [2008]), *Kultura Współczesna* quarterly monographic issue "Return to Archives," co-editor of *Antropologia ciała* (*Anthropology of the Body* [2008]), and *Antropologia kultury wizualnej* (*Anthropology of Visual Culture* [2012]). She also edits an online academic journal *View: Theories and Practices of Visual Culture*.

CHAPTER 5

The Postcard Never Sent
Guy de Maupassant and Rosalie Prudent's Cinematic Confession

Kamila Kuc

Figure 5.1   *Cher Maître* (2014), collage by Kamila Kuc

In reality every man is himself a piece of fate.
—The judge on the Rosalie Prudent trial

This text constitutes an exploration of the themes present in Guy de Maupassant's story "Rosalie Prudent," (1886) as prompted here by Walerian Borowczyk's eponymous adaptation (1966). My wish in this experiment is to propose a fictional dialogue between a few near-contemporary figures who shared an affinity with certain cultural trends and philosophical concerns; namely realism, fatalism, and the nature of man. Borowczyk's ascetic, clinical interpretation of "Rosalie" has brought my attention to some particular features of de Maupassant's story. Rosalie Prudent's suffering and the tragedy of her destiny are illuminated and enhanced by Borowczyk's use of camera and sound, as well as the employment of a rigorously minimalist mise en scène. All of this, as I will indicate in this chapter, injects de Maupassant's cruel realism with more contemporary appeal. What emerges is Borowczyk's take on motherhood, woven into an image of unflinching fatalism.

* * *

Nantes, the year 1886. Middle of the night. A small vegetable garden. Large lights behind a movie camera almost blind an eager coroner, while two small bundles of rags and newspaper — two little corpses — are being dug out by a group of local men. One was buried next to the artichokes; the other near the strawberries — away from each other "so they might not talk of their mother," confesses Rosalie Prudent, the defendant, in the most enigmatic trial that France had witnessed in the last century. For the first time, a trial in France was captured on a film reel and recorded for posterity.

Prohibited to all those under the age of eighteen, Rosalie Prudent's trial was surrounded by controversy. Mademoiselle Prudent, a servant at the Varambot household, "became pregnant without the knowledge of her masters, and had killed and buried her two newborn children in the garden," reported Le Figaro on the morning of the trial. Though it was "the usual story of infanticide committed by many a servant girl," there was "one inexplicable circumstance about this one." When the police searched the girl's room, "they discovered a complete infant's outfit, made by Mademoiselle Prudent herself, who for the last three months had spent her nights cutting and sewing it." Her entire wage paid for candles, which she purchased from the nearby grocer to make the late-night sewing feasible. "Rosalie — this fragile rose. What a savage misfortune," whispered one of the girl's neighbors present at the trial.

The judge was a rather large man with an extravagant moustache, who paid little attention to the meaning of names. Prudentia — the mother of all virtues. This meant very little to him. He considered himself, albeit secretly, the first immoralist. Taken back by Rosalie Prudent's beauty, he was more interested in the charm of indecency that constituted the subject of this case. Plain, filthy lust, he smiled to himself. His life had taught him that the male sex has a worse temperament than the female and thus he felt the deepest sympathy for this violated girl.

Numerous people attended the trial: a middle-class couple from the provinces, who voted for Rosalie Prudent to be guillotined without a trial. They fancied themselves moralists, much to the judge's discreet disapproval. The defendant, a pretty girl from Lower Normandy, wept continuously and would not answer to anything. Rosalie Prudent's tears obstructed her view of everything, testifying to the girl's innocence and vulnerability. It was as if Rosalie Prudent was responding to her own accusations; her own conscience acting the role of harsh prosecutor. "Do whatever you want with me," she kept repeating. "I am ready for anything." It was believed by Guy de Maupassant (he was among a number of important figures also present at the trial) that Rosalie Prudent "had committed this barbarous act in a moment of despair and madness, since there was every indication that she had expected to keep and bring up her child."

The judge knew what Rosalie Prudent and the witnesses didn't: that her fate had already been predestined. "God is dead and that there will be no greater judgment than Rosalie's own, since 'consciousness is only a surface. Call me a fatalist!'"

"All rise!"

Guy de Maupassant, named by the judge himself as one of France's most "inquisitive and delicate psychologists" (the two men often met in undefined circumstances in the company of mostly unidentifiable women), was joined at the trial by a certain Monsieur Walerian Borowczyk, a master film director whose attention to detail and montage skills were unparalleled. "*Quelle imagination fulgurante!*" shouted one of the distinguished guests during one of Monsieur Borowczyk's pictures some years ago.

"I have not yet heard your voice," said the judge to a tear-streaked Rosalie. Monsieur Borowczyk suddenly took to the stand, and with a swift movement of his hand closed the last button on her white shirt with its perfectly white polka dots. He also removed the Bible and the chair from her stand. Now Mademoiselle Prudent was up there entirely on her own. "Minimum décor for maximum emotional impact," whispered Monsieur Borowczyk to himself. The judge wondered why these men of cinema always had to be so precise. Rosalie Prudent began to feel more and more trapped, as if her back had suddenly been pushed against the wall. Closer and closer, the camera imperceptibly began to track her face. The public could now see each one of Rosalie's crystal tears streaking down her perfectly white, porcelain skin.

> *Exhibit One:* Rosalie Prudent kept sobbing in the background as Monsieur Borowczyk directed the witnesses' eyes to a photograph of a young,

handsome man in a military uniform (strangely resembling Monsieur de Maupassant in his early years). He then directs them to a white belt. (*Although the judge was fascinated by Monsieur Borowczyk's talent, he was starting to find his antics irritating.*) Monsieur Borowczyk's hardly subtle camera kept moving to the right as Rosalie, a helpless, fragile flower, sobbed with even more intensity, unable to utter a single word in her defense. As Monsieur Borowczyk tried to capture Mademoiselle Prudent's face, he began to wonder what kind of a mother she would have been anyway. Her innocence was lost. Her hands were gripping a tissue tightly. She had no desire to be identified by the drama-hungry spectators. Her eyes struggled to escape the camera. Monsieur Borowczyk's camera gaze was cruel. "Ah, cinema! It is pure movement! The mechanical apparatus is so superior to the written word. Cinema is life," whispered Leo Tolstoy, a famous Russian writer, who attended the trial only to compare his notes with those of de Maupassant. (The two men were considered rivals in some circles.)

This was a delight to the judge. "Monsieur Borowczyk, please move away." The Judge found a certain beauty in Rosalie Prudent's suffering. Possessed by his beliefs that God was dead (thus nobody could see anything), a view that he shared with de Maupassant, the judge gave way to his own imaginings of carnal pleasures that involved the defendant. "Beauty must be convulsive or will not be at all."

Exhibit Two: Madame Boudin's toolbox. A small white wool outfit, half-knitted. The sweet-tempered, delicate girl kept shedding her precious tears as the veil of her innocence was slowly being torn away. Le directeur Borowczyk now turned into an uncontrollable monster; the camera stared the poor girl right in the eyes.

Exhibit Three: A blood-stained pillow and a white wool sock. "What a morbid situation!" whispered some of the witnesses.

Exhibit Four: A long garden spade with remains of earth and dirt still clinging to it.

Exhibit Five: Two bundles of rags and newspaper, which had contained two little corpses. Rosalie swallowed her tears as she returned to her memories of the tragic night. As the knitting of Mademoiselle Prudent's little labored-over-at-night outfit was unraveled (thanks to the sublime and unique animation craft of Monsieur Borowczyk), the terrifying details of her story were revealed to the spectators.

"It was Monsieur Joseph, Monsieur Varambot's nephew," cried poor Rosalie. (It was brought to the judge's attention that Joseph Varambot was a non-commissioned officer in the artillery and had stayed at the house for a few months in the summer.) The soldier had looked at her as if he wanted to make love to her all day long, recalled the now very morose Rosalie, as she caught sight of Monsieur Borowczyk blushing. The cinematic master was trying to refrain from desiring her — it would distract him from his art.

'It was near the river that they had made love', notes Monsieur de Maupassant, who has been listening to Mademoiselle Prudent's words with great attention. Mademoiselle Prudent describes that she had struggled at first but then she had let herself "be taken in," she confessed sheepishly. "Then he went away" and she had not realized she was pregnant "until a month after." Monsieur Borowczyk's eyes opened wider and wider and the gaze of his camera was now permanently fixed on Rosalie Prudent.

The beauty of the girl Prudent was so seductive, that it did not matter to the judge what her crime was. Her eyes could have talked him into anything. These words could all be a lie ...

"I would have followed him to the ends of the world," cried the poor girl. Here Monsieur Borowczyk moved his camera closer, ever so clumsily, so the public could see every sinew of Rosalie's body, which was trembling like a leaf.

Intrigued by her confession, the judge urged the girl with more gentleness. He made Rosalie understand that all these men that had gathered here to pass judgment upon her were not anxious for her death and might even have pity on her.

As she began to talk freely, Monsieur Borowczyk failed to notice anything else. His camera focused on Rosalie and Rosalie only. Even de Maupassant himself seemed utterly taken by the girl's anguish, and his notes were becoming less and less coherent.

The judge was looking at Rosalie, thinking that her pure form had somehow been spoilt from being pregnant with a child by this pitiful soldier. He suddenly remembered a conversation he once had with a fellow judge about a similar case in which a pregnant woman had taken her own life: "Coitus, my dear friend, is a sign of the will to live," the judge's friend had said. "Maybe she wanted to die because of the shame it all caused her? After all, every woman who is surprised in the act of procreation would like to die of shame." The judge, who was convinced of the contrary, had thought this a strange notion. He believed that every woman surprised in the act of procreation displayed her pregnancy without a trace of shame and with a kind of pride. For the judge, female vanity was, in particular, at a low level of intelligence, always happy to receive alms. He quickly became ashamed of his own thoughts and returned to the trial.

"When I realized my condition I went to see Madame Boudin," continued the exhausted Rosalie. "Then I made the outfit, sewing night after night, until as late as one o'clock in the morning; and then I looked for another place, for I knew very well that I should be sent away, but I wanted to stay in the house until the very last, so as to save my pennies, for I have not got very much and I thought I should need my money for the little one."

"Wisdom consist infinitely more in multiplying one's pleasures than in compounding one's pains," said Miss Juliette to Miss Justine. The two were the youngest of all witnesses and unknown to most people present at the trial; at least to those who considered themselves "decent." They were the great granddaughters of Marquis de Sade, infamous for his orgies and pornographic novels. (De Sade was also a friend of the judge's grandfather.) The two women had lived their lives in the understanding that the man was the bearer of the looks and desires, while a woman was a mere tool for acting out his fantasies. A woman, they thought, was destined to carry the consequences of a man's actions. This is why Miss Juliette and Miss Justine had freed themselves from any notion of morality or social obligation. (It needs to be said that the judge was a quiet admirer of their lifestyle, which he personally expressed to them on numerous occasions.) One morning prior to the trial he was surprised to have found himself lying in between these two creatures' bodies, with Monsieur de Maupassant calmly gazing at them, scribbling something in his notebook.

"Oh, this pathetic Rosalie," moaned Justine raising her eyebrows.

"Then you did not intend to kill him?" asked the judge.

"Oh, certainly not, Monsieur!" explained Rosalie Prudent obediently.

"Why did you kill him, then?" "Evil soul!" cried one of the witnesses.

In the eyes of many, Rosalie Prudent was a more devastating whore than anyone could have ever dared to imagine.

The judge found himself overwhelmed by all this moralizing in the courtroom.

"Morality, my dear fellows," (the judge finally expressed his views) "is nothing more than a means of preserving the community and warding off its destruction."

"But Monsieur Judge," cried an old lady, "we must all have a conscience!" The judge took this opportunity to inform the elderly woman, not without sarcasm, that the content of her conscience was a mere compulsion. "You think, my dear lady, that you must do this and that, but do you ever ask yourself WHY must you do this?"

"Surely, there is such thing as good and evil!" shouted a young man from the corner of the room.

The judge could have sworn that he has seen this very same man embracing Miss Juliette on one of his hazy evenings. He did not concern himself with explaining to the man that good did not exist without evil and only in juxtaposition could we tell that either one meant anything or nothing at all; that both were part of the same coin.

At this very moment Rosalie "began to cry so bitterly that the judge, now slightly distracted by his thoughts, had to give her time to collect herself," de Maupassant's report stated. "It happened this way. It came sooner than I expected. It came upon me in the kitchen, while I was doing the dishes ... I had such pain; and then I pushed him out with all my strength. I felt that he came out and I picked him up."

"I did all that Madame Boudin told me to do," continued Rosalie, who had now calmed down a little. "And then I laid him on my bed." "Lui."

Murmurs were heard from the depths of the courtroom.

"Then such a pain gripped me again that I thought I should die." "I fell on my knees, and then toppled over backward on the floor; and it gripped me again, perhaps one hour, perhaps two." "I lay there all alone and then another one comes, another little one" "... I took him up as I did the first one, and then I put him on the bed, the two side by side." "Is it possible, tell me, two children, and I who get only twenty francs a month?" wept Rosalie Prudent. "One, yes, that can be managed by going without things, but not two. That turned my head. What do I know about it? Had I any choice, tell me?"

When would this poor girl gain sanctuary from life's storms? Such were the thoughts of an old, half-deaf nun to the right of the witness bench.

The judge began stroking his moustache slowly as Miss Juliette and Miss Justine giggled in a way that was familiar to him. There was some movement in the stalls.

"Quiet!" screamed the judge, "Continue, *s'il vous plaît*," he nodded at Mademoiselle Prudent.

"Monsieur Borowczyk, film the courtroom for once!" remarked the judge. Distracted by Mademoiselle Prudent's tragedy, Monsieur Borowczyk felt that his cinematic talent had momentarily escaped him, and he began directing his camera toward empty walls and a stand, as if he were blindfolded.

"What could I do?" Rosalie kept weeping. "I felt as if my last hour had come. I put the pillow over them, without knowing why. Both of them were quite dead under the pillow."

The judge closed his eyes momentarily with a certain relief.

"Then I took them under my arms and went down the stairs out in the vegetable garden. I took the gardener's spade and I buried them under the earth." Back in her bed Rosalie Prudent felt so sick that she could not get up. The doctor upon his arrival understood it all.

"I'm telling you the truth, Your Honor. Do what you like with me; I'm ready."

The whiteness of the white polka-dot of Rosalie's blouse, and the austerity and sterility of the courtroom seemed to mark her solitude in life. Half of the male jury were blowing their noses violently to keep from crying; many women in the courtroom were sobbing. Monsieur Borowczyk adjusted his lens for the judge's closing speech.

"This is a sorrowful tale of a girl in dire circumstances. Mademoiselle Rosalie Prudent was forced to surrender her innocence and abandon herself to her fate as a lost woman and a murderess," the judge began. Monsieur Borowczyk was still unable to get picture clarity. It was as if his emotional confusion concerning the fate of Rosalie Prudent had suddenly been transferred to his lens.

"Over the years we have seen similar cases all over the world. Some of you may even be familiar with the excellent reports of Mademoiselle Tristana's sorrowful life, so wonderfully recorded by Monsieurs Galdós and Buñuel (somewhat dreamily the judge recalled poor Tristana's amputated leg).

"Then there was Effi Briest of Monsieurs Fontane and Fassbinder." "All these women were entrapped by circumstance. We ought to be compassionate." "Oh, not to mention the black-haired flower Anna Karina, whose lifelong sufferings have granted her the faith of Joan of Arc; at least according to the man who called himself something along the lines of 'God'."

"What about Christianity? Has it outlived its usefulness in our society?" asked the nun.

"God is a crude answer, a piece of indelicacy against thinkers," responded the judge. "Christianity is the crime par excellence — the crime against life." "The Christian as a 'moral being,' this concept is more absurd," the judge continued. "Morality is the idiosyncrasy of decadents with the hidden intention of revenging themselves on life." "I thus declare morality a form of vampirism!" Monsieur Borowczyk had managed to capture the judge's devilish expression.

"Everything pure and good has perished and continues to perish in our society, because this society is corrupt, senseless and terrible," cried an old man as he was leaving the courtroom. "Rosalie Prudent *fut acquittée*," reported numerous newspapers the following morning.

Later that same year, both the judge and de Maupassant were noted to have died of "a disease of the youth," as syphilis was commonly referred to. On de Maupassant's desk, an unfinished postcard was found, addressed to Monsieur Borowczyk at his Paris apartment. "Cher Maître Borowczyk," it began. "When my words arrive upon you, with the weight of a pregnant Rosalie Prudent, you will understand why I could not allow her to be a m ..." From here onwards de Maupassant's words became unreadable, as if he had been writing with his last breath ...

Around the same time, Monsieur Borowczyk, then on his twentieth film, was spotted with Rosalie in one of the Montparnasse cafés by a local reporter. The great director was proud to announce that this poor little soul had become his wife. "She now enjoys the stardom, granted by the roles carefully designed by me, the great master of cinema." "Any children?" asked the interviewer. "Rosalie was already an impossible mother once," Monsieur Borowczyk replied bitterly. "Our films are our children," added Miss Prudent, now Branice (as per her artistic pseudonym), with a cryptic smile.

Sitting at a nearby table was Leo Tolstoy, the distinguished Russian writer, whose sympathy for Mademoiselle Prudent's life was evident during the trial, though he felt "de Maupassant's record of it was ambiguous," as he stated to the reporter. "Why do the demands of morality lay only on women, according to de Maupassant?" Tolstoy posed this rhetorical question to the reporter, Monsieur Borowczyk, and Mademoiselle Branice. Tolstoy remembered approaching de Maupassant's first report, *Maison Tellier* (1881), with "a certain indifference," as he recalled. (This flamboyant protégé of Flaubert and a distant friend of Zola? Tolstoy thought, not without envy at the time.) Later Tolstoy remarked in the Russian press that the author of the report on the Rosalie Prudent trial was endowed with that particular gift of writing that enabled him to "direct, according to his tastes, his intensified but stained attention to this or that subject."

"It was almost as though it was written for Monsieur Borowczyk's camera," Tolstoy remarked, smiling to both men. "Although, de Maupassant possessed the clearness of exposition, the beauty of form, and sincerity," continued the Russian writer, "he did not have a moral relation to the subject." "De Maupassant loved and hated what he described, but why was he so incapable of distinguishing between good and evil?"

Over the years Tolstoy had come to the conclusion that the problem was, as he cared to share, "that de Maupassant looked at the most uninteresting, physical side and completely overlooked the most important, spiritual side."

"But surely the two are connected?" asked Monsieur Borowczyk somewhat provocatively. "Certain things should simply be left unspoken," responded Tolstoy, and "debauched persons belong to that category." "And you, Monsieur Borowczyk, if you do not wish to return to the subtlety of your early expression, you must be aware that you will soon be labeled none other than a pornographer. What a shame this would be! Such talent and sophistication are rare in the cinema!" "Why, Monsieur Borowczyk," continued a concerned Tolstoy, "why must you believe that all women are loose in morals and that all mothers are holy?"

"Please allow me a careful observation", Tolstoy remarked for the last time that night, "there exist no mothers in your films." The great director paused for a minute and looked straight into the lens of his camera: "I never understood the virtue of motherhood." He quickly gulped his last sip of red wine.

Actors

Rosalie Prudent — Ligia Branice
The judge — Friedrich Nietzsche

Monsieur Walerian Borowczyk — Himself
Monsieur Guy de Maupassant — Himself
The judge's Friend — Arthur Schopenhauer
Miss Juliette and Miss Justine — Themselves

Bibliography

Bartes, R. 1976 [1971]. "The Life of Sade." In *Sade Fourier Loyola*, trans. by R. Miller. New York: Straus and Giroux.
Breton, A. 1960 [1928]. *Nadja*, trans. R. Howard. New York: Grove Press.
de Maupassant, G. 2004. *A Parisian Affair and Other Stories*, trans. S. Miles. London: Penguin.
———. 2014 [1886]. "Rosalie Prudent," *ReadBookOnline*. Retrieved on 4 June 2014 from http://www.readbookonline.net/readOnLine/1605/
de Sade, M. 2008 [1797]. "Justine" and "Juliette." In P. J. Gilette (ed.), *The Complete Marquis de Sade*. Los Angeles: Holloway House Publishing Co.
Durgnat, R. 1996. *Eros in the Cinema*. London: Calder and Boyars.
Mikurda, Kuba and Jakub Woynarowski. 2013. *Corpus Delicti*. Warszawa, Kraków: korporacja Ha!art.
Nietzsche, F. 1986 [1878]. *Human, All Too Human: A Book for Free Spirits*, trans. by R. J. Hollingdale. Cambridge: Cambridge University Press.
———. 1988 [1888]. *Ecce Homo: How One Becomes What One Is*, trans. R. J. Hollingdale. London: Penguin Books.
O'Pray, M. 2010. "Walerian Borowczyk's Blanche: Courtly Love, Lacan and Surrealism." In K. Wielebska and K. Mikurda (eds.), *A Story of Sin: Surrealism in Polish Cinema*. Warszawa, Kraków: korporacja Ha!art.
Tolstoy, L. 1904 [1894]. "The Works of Guy de Maupassant." In *The Complete Works of Count Tolstoy,* volume XX, trans. L. Wiener. New York and Boston: Colonial Press.
———. "Lew Tolstoj o Kinematografie." 1923. *Film Polski* 3.

Kamila Kuc, Ph.D. is a multimedia artist, curator, and writer. Her films have screened in venues and at film festivals nationally and internationally, including: Whitechapel Gallery, British Film Institute, Institute of Contemporary Arts London, Anthology Film Archives New York, and Ann Arbor Film Festival. She is the author and editor of numerous books and articles on experimental media, including *Visions of Avant-Garde Film* (Indiana University Press, 2016) and the first study of Polish avant-garde film, *The Struggle for Form: Perspectives on Polish Avant-Garde Film 1916–1989*, co-edited with Michael O'Pray (Columbia University Press, 2014). She is also the co-founder, with Sam Jury, of *Disasters of Peace* — a creative initiative that encompasses research, writing, making, and curating.

CHAPTER 6
Boro
The Guide for the Perplexed

Fernando F. Croce

Goto, Isle of Love (1968)

"The main thing is the optical effect" — heard as the despot's portrait is exhibited in school. Like Frank Tashlin, Walerian Borowczyk displays the animator's repulsion toward realism; the central image finds a pair of dolts pushing each other against a concrete wall, but the flat perspective is adorned by ravishingly soiled bric-a-brac (the glass cabinet at the back of the classroom holds a pistol and a dummy's painted noggin). The island takes its name from the aging dictator (Pierre Brasseur), a squashed satyr in generalissimo uniform who holds gladiatorial bouts to decide the fate of his prisoners. His wife Glossia (Ligia Branice) is a sad swan who rolls in the hay with her horse riding instructor, Gono (Jean-Pierre Andréani), and gazes at the horizon across the waters: the ocean may promise new things ("Not better ... different"), but it's also where bodies are dumped because "salt devours everything." Grozo (Guy Saint-Jean), a convict with mean eyes, is pardoned and becomes the dictator's personal boot polisher and kennel keeper, and the island's chief hunter of flies. The tenor of the film is rather close to Kafka (and also, fortuitously, to George Franju's *Eyes Without a Face* [1959]); the universe is boiled down to crawling desire and neurosis. The terse filmmaking expands the visions Borowczyk can't get out of his head (galloping horses, apples, binoculars, flies, flies, and more flies). Given a gun to take down the unfaithful Glossia, Grozo shoots Goto instead and usurps the throne before going after Glossia for himself. When the trappings of ambition and the release of lust cancel each other out, is it any wonder that the world looks like a tattered penal colony and sounds like an organ grinder's version of Händel? The characters remain locked in their subterranean circles, yet Borowczyk finds transcendence amid the grime by insisting on the mystical force of longing: Glossia's body is laid out before an ardent camera, and the missing link between the endings of *Ordet* (1955) and *Sweet Movie* (1974) suddenly materializes.

Immoral Tales (1974)

La Rochefoucauld is evoked at the outset ("love pleases more by the manner in which it shows itself than by itself"), but Walerian Borowczyk's tool for disarming prurient criticism is his sly humor, already evident in the title. Rohmer's moral tales, Borowczyk's immoral ones: Fabrice Luchini is plucked from *Claire's Knee* for "The Tide," the first short in the quartet, pumping air into his bicycle tire as his lissome young cousin (Lise Danvers) pops up wearing a bikini under a diaphanous white dress, ready for the beach. The two are stranded on a rocky isle; he wants her to orally illustrate the "mechanism of the sea," so the blow job montage is attuned to the cosmic rise of the tide. The girl's pink mouth is at the center, going from blankly apprehensive to briefly blissful and back when her own pleasure is denied. Sexuality is blessed in the next short, "Thérese the Philosopher," where the fin-de-siècle, pubescent heroine (Charlotte Alexandra) hears the Holy Ghost while fondling the church organ pipes, and, locked in a room, rummages through the bric-a-brac to find volcanic ecstasy by blending the Gospel and De Sade. By the end, she's a still life of exhausted, aroused flesh, locked up yet freed carnally. Going back in time, "Erzsébet Bathory" contemplates Paloma Picasso as the Blood Countess, a saturnine vulturette on horseback; she rounds up medieval lasses for extended shower scenes in her castle, followed by sanguine frenzies. This is a pearly study of fluids and skin, with Borowczyk forcing himself to switch from sex to death for the punch line; the great painter's daughter becoming an object d'art in a vat of thick blood after having disapproved of the girls' salacious sketches on the lavatory walls. Finally, "Lucrezia" — the Borgia epoch — lavishes us with ecclesiastical pomp and wicked reflections on Russell and Pasolini. Lucrezia (Florence Bellamy) and her family (Jacopo and Lorenzo Berinizi) romp in the chamber while Savonarola (Philippe Desboeuf) preaches from the pulpit; his burning at the stake mingles with their climax. "*Quel sacrilege!*" Borowczyk would concur, only to reverse another Le Rochefoucauld maxim: "Our virtues are most frequently but vices in disguise."

The Beast (1975)

In full command, Walerian Borowczyk promptly stakes his turf — a Voltaire quote (troubled dreams and fleeting madness) segues into an erect horse cock. Equine fucking is documented outdoors, while wily old Marcel Dalio nourishes his "morbid fear of womanhood" in his wheelchair inside the chalet. The family fortune has long dissipated, so patriarch Guy Tréjan invites a lissome heiress (Lisbeth Hummel) to marry his son (Pierre Benedetti). Benedetti is taken out of the barn, sheared, and baptized into the human world, while Hummel rides swathed in furs and carnal curiosity. Both are newborn creatures; he forced into society and she catapulted into the animal realm. Dalio waits in vain for a call from the Vatican, banquet preparations take the servant away from the boss' horny daughter, who in frustration straddles the bed rail and rides away to completion; dinner suggests the slightly later *Eraserhead* (1977), for, as the wizened priest sighs, "we suffer the laws of nature, alas." Hummel is a sunny gal, who believes that nature is serious but not tragic and that champagne doesn't change the cosmos. She becomes fascinated by the mysteries of the place, principally an ancestor's fairy tale dalliance. Dissolve to Borowczyk's stupefying centerpiece — harpsichord tinkling competing with animalistic roars as a bewigged maiden (Sirpa Lane) is ravished by The Beast, a furry behemoth with a raging hard-on (the intense erotic wackiness is punctuated impishly with a snapshot of a snail crawling over her dainty shoe). Lane takes to the critter's geysering ejaculations and drains him of cum and life. Flashback? Dream? A deleted segment from *Immoral Tales*? In any case, bestial bluntness has unchained desire from civilized machinations, and at the chateau the heroine diddles herself with the rose originally employed by Tréjan to seal monetary matters. The beast's heritage is finally uncovered. The movie itself is a missing link, bridging Cocteau with the gonzo porn of Perverted Stories, illuminating not only *La Belle et la Bête* but also Charles Perrault, the Brothers Grimm, and King Kong. Beauty killed the beast, Borowczyk says, and erotic poetry freed the screen.

The Strange Case of Dr. Jekyll and Miss Osbourne (1981)

This is Walerian Borowczyk on Robert Louis Stevenson like Ulmer on Poe (*The Black Cat*): the obsessive travesty cuts closer to the original author's soul than any of the faithful adaptations. Victorian England is sketched with stark ease: a dark blue filter on the cobblestone streets outside, and indoors — creaking wood floors, cabinets, and frosted glass; a subtle, baleful shiver runs through them all. The event is the engagement party of Henry Jekyll (Udo Kier) and Fanny Osbourne (Marina Pierro), the topic of discussion is the doctor's controversial manifesto *The Laboratory and Transcendental Medicine*. Order stifles from the very start; horny hands grope frantically for the flesh beneath corsets while hunched-over figures of authority (Patrick Magee's glowering general, Howard Vernon's pragmatic scientist) smirk and skulk. A Vermeer canvas is heralded as the height of artistic achievement, though Fuseli's nightmares are clearly nearer Borowczyk's heart, as seen in the bloodthirsty goblin named Hyde (Gérard Zalcberg), who rises out of the bubbling slime in the doctor's bathtub to gleefully molest the guests. Jekyll's search is for new realms of consciousness; his fiendish alter ego sees gentility as little more than a barrier and, omnivorous spiked phallus at the ready, tramples it accordingly. ("You've committed worse atrocities in your dreams," the goblin retorts to an accusatory victim.) This is a work of astoundingly peculiar, eroticized textures: a mauled tawny ingénue sprawled under a lacy curtain, a wound staunched with perfume, a scarlet military coat studded with poison-tipped arrows, and even the scratchy sounds of a quill on paper. (Noël Véry's cinematography exudes moist enchantment, while Bernard Parmegiani's synthesizer score is like an electronic version of one of Popol Vuh's Herzog trances.) The ferocious climax, with Jekyll's and Fanny's monstrous selves laying waste to everything and everyone around them, reveals nothing less than the dinner soirée from Buñuel's *L'Age D'Or* as Borowczyk's inspiration and becomes a similarly high-pitched howl of barbarous exaltation. Mamoulian's 1932 version is an anxious bachelor comedy; here is a capital portrait of unholy matrimony pushed to its consummation and beyond.

Fernando F. Croce is a Brazilian-born film writer based in California. His writing has appeared in *Slant Magazine, The Mubi Notebook, Reverse Shot, Movie Mezzanine,* and *Film Comment,* as well as on his personal site *Cinepassion.org.*

CHAPTER 7
Borowczyk's Serial Labyrinth
From *Goto, Isle of Love* (1968) to *Behind Convent Walls* (1977)

James Snazell

> She said, "It's not life or death, the labyrinth."
> "Um, okay. So what is it?"
> "Suffering," she said. "Doing wrong and having wrong things happen to you. That's the problem. Bolivar was talking about the pain, not about the living or dying. How do you get out of the labyrinth of suffering?"
> —John Green in *Looking for Alaska*

Borowczyk's work can be seen to evolve from poster design in the mid to late 1950s to the production of full feature length films toward the end of the 1960s. Borowczyk gained recognition during a decade that saw the development of a counter-cultural freedom and an expansion of the popular arts, which included the development of an aesthetic mixing of what was considered high and low art. On one level, such an aesthetic manifested itself in Borowczyk's work by way of a focus on the flattened pictorial plane, which can be seen as having developed from his training in classical fine art painting as well as graphic design and printing.

This focus on flat 2D space throws up a range of aesthetic considerations and compositional techniques that come to form, in one sense, a foundation for his work and show an aesthetic sensibility that is distinctive to Borowczyk. In understanding Borowczyk's animation and film work we can come to see the way in which essentially graphic and painterly composition techniques are translated by Borowczyk into cinematic space. I particularly want to highlight in this chapter the twofold capacity of his films in the sense that they work by way of a series of shots as a 2D sequence and also by way of individual frames, which can be isolated and highlighted as flat 2D iconic images. This can be seen, particularly, in seven feature films from *Goto, Isle of Love* (1968) to *Behind Convent Walls* (1977) made over a ten-year period.[1]

Borowczyk studied at the Academy of Fine Arts in Kraków, where he practiced painting and lithography, which led him into the graphic arts profession, designing and creating posters for cinema. An example of such design work is the 1956 poster for the Mexican film *Roots* (*Raíces* [1955]). It shows a sequence of stills from the film bordering a main, central still. Such a framing device works to flatten the whole composition; a technique that was used many centuries previous within orthodox icon painting. In learning the craft of poster design, Borowczyk established a range of skills that he then took into animation and then film: the ability to catch the viewer's eye through the absurd, surreal, and bizarre; the use of omission and suggestion; the use of objects placed within the frame; the juxtaposition of these objects; the ability to tell a story through an image, etc.

As Michael Goddard explains, Borowczyk's work is based more in the Polish poster school (as pioneered by Henryk Tomaszewski) than anything else — and such a starting point was used by Borowczyk as an entry into the cultural production of cinema and animation.

> Both Lenica and Borowczyk were designers with a background in producing such posters: and their earliest animations can be seen largely as animated posters, a quality bringing them closer to the French and international new wave movements' interests in revaluing the popular and the contemporary over even avant-garde traditions. This was only intensified by Borowczyk's increasing interest in animating photographs, evident in House and even more so in School *(1958)*, which animates a series of still photographs ... (Goddard 2012: 292)

Innovative poster design in 1950s Poland can be seen partly as the result of designers having translated various trends in Western modernism, including, for Borowczyk, the styles of John Heartfield and Max Ernst, which highlight the collaging and cutting out of individual images to form a collection and sequence of diverse images. The achievement of Borowczyk and Lenica was to take the innovations of the Polish poster particularly in terms of aesthetic and compositional techniques into animation and then into film. The transition from poster design to animation for both Borowczyk and Lenica makes sense, because, essentially, animation is about the fascination of a single frame in terms of how it looks and works so that it can then relate and connect to a whole series of frames to form a storyboard, which then goes into creating the animation as moving image.

This skill of working with a series of images is one Borowczyk would have developed through designing posters. When undertaking poster design, a graphic designer will often work to produce a series of mock-ups that are a variation on one particular design. The client may ultimately only select one design to be printed or it might be that a series of posters, such as a set of three, go to print in order to advertise the same thing. This skill of working in series can be seen translated into the majority of Borowczyk animations, in terms of the way he works a short narrative as a set or series of sequences or scenes and likewise a number of his films can be seen as a series or set of short stories. Such serialism is also reflected in the structure of his work by way of seeing his animations and films as a series of shots joined together, like a set of photographs or collaged images. Borowczyk doesn't often use dissolves or fades, particularly in his feature films, preferring simple cuts; often one encounters a still shot with some movement within the frame — sometimes you will see him pan either horizontally or vertically then cut to the next shot. An example of such a technique can be seen in *Behind Convent Walls*; Borowczyk and cinematographer Luciano Tovoli filmed the scene of the nuns in high spirits in the chapel with rapid, loose, handheld shots that were cut together and that scan the action both horizontally and vertically. Such a way of working emphasizes the flatness of the objects, color and shapes within the composition and emphasizes the interconnectedness of the forms. Often the narrative is developed by the build-up of these sequences rather than the focus being on the actor. The actor fits into Borowczyk's fascination with the visual and his use of composition, which is then structured within animation by way of the form and movement of the composition — this takes the lead in Borowczyk's work to get across a sense of the inanimate becoming animated and the animate becoming inanimate.

Editing as such can be defined as the process of fitting sequences together to form a new whole as a series of edits. However, There is something pronounced about Borowczyk's use of the series; for example the use of photographs collaged together in *School* (1958) or *Behind Convent Walls,* which on one level works as a series of scenes and sequences that are spliced together, but which, as it could be argued, gives no sense of a clear beginning, middle, or end. This use of a series can be said to produce the sense of a maze — so indicative of the Baroque — of endless variation and decoration, which is used not only to produce grandeur but drama and tension. Angela Ndalianis (2005: 34) relates the idea of serialism to a labyrinthine meandering, which she describes as occurring within entertainment media, deriving such an analysis from Gilles Deleuze's reading of Leibniz, the Baroque, and the fold. In understanding the labyrinth in relation to the Baroque, Deleuze takes Leibniz's understanding of the fold, which he describes as never being a singular event but rather to be seen as a series of many folds:

> *Thus a continuous labyrinth is not a line dissolving into independent points, as flowing sand might dissolve into grains, but resembles a sheet of paper divided into infinite folds or separated into bending movements, each one determined by the consistent or conspiring surrounding ... A fold is always folded within a fold, like a cavern in a cavern. The unit of matter, the smallest element of the labyrinth, is the fold, not the point which is never a part, but a simple extremity of the line. (Deleuze 1993: 6)*

Such an analysis of the maze is indicative of the use of space within much of Borowczyk's work. For instance in *Goto, Isle of Love*, *Blanche* (1971), and *Behind Convent Walls*, long establishing shots of the surroundings are simply not present. Instead, there are views outwards from the strongholds that contain the characters, to the fields and trees, or to the distant shore. This helps to give the spaces within these films a particular quality. The fortress, the castle, the convent, the city are all seen as parts of a maze; a labyrinthine interior of passages, doors, windows, and various connecting rooms. In other words, they are depicted as a series of spaces, with each one joining the next to form a patchwork sequence reflecting Borowczyk's style of constructing animations and films. Jeremy Mark Robinson in talking about *The Beast* mentions the way Borowczyk uses the editing process to organize a network of connections in order to bring together all the characters, with such a process becoming obscured by the action taking place on screen (Robinson 2008: 108).

Such a use of space must surely connect Borowczyk's work to films such as Orson Welles' *The Trial* (1962), Chris Marker's *La Jetée* (1962), and Jean-Luc Godard's *Alphaville* (1965) where unreal and non-spaces — as compelling as those in *Goto, Isle of Love* — give a sense of narrative space that reflects an environment like a labyrinth: both warped and uncanny. Borowczyk's work also relates to *Alphaville* in terms of the way compositional technique becomes of equal importance to any inherent structured message. In his book about *Alphaville*, Chris Darke describes Godard's use of space as being as much about geometry and the way it relates to the cinematic process as it is about being a futuristic sci-fi dystopia:

> *For it is not just that Alphaville creates the future from the present, hence constructing Alphaville from Paris. Rather, the film is a demonstration that such a transformation is inherently cinematic, that, even in revealing the presence of the future, the cinematic process transforms, distorts, "dislocates" a three-dimensional space into a two-dimensional representation.* (Darke 2005: 66)

Darke's analysis describes how Godard mixes shots of particular kinds of architecture, which give a sense of depth through 3D perspective — such as stairwells and corridors that show images of various advertising signs in which the lack of "depth" reminds us that cinema essentially presents an illusion of space. Godard shuttles back and forth between depth and lack of depth in the image, reminding viewers that what they are watching is "only a movie."[2] Borowczyk, like Godard, plays with cinematic space, invariably using the past as opposed to *Alphaville's* futurism, and as a result gives great emphasis to creating flat tableaux compositions that show a definite lack of depth. Borowczyk's work can be seen as heavily influenced by painting, but through the use of light, line, color, texture, and shape, he creates (much like Godard did) a space that is essentially cinematic and achieved by the use of movement and time (which Borowczyk further explores by way of sequences and series).

Of course, such an analysis of the use of the series and the maze in relation to Borowczyk's work has a deeper connection to the way his films often get talked about in relation to eroticism. Many of his films are described as mere titillation, but delve beneath such a surface reading and there is a range of issues being explored — such as tension, frustration, and destructive sexual energy. In short, it is an exploration of eroticism that leads to relief, escape and a sense of freedom, but which also leads to a sense of being trapped within a maze. This holds true both in terms of those who look to trap, control and direct others by way of some kind of authoritarian structure, and of those who look to escape such a structure using the erotic in some shape or form. Daniel Bird describes Borowczyk's *The Margin* (1976) and Joe Dallesandro's character within the film:

> ... it's about a guy who gets lost in a fantasy, only to find it crumbling around him. Far from being an "erotic" film, it's actually a study of grief and suicide. (Bird 2011)

To describe someone as getting lost in a fantasy is to describe that person as getting lost or trapped in a maze. Borowczyk himself couldn't escape the maze formed by the accusations of film critics, who merely focused on the eroticism and titillation and helped to pigeonhole his films. By the late 1970s the popular view of his work as having declined into mere pornography had largely trapped Borowczyk and worked like a whirlpool, sucking him away from wide recognition and critical acclaim.

The theme of being trapped is one that Borowczyk himself explored by way of characters in his films who are trapped within spaces and as a result are prisoners of their own existences. We can also examine this in terms of the view of the camera and the way it frames and traps a character within a composition and within a scene. There is the sense that when you watch a number of Borowczyk's films there is only ever one camera on the set and that this single camera has Borowczyk standing behind it and directing the action. If the shot moves to a different position it's because that one camera has been moved by Borowczyk; in other words, he is always positioned at the center from which the action happens and at the heart of the maze that he creates, with his camera working like a closed-circuit security device in terms of its fixed, slightly artificial positioning. It might pan horizontally or vertically but it doesn't glide around a set. This fixed position also relates to what is seen and how it is seen, since the camera usually treats everything within the frame the same whether animate or inanimate. Often the camera sits back as it captures a scene, flattening out the elements within the frame by use of composition and bright, even-handed lighting.[3]

Such a cinematic approach relates to Borowczyk's training as a fine artist as well as his love and fascination for classical painting. For instance, in the second segment of *Immoral Tales* — "Therese the Philosopher" (1974) — the character of Therese lies face down, nude on a bed, locked in a room.[4] The scene and the way it is presented recalls seventeenth and eighteenth century canvases of reclining nude women: in particular, François Boucher's *Mademoiselle O'Murphy* (1751). The more one visually analyzes this painting the more the distinction between figure and objects — the animate and the inanimate — becomes blurred to the point where one comes to realize that it consists of the interplay of curves, creases, outlines and overlaps between the figure, the pillows, the curtain, and the fine linen that the figure relaxes upon.

Borowczyk initially does a similar thing regarding shape and form in the sequence of Therese on the bed in the locked room. But firstly, like Boucher, he looks to utilize his fondness for flattened perspective, dissolving the distinction between foreground and background by setting the bed against the wall, with the camera set back flattening the elements within the composition and the frame. But Borowczyk also does something else in that he doesn't just translate the aesthetic of painting into film; he looks to translate it into cinematic space. In the scene with Therese on the bed, Borowczyk uses a series of close up shots of Therese, with the camera panning her body closely enough for her figure to become flattened. The shots are cut and edited together to form a series of shots that fit together to give an abstracted interplay of shape and form through cinematic space. At the same time, such a series of shots is intermixed with another series of shots, some of which are set as fixed images of objects, including paintings, a lithographic print, photographs, books (including pages from a book), etc. Such a technique is often used by Borowczyk in his feature films: that of having a series of quick snapshots that act almost as still images, and which relate to a main series of shots.

In understanding the way in which essentially painterly composition techniques are translated into the language of Borowczyk's films, we can come to realize that parts of his films have a twofold capacity in the sense that they work in terms of the idea of the series — of sequences of shots — but also in terms of certain frames working as individual still images, which have an iconic, poster-like quality to their composition. One could look at the paintings of seventeenth-century Dutch painter Johannes Vermeer and argue that the majority of his work relates to a series with variations and that within such a body of work there are particular paintings that stand out as iconic. Borowczyk was no exception when it came to this skill of producing iconic images within a series of images that link up. Who could not notice in *The Beast* the incredible iconic image of the snail crawling over the shoe, evocative of the delicacy of the natural contrasting with the delicacy of the man-made; the juxtaposition of the two giving a sense of the surreal, with the animate and the inanimate both having an element of similarity in terms of their ornateness. In being discarded, the shoe gives a sense of being lost and the snail gives the first sign that this object has been claimed and taken over to become part of the forest and the labyrinth of the wilderness. Whilst such an image can certainly be looked at in isolation in terms of its iconic display, it also relates, within the film, to a series of quick snapshots that include a lake, trees, and discarded clothes, which fit into and run alongside the primary edits of the scene.

At first one might think that his series of feature films from *Goto, Isle of Love* to *Behind Convent Walls* can easily be categorized as surrealism or eroticism, but on closer analysis you realize that such definitions fall apart, as Borowczyk's work slips and slides when you attempt to shoehorn his work into neat categories. These works can be seen in terms of a compositional interplay of shape and form and the flattened pictorial plane, and there is a relationship between isolated individual shots and the whole series. This is fascinating because of the way Borowczyk relays this interplay in cinematic space, creating what is essentially a cinematic maze. One cannot ignore many of the issues that Borowczyk himself was no doubt trying to deal with by way of constructing his labyrinthine series of animations and films and in particular the feature length films he made from the time of *Goto, Isle of Love* to *Behind Convent Walls*. Many of his films give a sense of being trapped within a maze and we have seen how this relates to Borowczyk in the sense that he couldn't escape from the criticism that pigeonholed his work as being merely erotic titillation — and there is no sense that Borowczyk ever escaped from this; at a certain point in his life he simply stopped making feature length films.

Notes

1. The film that best demonstrates Borowczyk's use of a series of sequences or scenes is *A Private Collection* (1973), which was originally going to be part of the series of shorts that would become *Immoral Tales* but was released separately. It is seen as a midway point between a whole series of shorts that Borowczyk made starting from *August* (1946) and ending with *Scherzo Infernal* (1984). The short consists of a catalog of shots of Borowczyk's own collection of erotic objects. There is no sense of a defining moment within the film and each object is focused on for roughly the same amount of time. There is an intensity about this, which is heightened by the fact that each object is filmed fairly close up, giving little sense of the surrounding space or room in which it is situated.
2. Comparisons can also be made between Borowczyk and Andrei Tarkovsky Sergei Parajanov regarding the use of compositional technique to create cinematic space. In Tarkovsky's *Andrei Rublev* (1966), a meditative color slideshow of icons painted by the fourteenth-century Russian monk (Rublev) follows almost 200 minutes

of black and white narrative. Tarkovsky is clearly influenced by Rublev in terms of aesthetic and compositional technique but what he achieves is something inherently cinematic. In *The Color of Pomegranates* (1968) Parajanov — who was influenced by Tarkovsky — attempts to reveal a poet's life visually and poetically rather than literally. He does so by presenting the film in the form of static tableaux, with the actors moving as if by some strange clockwork, performing repetitive stylized gestures.

3. Such a process of flattening compositions recalls theater as well as Italian Renaissance fresco painting, including the early Quattrocento painters, such as Giotto and Duccio, as well as the mystical, geometry plane based painting of Piero della Francesca. Often in Borowczyk's films actors are shot against flat backgrounds of doors and walls, often with long lenses moving parallel to walls, moving only on the right angle axis of the camera. The development of Baroque and Rococo theater is interesting in relation to Borowczyk in the sense that it was during the sixteen hundreds that painted flats were developed whereby a perspective painting was transferred onto a series of flat surfaces. Such techniques saw the development of the interplay between 2D and 3D surfaces and the creation of space that deals with flattened perspective and the dissolution between foreground and background. It was also the period when set design whether it was wings, boarders or backdrops could be changed easily from one set to another while any number of special effects took place simultaneously. This theater was described as the clockwork stage because of the development of pulleys, levers and cogs to make such changes happen; such developments dominated theater for the next 200 years. Borowczyk was fascinated by mechanisms that predated cinema as can be seen in *A Private Collection*.

4. There are so many instances in Borowczyk's work of individuals either locked in rooms, walled into rooms, as well as instances of people spying on others in rooms.

Bibliography

Bird, D. 2011. "Moon in the Gutter: Q&A with Writer and Director Daniel Bird." Retrieved 13 July 2014 from http://moooninthegutter.blogspot.co.uk/2011/01/moon-in-gutter-q-with-writer-and.html.Darke, C. 2005. *Alphaville: French Film Guide*. London: I. B.Tauris.
Deleuze, G. 1993. *The Fold – Leibniz and the Baroque*. London: Athlone Press.
Goddard, M. 2012. *The Impossible Polish New Wave and its Accursed Émigré Auteurs: Borowczyk, Polański, Skolimowski, and Żuławski*. In A. Imre (ed.), *A Companion to Eastern European Cinemas*. London: Wiley-Blackwell.
Green, J. 2011. *Looking for Alaska*. London: Harper Collins Children's Books.
Ndalianis, A. 2005. *Neo-Baroque Aesthetics and Contemporary Entertainment* Massachusetts: MIT Press.

Robinson, J. M. 2008. *Walerian Borowczyk: Cinema of Erotic Dreams*. Maidstone: Crescent Moon Publishing.

James Snazell is an experimental filmmaker and lecturer and is currently teaching Animation and Visual Effects at Edge Hill University, UK. He has had his moving image work screened at a range of experimental film festivals including the Berlin Directors Lounge Film Festival, Australian International Experimental Film Festival, The Athens Video Art Festival, Da Fest Digital Art Festival Sofia Bulgaria, Punto y Raya Festival Madrid, and the Lausanne Underground Film & Music Festival in Switzerland.

CHAPTER 8
Immoral Toys
On Borowczyk's *A Private Collection* (1973)

Edwin Carels

> *Making a film, equals constructing an object that carries a philosophy within, but before anything else, a film is a load of celluloid in a can!*
> —Borowczyk in *Contes Immoraux – Dossier de Presse* (1975)

A Private Collection (1973) is not usually considered among the canonical titles in Borowczyk's filmography. This seemingly straightforward documentation of a collection of erotic toys does not contain any of his trademark animations, stylized acting, surprising editing or ingenious mise en scène. All we see is a pair of male hands manipulating various objects, such as a peep box, a shadow play theater, a magic lantern, and some other vintage media curiosities. What unites them is their pornographic content: from a dildo adorned with a photograph to a wooden slot machine whereby each coin inserted triggers the mechanic representation of a fellatio act. Borowczyk reputedly borrowed the objects from a private collector, the surrealist writer André Paul Édouard Pieyre de Mandiargues. After the writer's death they ended up in the filmmaker's possession, although he did not particularly consider these objects "part of his universe," nor did he rank the film itself as anything more than "a simple amusement."[1] In spite of its deceptive simplicity, however, *A Private Collection* can be read as a manifesto that unveils Borowczyk's philosophy as an ambimodern filmmaker.

Made in between the feature films *Blanche* (1971) and *Immoral Tales* (1974), it could easily have been integrated into the latter, as it is a film à sketch, illustrating four distinct cases and different degrees of perversion through the ages. For it to function as an additional fifth episode or even better as a coda, some formal diversions are too strong: not only is its duration shorter, the approach is also more descriptive and factual than the four very literary adaptations in *Immoral*

Tales. A Private Collection is based around a contemporary man instead of a historical female persona. On the other hand, *A Private Collection* quite explicitly announces that Borowczyk's aesthetic strategy would forevermore include an insistent attack on the hypocrisy surrounding sex and pornography. As he stated in the mid 80s:

> *Pornography is a legal term, not a critical or artistic one. One can't talk about pornography as the curse of society because in every country it is expressed as being different in the penal code. As for the censorship boards, I have never heard of one of the judges rushing from a screening to rape and kill because he saw it in a film, so why on earth should they suppose that someone else would behave like that?* (Borowczyk 1985: 25)

In the film we repeatedly see the hands of the private collector turn a wooden toy box with the depiction of a uniformed member of the vice squad (*police des mœurs*) away from sight and put it in a corner, no longer facing the camera. Such playful attacks against legal authorities also structured the earlier short films *School* (1958) and *Autumn* (1954), the latter even demonstrating a similarly repetitive ritual of a voyeurist guard in a public park. This insistence on the evasion of the eye of the law already turns *A Private Collection* into more than a straightforward documentation. Like in all his work, Borowczyk carefully composes each frame, consistently hiding the identity of the male guide in a private cabinet. As the critic Robert Benayoun remarked: "Borowczyk shoots his work with in each second the voyeurism of an aristocrat, and he manifests a fanatic curiosity, anticipating the same condition from his viewer" (Benayoun 1997: 20). Trained as a graphic artist, Borowczyk thematizes the framing of the gaze in all his work. To a large extent, *A Private Collection* is a mise en abyme of peep boxes and miniature dioramas, reminiscent of the glass-cased collages and toy boxes by Joseph Cornell, yet of a more salacious kind. Each manipulation triggers an erotic action, such as the finger puppet of a masturbating acolyte, or the shadow play of a professor penetrating a female student. The libidinous allure of a self-contained universe is also manifest in another category of objects, which need to be taken out of their box before they can stimulate the senses. Like Buñuel and his mysterious striped box from *Un Chien Andalou* (1929), Borowczyk toys with the viewer's fetishist gaze, returning cinema back to what it essentially is: an optical contraption that stimulates the curiosity; a guilty pleasure.

André Pieyre de Mandiargues, the instigator of this particular collection of erotica, also provided the literary inspiration for the first episode of *Immoral Tales*, with his short story "The Tide." This text was originally commissioned by André Breton to be included in the deluxe catalog accompanying the *Exposition Internationale du Surréalisme*, organized by André Breton and Marcel Duchamp at the end of 1959 in Paris and commonly known as "EROS." Borowczyk would affirm his affinity with the surrealists by using a complimentary quote from Breton as the title for his 1997 solo exhibition in Annecy: "L'imagination fulgurante" (The dazzling imagination). And just like Duchamp so often did, Borowczyk alternates in *A Private Collection* authentic, found objects with emulations and appropriations. An important difference is of course that Duchamp took his cue from more common household utensils, instead of uniquely crafted examples of folk erotica. Although in later years Borowczyk denied that the objects in the film really belonged to "his universe," at least some were definitely made by his own hands. There is the furtive appearance of a singular, more abstracted phallic shape in a wooden holder — an item we find back in the catalog of Borowczyk's own sculpture art under the title *Cylindre Sauterelle (Cylinder Grasshopper)*.[2] The only function of the cylinder is indeed to hop up and down, which produces a vibrating sound. Another artwork by Borowczyk himself is featured, even more discretely, in the background on the wall of the collector's private cabinet. It is a painted study for the same cylindrical object, but more than a rudimentary technical drawing, it emulates an old calligraphic text that is written on top of the colorful sketch. For the occasion of the Annecy exhibition, Borowczyk particularly foregrounded this drawing, notably as the campaign image for the invitation card, poster, and catalog. The title of this graphic work is, again, derived from a short story by de Mandiargues: "L'Anglais Décrit dans le Château Fermé."[3]

After the Annecy exhibition, Borowczyk created at least a dozen more of these highly stylized wooden sculptures. Each of them is an enigmatic piece of organic material, designed with minimalist grace, like a three-dimensional form of graphic art. However ephemeral the outlines, their material qualities were obviously crucial for Borowczyk. He proudly mentions "without nails" in their descriptions and sometimes even adds the type of wood and its origin in the subtitles. With these sculptures, Borowczyk, in his own particular way, ties in with the tradition of tactile art; like for instance with *La Grande Crécelle (The Big Rattle)*, which he describes as "a useless yet indispensable machine, a sonoric sculpture to be animated with a single finger (the digit)" (Borowczyk 2009: 87).

The sound produced enhances the tactile quality, as it is a response that directly touches the ear. The vibrations produced can be understood as a kinetic characteristic. The most subtle of his sculptures is *Silence*, a flat rectangular board with two triangular shapes symmetrically attached to them, evoking a stylized angel figure. In his description, Borowczyk mentions a supplementary function of the contraption as a barometer. When the air becomes dry, the wings are deployed in an inaudible exhalation. The energy of such latent sounds matches the impact of latent images, lurking underneath what Borowczyk is allowing his viewers to experience at first glance. Their dynamic is often implicit.

In a more sublimated sense than the optical erotica of *A Private Collection*, Borowczyk's sculptures can be understood as variations on the concept of the *machine célibataire* (bachelor machine). Their iconography is often mechanic, like the evocation of cogwheels in *Tourne-disque de haute précision* or *Pièce détachée femelle*, but they are redeemed by material qualities and the utter lack of any functionality. Their sole purpose is to be touched and to produce vibrations that massage the ears of whoever is manipulating them. Thus *A Private Collection* foregrounds what is usually only furtively present in his feature films: objects that are much more than props; that are non-human agents in their own right. "Alternately inventor and saboteur," as Benayoun labeled him, Borowczyk stages their agency as provocatively counterproductive: his contraptions generate pleasure, but do not produce any material results. Accordingly, in *A Private Collection* as well as in *Immoral Tales* no sexual act is aimed at procreation.

The short film that preceded this allusive visual essay on pornography was *Phonograph* (1969) in homage to the earliest type of this acoustic machine, operating with a wax cylinder. Lovingly photographed, Borowczyk ends his homage to the phonograph with the self-destruction of the device. In *A Private Collection* the scratchy, thin sound originates from this same type of machine. The paradoxical combination of nostalgic attention to vintage objects and a brutal celebration of destruction were already present at the heart of *Renaissance* (1963). Daniel Bird considers that these regressive demonstrations of "catastrophism" are motivated by "a worry that craftsmanship is dying and that 'vivacity' is being displaced by a 'mechanical society' based on excess" (Bird 2006). A similar love for pre-modernist craftsmanship is indeed manifested in the press release that accompanied *A Private Collection*:

> *The particular collection of erotic objects displays the naive and creative invention which nowadays has disappeared a [sic] the stage of the*

sex shop's industry. This naive art underlines the degeneration of a commercial and common production deprived of any expression. Motion picture had to record these unpublished forms of a culture in process [sic] of extinction.[4]

But then again, is the cinema industry not equally a "degenerated" form of mass produced images? Isn't *A Private Collection* itself a media-archaeological statement about handcrafted cinema before the cinema? Most of the featured objects can be labeled as proto-cinematic, as they produce motion pictures that stem from the days before the film industry, each of them demonstrating how an image can be animated through simple manipulation. As a filmmaker just starting out, Borowczyk was already aware of his ambivalent approach to the medium. In a joint interview with his colleague Jan Lenica he stated: "We consider that cinema perished with the death of the French avant-garde. More than anything we wish to return to Méliès, when the image prevailed on the movement. It is our aspiration to give to animation its letters of nobility" (Giżycki 2009: 91).

This statement dates from 1957, during the boom of postwar modernism. Borowczyk's innovative film language was repeatedly hailed as typically modernist. And yet at the core of so many of his films lies a profound skepticism about the industrialized society that achieved both mass production and mass slaughter. In the wake of Hiroshima and the Holocaust, Borowczyk seems to plead for a similar strategy as applied earlier by Duchamp, Max Ernst and many other surrealists. Already after the First World War they tapped back into nineteenth-century iconography and vernacular culture as ingredients for their iconoclast art. In the nascent years of film production — the time of Méliès — a similar paradox between innovation and traditionalism immediately became manifest. To explain this apparent contradiction in many films from the first decade, Ben Singer coined the neologism "ambimodern" (Singer 2009: 39). He observes that the modernity of early cinema has too often been narrowed down and characterized in terms of novelty, velocity, mobility, instability, flux, and so on. The logical result was the dismissal of anything that did not epitomize modernity and that was categorized as "anti-modern." And yet, as the cases of, for instance, Émile Cohl, Segundo de Chomón and Georges Méliès illustrate: the fastest, most attractive and innovative films were often the ones with the most "regressive" narrative settings. And as Tom Gunning has argued: during this pioneering era of the so-called "cinema of attractions" the machine producing the movement was often regarded as part of the spectacle itself (Gunning 1990).

What was lost with the industrialization of the cinema — as *A Private Collection* seems to suggest — is the personal touch: intimate relationships during the production of the image, and the direct contact when experiencing it. A common characteristic of most proto-cinematic devices, from the thaumatrope and the phenakistiscope to the mutoscope and the cinematograph, was indeed their requirement to be activated by hand. Every movement corresponded with the rhythm, the heartbeat, of the operator behind it. Even when not functioning, all these nineteenth-century formats of cinematic entertainment — like peep boxes, silhouette cards, shadow theaters, and lantern slides — offered their owners a particular joy, as they could become part of a larger personal collection. In the original French title, the world *'particulière'* not only suggests a 'curious' but also a 'personal', a 'private' collection, which opposes it to the public collections of musea and other institutions.

There exist two versions of *A Private Collection*: one for distribution, and a director's cut (also called the "Oberhausen version," where the film premiered). The former has the voice of de Mandiargues as a quirky narrator offering occasional commentaries and thus adding a twisted sense of documentary codification to the film. With similar irony in this version, the index finger of the demonstrator covers every close up of sexual organs in the sequence with vintage pornographic photographs. The original festival version, however, is altogether more straightforward, with no words distracting from the music, no flesh tones covering the black and white poses, and most tellingly it lasts two minutes longer, as it includes a pornographic home movie of a woman having intercourse with a dog.

Arranging his short anthology of proto-cinematic toys, Borowczyk thus jumps from the magic lantern and shadow play to the projection of live action. The murky gray footage of this hardcore scene is intercut with surprisingly colorful loops of vintage drawn animation. Their iconography displays childlike naïveté, although by now every image in the film is obviously tainted by sexual innuendo. One particular looped image shows a magician, who clearly carries the features of Georges Méliès. In the first decade of cinema, toy versions of the earliest films were circulated, made for a convertible magic lantern and adapted for so-called "chromolitographic films" that were drawn by rotoscope from live action scenes and then reproduced on 35mm film (Mannoni 2009: 249). Perhaps Borowczyk's point in contrasting the grainy live action images with such bright and colorful sequences of the earliest form of animated film was only meant as an illustration of the range of domestic entertainment then in circulation. But the final sounds and images of the original film make clear that he did put more composition and conceptualization into the project than he would later admit. The purring sound of the mechanical windup toy with the police officer blends with the characteristic noise of a film projector. With *A Private Collection* and the feature films that followed, Borowczyk explicitly cultivated cinema's paradox of public privacy and exhibited intimacy.

And thus, labeling this film as "for personal amusement" was perhaps Borowczyk's elegant way of making a statement about cinema as a *machine célibataire* in its own right: an unproductive, immoral toy that is essentially there to touch the viewer's senses. As with each of his consecutive films, but never more explicitly so, Borowczyk celebrated with *A Private Collection* an intimate, more personal, complicit relationship with the moving image and its machinery. At the end of the film, even the policeman can no longer hide his erection, the embodied manifestation of his arousal. Instead of functioning as an exponent of the culture of surveillance and punishment, Borowczyk suggests that the cinema should be there to cater to our most particular and private pleasures.

Notes

1. The author's correspondence with Borowczyk dated 29 March 1998 in response to the author's proposal to curate an exhibition with these particular objects. Borowczyk declined the proposal, and confessed he was considering selling them.
2. For a reproduction of *Cylindre Sauterelle* (Cylinder Grasshopper) and other wooden sculptures see Vimenet (2009: 86).
3. This erotic novel was first published in 1953 in Oxford and Cambridge under the pseudonym of Pierre Morion, and published in Paris only in 1979 under his own name. In 1976 Borowczyk also adopted de Mandiargues's novel *The Margin*; in 1979 the short story "Le Sang de L'Agneau" inspired Borowczyk for the episode "Marceline" in his film *Heroines of Evil*, and in 1988 he turned his novel *Tout doit Disparaître* into the film *Love Rites*. As a literary colleague, de Mandiargues wrote the introduction to Borowczyk's own publication of short stories: *Anatomy of the Devil* (1992).
4. Press release leaflet, Argos distribution, obtained by the author through correspondence with Borowczyk. This is the author's direct translation. The original French verion reads: "Une invention naive et toujours créatrice qui de nos jours a

disparu au stade de l'industrie du sex shop. Cet art naif manifest la dégénérescence d'une production banale et commerciale privée de tout caractère poétique. Le cinéma se devrait d'enregistrer ces formes inédites d'une culture en voie de disparition."

Bibliography

Benayoun, R. 1997. "Walerian Borowczyk, the Fangs of the Dolly Man." In M. Corbet (ed.), *Boro, L'Imagination Fulgurante*. Annecy: Centre international du cinéma d'animation.

Bird, D. 2006. "The Ghost of Goto, Walerian Borowczyk Remembered." In *Vertigo* 3(1). Retrieved on 10 April 2014 from http://www.closeupfilmcentre.com/vertigo_magazine/volume-3-issue-1-spring-2006/.

Borowczyk, W. 1975. *Contes Immoraux – Dossier de Presse*. Paris: Argos Films.

———. 1985. "Enticements to Voyeurism." In *Cinema Papers* 50, February–March.

Carrouges, M. 1954. *Les Machines Célibataires*. Paris: Arcanes.

Giżycki, M. 2009. "Borowczyk, Années Polonaises." In P. Vimenet (ed.), *Walerian Borowczyk – Les Animés*. Montreuil: Éditions de l'œil.

Gunning, T. 1990. "Cinema of Attractions." In T. Elsaesser (ed.), *Early Cinema: Space Frame Narrative*. London: British Film Institute.

Mannoni, L. 2009. *Lanterne Magique et Film Peint, 400 ans de Cinema*. Paris: Éditions de la Martinière.

Singer, B. 2009. "The Ambimodernity of Early Cinema: Problems and Paradoxes in Film-and-Modernity Discourse." In A. Ligensa and K. Kreimeier (eds.), *Film 1900: Technology, Perception, Culture*. New Barnet: John Libbey co.

Vimenet, P. (ed.). 2009. *Walerian Borowczyk – Les Animés*. Montreuil: Éditions de l'œil.

Edwin Carels is a teacher and researcher in the arts at the School of Arts KASK/HoGent (University College Ghent — Faculty of Fine Arts). His Ph.D. is titled "Animation beyond Animation — a media-archeological approach to the use of animation in contemporary art." For more than a decade, Edwin Carels has been active as a film programmer and curator for the International Film Festival of Rotterdam. Carels publishes essays on media-archeology, visual arts, film and animation. He is also affiliated with the Museum of Contemporary Art in Antwerp (the M HKA) where he has curated thematic shows such as *El Hotel Eléctrico* (2014), *Graphology* (2011), *Animism* (2010) and *The Projection Project* (2006). Recent exhibitions have involved collaborations with Dora Garcia, Luc Tuymans, Chris Marker, The Quay Brothers, Robert Breer, Jan Švankmajer, Zoe Beloff, and Julien and Ken Jacobs, among many others.

CHAPTER 9
The Beast with Two Backs
On Borowczyk's *The Beast* (1975)

Phillip Warnell

> *What profane wretch art thou? I am one, sir, that comes to tell you your daughter and the Moor are now making the beast with two backs.*
> —William Shakespeare, *Othello* (Act One, Scene I, 117–118)

The strangeness of bodily form, the silent taboo of zoophilia, the eternal palimpsest of the monarch and the beast. A tale of haunting bestiality traverses Borowczyk's *The Beast* (1975) — his take on *Beauty and the Beast* — harking back to Shakespeare and the coining of a phrase by which the endless shapes of coitus were intrinsically linked to beast-like behavior and sexual performance.[1]

Borowczyk's *The Beast* is a tale of tails, located somewhere between a story and an oddity. It concerns an heiress, Lucy Broadhurst (Lisbeth Hummel), whose inheritance depends on a frantically arranged marriage to a marquis named Mathurin (Pierre Benedetti), son of her late father's closest friend, whom she has never met. He turns out to be of lamentable and diminished character, a living Wolpertinger, suspended in an uncomfortable, improbable state of bodily disassembly: between species, as it were. His chief preoccupation is with the intensity of horse copulation at a family stud farm, where he marvels at the spectacle of equine interbreeding: the pulsing sex of the species is accompanied by its shrieking cries uttered in the act of conjoining, which pre-empt the Beast's own later mating vocalizations.

Amidst all graphic intent and definite sexual transgression, Borowczyk's film also develops more discreet, underlying themes concerning the relationship between the passions of landed gentry and latent animal impulses, with the whole narrative presented as one of sexual awakening (as supported by continual interracial household transgressions, namely the *Othello*-like encounters of the aristocratic white heiress with the largely silent black servant). The Beast, which makes its appearance in the second half of the film, is explored in unison with the landed gentry as a sort of palimpsest: a duo of refinement and perversion where coiffure meets hairiness. This relationship is witnessed repeatedly by Lucy, firstly through literature (a jealous potential in-law seeks to ward her off by introducing her to tales of the beast's mythical associations), and then in a succession of flashbacks to a period centuries prior, where she dreams she is Romilda (Sirpa Lane), ancestor of Mathurin. It is during these sequences that the eponymous mythical creature returns: its prodigious, de-territorialized roaming continuing, set, as ever, across a vast range of literature, cinema, and the unconscious, all representing truer worlds of its habitation and inevitable conquests. As it goes, the film mythologizes, thus devouring and flavoring centuries past and those yet to come. The beast's appearances in Lucy's dreams are presented in concomitance with the heiress' projection of embodied omnipotence onto her sleeping, woeful husband-to-be. She repeatedly, surreptitiously, visits his room in the process of her own gathering arousal, only to discover an unresponsive, slowly disappearing soul, whose restless dreams remain unshared and unscreened.

As her staged dream advances she empathizes in full affection with Romilda, who, dressed in full, frilly period regalia, leaves the safety of a stately summer house to follow a straying lamb. She encounters the Beast's prowess in a forest, during its devouring of the stray, in a scene that progressively unfolds as both a comic and disturbing horror escapade. Accompanied by her own insistent harpsichord playing, a chase sequence develops during which her layers of bodice and garment are ripped piece by piece from her; the beast eventually violating her in full depravity, commencing with mouth to sex organ. Eventually, however, as the dream plays out, prowess turns to mutuality, shown in savage, primordial and full-blown intercourse — noblewoman and fiend making "the beast with two backs." The libidinal excesses of the woman, however, continue to drive her ignoble prurience during a complete about-turn; the beast's increasing, even worrying, signs of savage-tenderness are expended beyond exhaustion, at which point, frenzy over, he expires — a salient and less than poignant reminder of those species for whom the excesses of sexual transgression culminate only in death. The realization of this B-movie scene is also memorable for an overblown, somewhat extraordinarily modeled phallus that at a certain point appears to be in an almost constant state of ejaculation. Awkward and extended, this strap-on meets percolator produces continual, milky, ejaculatory surges. Horror meets art department with this cumbersome comic cock, which offers only the faintest echo of nature's sleek, equine-like instrument for sexual engagement.

The heiress' sweaty hallucinations and hypnotic dreams bring sex and seduction into what arguably becomes a genuinely erotic scene in the house. Rightly giving up on Mathurin, Lucy eventually masturbates. She inserts a rose into herself in a close-up that becomes a Bataille-like image full of metonymic association (Barthes 1978). The rosebud and flower petals offer a strangely exemplary counterpoint to her enraptured, landscaped and disembodied sexual encounter with the beast. Sleeping on, she tugs at both myth and bedclothes to unconscious, sensory effect. In the apparent race against time to consolidate estate, property, and power, she in fact encounters not an estate, but an ecstatic-state, whereby the lineage of her past-life transgressions return and transfix and consume her. Equally compelled toward an immediate futurity, she becomes disoriented, wandering Beauty-like through corridors and confusing her dream arousal with what she perceives must have been the actual interventions of her future husband. Spirited intent and erotic drive ultimately prevail, as Lucy checks whether Mathurin is awake. To her horror, she discovers that he sleeps on, and he eventually mirrors the decline and demise of the beast, expiring in his sleep.

Furthermore, the film exposes Mathurin as the beast's unlikely, distant descendent when his post-mortal, mutant corpse is finally unmasked. Upon the removal of a plaster cast he had worn throughout, the extent of his mutation is thus disclosed: a clawed hand and hairy spinal curvature complete with a pathetic tail. Even in death, Mathurin's unrequited, disavowed body is outlawed — castigated by attendant priests citing Leviticus' biblical laws that condemn bestiality. Thus the bio-politics of man, beast and judicial protocol all come into sharp, disapproving focus.

Borowczyk deals uncannily with absurdity, employing both corporeality and horror-erotic tone, as the events descend into a Buñuelesque, use-diacritics-wherever-necessary, sexually charged fiasco, which melds ritual time and phantasmatic sexual energy, reminiscent of the revelry and catharsis of Franz Mesmer's bizarre concoction, *The Discovery of Animal Magnetism* (1779). During these seances, discomforted nobles were tethered to a strange bathtub containing magnetized water and were required to grip a protruding, metallic skeletal arm. The resulting, tingling sensation of their group therapy induced a hypnotic, hallucinogenic and revelatory state of self-diagnosis and bodily transparency, its catharsis recalibrating one's urges and drives and reputedly providing equilibrium between all living matter in the universe. Whilst Mesmer was famously depicted as a charlatan, half nobleman, half donkey, the Beast's own pseudo-violation turns into mutual lust, (therapeutic) seduction, and inevitable death. Sovereign and the Beast unite, reversing their respective roles — Lucy gorged with her own form of psycho-ceremonial, beast-like becomings, borne of a desire both imagined and inherited. Conversely, Mathurin falls pathetically into a silent, unresponsive eternity due to his quasi-animality and physical distortions. The upshot being that the attempted match of husband and wife is sacrificed, falling to that other eternal prerequisite — a ubiquitous need for the continual updating of a timeless formation, a geometry cut and set between monarch, beast, and dominion. The phantasmatic coordinates of eternal desire are presented by Borowczyk in startling opposition to their temporal and distant cousin: marriage — that familial constellation of corporeal alignment that can only culminate in exasperation, frustration, and loss.

In distilled moments of virtual intimacy between the beast and the aristocrat, the film traverses pornography and eroticism, horror and pastiche, thus uncovering a strange avowal, which summons the beast into the service of the landed gentry. This tendency of the sovereign toward the beast and vice versa offers an uncanny association, endlessly and variously played out through art, literature, and film. The kingdom, the one who reigns over it and the prodigious nature of the beast who transgresses it all interact with one another. Their contact permeates all worlds: the bodily, the territorial, and the psychological, with each of them perceived through the other's transparency. Thresholds and limits dissolve into a flurry of ritual, primordial and magnetic effects. Scripts are rewritten and the cinematic emerges. In Jean Cocteau's *Beauty and the Beast* (1946), Beauty effortlessly traverses a seemingly endless corridor, which constitutes a parallel dominion. Her encounter with the horrific refinement and bizarre makeup of actor Jean Marais provides an astonishing, enchanted set of episodes culminating in the death of the beast, who becomes a prince in the very moment of his death. Palace, pavilion, glove, key, arrow, mirror are the glossy material, spatial and magical trappings of Cocteau's own take on sovereign-beast transcendentalism and corporeal convergence. The transfiguration from beast to prince — their union — further reminds us of Derrida's exploration of sovereign and beast. It brings into question, as does *Othello*, the friction between what might be considered the laws of nature versus those of society, as well as the continuing mystery of man's and animals' borders: this troubling resemblance, this worrying superposition of these two beings outside the law, which beast and sovereign both are when viewed from a certain angle, I believe resembles, explains and engenders a sort of hypnotic fascination or irresistible hallucination, which makes us see, project and perceive as in an X-ray the face of the beast under the features of the sovereign. Or conversely, if you prefer, it is as though through the maw of the untamable beast a figure of the sovereign might appear.[2]

Derrida refers to the extraordinary situation whereby the sovereign is the one who does not have to respond, in accordance with their status as the one who is placed above the law. And this is as per the beast: castigated by humanity as beneath the law, it is a creature that, whilst it can react, is (purportedly) unable to respond. Further to this, Derrida reminds us that even God himself does not respond, emphasizing the shared ability of the savage outlander and Him, endlessly worshipped through the sacred animal and its sacrifice (Derrida 2009: 18). The monarch resides above humanity — it is God-like, yet prone to a certain irresponsibility like the beast, and is regularly nicknamed as one; one thinks of the derisory naming of Saddam Hussein as the "Beast of Baghdad," for example. Their co-existence as a palimpsest confirms the requirement for a role interplay in representation, whereby, as directed by Borowczyk, beauty and the beast becomes beauty as the beast.

These tones also suggest the unfortunate philosophical history — the Derridean and others' view of which is ongoing — which still displaces and degrades the "animal," devoid of language or response, lacking consciousness, or oblivious to the concept of its own mortality. The manner of this ridiculous split between the human animal and all other species as written into such esteemed tradition remains a sweeping, mystifying and bizarre assumption — emblematic of our violence toward all other creatures, while as Deleuze suggests, "It is animals (contrary to what's written) who know how to die" (Deleuze 1996).

The ability of a species to "know their time is coming," to seek a place, a corner, a territory or secret spot to die in, offers a compensatory restitution, presenting an animal-machine that fills in for our inability to successfully conquer other species. Phillippe Ariés' *The Hour of Our Death* (1981) reminds us how we have banished our own understanding of what he describes as a "tame" death. Perceived in earlier ages as quite simply a transition point toward an eternal life, it has become something more of an unendurable truth in our times. This chimes with the forest as a plentiful, territorial dominion of banishment and redress, where the shady figures of sex and death come in and out of proximity as emergent forms of bodily secrecy and constitution. Caught in the throes of their zoophilia in all its strange potential, Lucy's unconscious desire is unleashed, taming and ultimately sacrificing the Beast's initially unsolicited sexual pursuit of her. The tame, silent and perhaps wished-for passing of the Beast is thus the culmination of a primordial, ritualistic state, witnessed in concomitance with Lucy's burgeoning realization of her own animality, metamorphosis, and bestial assimilation.

The ability to place oneself in preparation for death offers a kind of geometry for all creatures passing from this world, where the curvature of bodily form is positioned within a corner or some other particularity of the spatial, reminiscent of the overlooked notion of someone or something as, indeed, having "taken place." Ariés even describes death itself as a wild beast, as mysterious and overwhelming as the meaningless monster eventually (lovingly) buried by Lucy in a shallow grave. In contemporary life, our fearful encounters with death's invisible indifference allow that particular wild beast free rein, lording it over us somewhat. Perhaps Borowczyk's insatiable beast is just such a being; the film providing death with a mirror to itself — a paradoxical, unbearable encounter with its own immortality and mutated, beast-like form, while Mathurin's mortal coil echoes that of the eternally re-enacted anniversary of death's strange familiarity.

The cadaveric condition of our death and the dimensionality of our form were recently reconsidered by Jean-Luc Nancy as a timeless formation, and the only state in which the body can truly be seen to its full extent; in its full effect, as it were:

> ... body is itself in its integrity only when it is dissected and found anatomized. Finally presented in death, in the absence of an inspiration, soul or visitation, each body can be seen resting, "a stranger to end in the world, whose secret it takes with it, each body, coiled up, deployed in world secret." (Warnell 2010)

Sleep well, Mathurin.

Notes

1. The book was adapted and directed for screen by Jean Cocteau in 1946.
2. Othello himself is described by Iago as a "Barbary Horse" and "old black Ram," connoting the notion of savagery in the Moor.

Bibliography

Aries, P. 1981. *The Hour of our Death*. Oxford: Oxford University Press.
Barthes, R. 1962. *Metaphor of the Eye*. Paris: Critique.
De Beaumont, J. M. L. P. 1757. *Beauty and the Beast*. Paris.
Deleuze, G. 1996. *L'Abécédaire de Gilles Deleuze*. Editions Montparnasse.
Derrida, J. 2009. *The Beast and the Sovereign*, volume 1. Chicago: Chicago University Press.
Mesmer, F. A. 1779. *The Discovery of Animal Magnetism*. Vienna.
Nancy, Jean-Luc and Phillip Warnell. 2010. *Étranges Corps Étrangers*. London: Wellcome Trust.
Shakespeare, W. 1603. *Othello*. London: Penguin.

Phillip Warnell is a filmmaker (www.phillipwarnell.com) and academic based in London. His films traverse philosophy, human-animal studies, and cinematic experimentation; most recently he produced and directed two films in collaboration with philosopher Jean-Luc Nancy. His films have been screened, exhibited and curated internationally, most recently at New York (NYFF), Marseille (FID), Vienna (Viennale), Amsterdam (IDFA), Copenhagen (CPH-Dox), Montreal (FNC), Jihlava (Prague), and Extra City (Antwerp), all in 2014. Phillip is a professional mentor and Associate Programmer at BFI Southbank, where he established and co-curated "Essential Experiments" between 2009 and 2013. His associated academic work includes delivering essays on "projections of animality," the "life-like," and human-animal relations, and he has published articles in academic journals and artists' publications. He is currently writing a chapter for *Jean-Luc Nancy and Visual Culture* (Edinburgh University Press, 2015). Phillip is Director of Studies in Film & Experimental Film at Kingston University, London and has further research affiliations with The Wellcome Trust and Cambridge University.

CHAPTER 10
Laugh in the Doll House
On Victorian Surrealism in the Films of Walerian Borowczyk

Kamila Wielebska

> *In this world let me have my world, to be damned with it or to be saved.*
> —Richard Wagner, *Tristan and Isolde*

> *It's in the trees, it's coming!*
> —Jacques Tourneur, *Night of the Demon* (1957) /
> Kate Bush, *Hounds of Love* (1985)

My story, just like the story of life on Earth, ought to begin by the sea. And because I lay no claim to being able to grasp the things I will be talking about in their entirety, the text can be treated as a suddenly-found-on-the-sand-during-a-walk-by-the-sea-scribbled-by-some-hand fragment; a part of something only, which we manage to hastily read before it gets licked off by the salty, glimmering waves. Or perhaps as a fragment of a-text-placed-by-someone-in-an-empty-bottle-and-drifting-peacefully-on, which we, immersed in the thoughts of a late afternoon walk, suddenly fish out ... We catch it with uncertainty, as we cannot immerse ourselves in certainty right from the start that it was addressed to us. What is behind the text? Can we penetrate it?

This sea-side (or even the sea itself) landscape is one of those typical to surrealism (Taborska 2007). It is also here that *Immoral Tales* by Walerian Borowczyk begin. The first part of the film, made in 1974, is entitled "The Tide" and is based on a short story by André Pieyre De Mandiargues. It opens with the words: "Julie, my cousin, was sixteen, I was twenty, and that tiny difference in age made her docile to my commandments." These words seem a perfect introduction to a text devoted to Borowczyk's output, since — like most of his works — they inspire ambivalence: unnerving and repulsive, yet rousing interest, drawing you somewhere deeper into the depths of a strange, unpredictable world. Will we find something for ourselves?

I focus here mostly on full-length feature films made between the late 60s and the late 80s. I would also like to highlight the discussions that took place at the Ujazdowski Castle in Warsaw between the 23 and 26 of January 2008 around a Borowczyk showcase and exhibition opening, and in which I had the pleasure to participate. For those who took part it became clear that the entire oeuvre of this artist represents a certain vision, manifesting itself in many guises. That is also why I have chosen for my deliberations an epigraph from an opera libretto (presented first in Munich in 1865) based on the Celtic legend about the sad Tristan and golden-haired Iseult.

Because Walerian Borowczyk's films usually have a woman as their protagonist, my journey through his output will be accompanied by a text, *The Laugh of the Medusa* by Hélène Cixous, which I will weave into the fabric of my own writing. It was first published in 1975 in the *Arche* journal, and in which Cixous confesses: "I write this as a woman, toward women."

These films, of which the main theme is the dense intertwining of love and erotica, lead us deep into the history of European culture, carrying us away on a serpent-like, velvety coil toward the songs of the twelfth-century troubadours. But this rootedness in tradition does not mean a contemplative calm sanctified by the blessed canon. Never! Looking for the source of contemporary love we arrive at the center of an outrageous rebellion, into the heart of a radical revolt, known in those monastic times as heresy.

Provençal troubadours, who, according to Joseph Campbell, were "the first ones in the West who really thought of love the way we do now – as a person-to-person relationship" joined the Manichaean heresy of the Albigenses (Campbell and Moyers 1991: 162). The delicate culture of their poetry was destroyed in one of the most cruel carnages on the European continent. Initiated in 1209 by Pope Innocent III, it was part of a crusade carried out by inhabitants of Provence on its own people.[1] To the arranged marriages forming part of the structure of the system, the troubadours responded with an idea of love as a selfless, sudden elation of the heart. This idea was aimed against an economic policy in which a woman was but an object exchanged between men, a custom upheld by the church. As Campbell notices, AMOR is ROMA, the Roman Catholic church spelled backwards (Campbell and Moyers 1991: 164).

> *There have been poets who would go to any lengths to slip something by at odds with tradition – men capable of loving love and hence capable of loving others and of wanting them, of imagining the woman who would hold against oppression and constitute herself as a superb, equal, hence 'impossible' subject, untenable in a real social framework. Such a woman the poet could desire only by breaking codes that negate her. ... But only the poets – not the novelists, allies of representationalism. Because poetry involves gaining strength through the unconscious and because the unconscious, that other limitless country, is a place where the repressed manage to survive: women, or as Hoffmann would say, fairies. (Cixous 1997: 350)*

Since we are in this strange place, a mysterious space without boundaries, it should not pose as a difficulty to follow (using French poets as our guides) another trail and visit another "epoch" — that of Surrealism. It is here that Bertrand Mandico and Pascal Vimenet, the French curators of the Warsaw exhibition, placed the "starting point" of Walerian Borowczyk's oeuvre, giving the first night of discussion the title "Avant-garde, Surrealism: Is Everything Cinema?" During this debate there were great differences between the participants in their general reading of surrealism. The disagreements concerned the issue of love — so important for the surrealists — and also their approach toward women.

French surrealism took up the characteristic traits of the avant-garde, which meant that radicalism and revolutionary zeal also had to measure up to its great myths, including faith in the innovativeness of artistic means and themes as well as the possibility of creating a better world. To the surrealists, the things that could abolish the rules that had so far held true were love and desire. But the object of surrealist love, mad love — *l'amour fou* — was to the male surrealists a woman — a strange and astonishing creature, identified in their dreams and poetry with mysterious, wild nature, and with that which resides in the subconscious. The image that springs to mind is one of the scenes from Borowczyk's 1987 film *Emmanuelle 5*: on a hot summer's day, during the Cannes film festival, an actress leaving a building is being hounded by a pack of hungry men, who, after ripping apart consecutive layers of her clothing, chase her all the way to the marina, where she saves herself by desperately jumping aboard the yacht of a random, romantic millionaire.[2] Paradoxically, while opposing the misogyny of their time, the bourgeois mores, and the social order, the surrealists were in their majority misogynistic themselves and in many cases also homophobic. The type of woman they desired was condemned to their fetishizing, voyeuristic gaze, to which, reduced to the role of an exciting object, a fetish, she could not respond. As Sarah Wilson writes:

> *Despite the Surrealists' proclaimed desires for revolution, emancipation, free love, they resoundingly rejected the threatening New Woman of Paris, the Amazone, the garçonne, preferring their Muses, from Kiki de Montparnasse to Gala – and only the most compliant "Americaines" (Lee Miller), whose modest, downcast eyes preluded the sexually ecstatic. (Wilson 1995: 5)*

There were of course artists such as Claude Cahun, whom Wilson calls "a surrealist woman who was never a Muse" and "a pioneering code-scrambler" (Wilson 1995: 7). Claude Cahun, aware of the meaning of the photographic situation of "imprisonment" in a random frame, the reduction of the human being to their image, and playing with it.

> *And why don't you write? Write! Writing is for you, you are for you; your body is yours, take it. I know why you haven't written. (And why I didn't write before the age of twenty-seven.). (Cixous 1997: 348)*

Yet in 1944 the misogynistic Breton writes:

> *The time might have come to valorize woman's ideas at the expense of those of man, whose bankruptcy has achieved a tumultuous climax today. (Breton 1944: 1)*

The surrealists identified women with the figure of a doll/mannequin, which — "from a subject turned into an object" (Hussakowska 1973: 103) — slowly came to life and stepped onto the stage. Forty years on, in 1984, Donna Haraway (an art historian and primatologist) wrote her jocular but seriously presented "Cyborg Manifesto," "an ironic dream of a common language for women in the integrated circuit" (Haraway 1983). As the author puts it:

> *By the late twentieth century, our time, a mythic time, we are all chimeras, theorized and fabricated hybrids of machine and organism; in short, we are*

> cyborgs. Thus cyborg is our ontology; it gives us our politics. The cyborg is a condensed image of both imagination and material reality, the two joined centers structuring any possibility of historical transformation. (Haraway 1983)

In Ridley Scott's *Blade Runner*, made two years earlier, the replicant slaves rebel when they achieve a level of development at which they are able to have so-called higher feelings. The moral implications of their presence are but another form of asking the age old questions about the provenience of the right of some species and races to rule others. Does there always have to be a two-caste system of masters and slaves?

The story of that thought began in Switzerland, by Lake Geneva, where Mary Shelley (the daughter of Mary Wollstonecraft, the forerunner of feminism and author of *A Vindication of the Rights of Woman*, and William Godwin, the forefather of anarchism), her husband Percy Bysshe Shelley and Lord George Byron, both outstanding English romantic poets, would pass their evenings telling each other ghost stories. From those tales *Frankenstein, or the Modern Prometheus* was born. Written in 1818, the book not only started the whole genre of horror, but — to quote Haraway once more — directed its criticism against

> the ... racist, male-dominant capitalism; the tradition of progress; the tradition of the appropriation of nature as resource for the productions of culture; the tradition of reproduction of the self from the reflections of the other. (Haraway 1983)

The Victorian era, which I call up here, is of paramount importance to the works of Walerian Borowczyk. His films were created as total works over which he wanted full control, and for which he built the stage design; also, as his close collaborators ascertain, he often dubbed the films himself with the exact desired voices of men, women, and animals. The fascination with the turn of the nineteenth century is clear; the films are full of strange Victorian objects (*A Private Collection*, 1973), tightly laced-up corsets, lace-up shoes with elongated, rounded tips. In *Goto, Isle of Love* (1968) the sight of shapely Victorian footwear does not leave us for even a second, and we see it even in the moments of the protagonist's highest distress. Beautiful young women fall head over heels in love with stiff-looking, refined Victorians in photographs, complete with their ridiculous moustaches ("Thérèse the Philosopher," a segment of *Immoral Tales* [1974]). Is this only a kind of esthetic fascination?

In 1886 the Scottish writer Robert Louis Stevenson published his *Strange Case of Dr. Jekyll and Mr. Hyde*. The dramatic tale of the human double nature and the impenetrable darkness of the soul have been the inspiration for many films, including Borowczyk's *The Strange Case of Dr. Jekyll and Miss Osbourne* (1981). In the 95 minutes of its duration, Borowczyk manages to settle matters with the Victorian era, deconstructing this matrix of which we are the lost children. Under the influence of a magic potion prepared in a laboratory, the protagonist turns into a havoc-wreaking, criminal beast. The combination of science and mystery is characteristic of the times, where the technical achievements perfectly coexist with a belief in the supernatural in such a way that it becomes possible to photograph beings arriving from the astral plane.

Miss Osbourne, Dr. Jekyll's fiancée, is the one to discover the dark secret of her lover, who under the influence of the mysterious concoction lets all his criminal drives run wild. When Jekyll transforms himself into the monster no one is safe and everything terrifying is possible. The story is first and foremost the tale of the tragedy of the protagonist, a part played by the great German actor Udo Kier. We should also note that while Udo Kier has many times played the role of demonic villains, including Dracula himself, Borowczyk might have been the first to note this psychopathic trait in the physiognomy of Sir Anthony Hopkins, who was originally the choice for this part. *The Strange Case of Dr. Jekyll and Mr. Hyde* shows the dilemma of the contemporary man, who having torn himself apart in his own head finds no place to hide from his own self. No one to turn to, nowhere to hide. "No, don't do this! There is no way back" — shouts the doctor to Miss Osbourne when she decides to follow her beloved. He cannot stop her, and she delights in the bath she takes in the strange brown liquid, stronger than the most potent drug, which releases the beast within. Can nothing protect us from the terror of the brown depth we have entered without any hope for redemption? Like the lovers in Liliana Cavani's *Night Porter* (1974), who in their last convulsions of passion deplete their famished bodies, Dr. Jekyll and Miss Osbourne ruin the grim Victorian house together. We then see them get into a carriage and drive off into the night; speeding off ahead with tousled hair, eyes aglow, smeared in blood, and biting each other (Cavani's main characters also resemble vampires). When they take their last walk — like two apparitions, two undead creatures — across the bridge (perhaps the very same bridge painted in 1893 by Edward Munch) we can hear a terrifying howl of an accursed dog. A sound of a werewolf wandering on the moor with a burning wound in his heart.

It seems strange that despite all the horror of this heavy psychedelic film by Borowczyk, it is also for the majority of its duration rather funny. Watching it one cannot help but laugh, almost incessantly. And our laughter accompanies the subsequent deaths of the monster's victims. One could think of Victor Hugo's novel *The Man Who Laughs* (1869) about a man whose face is deformed; his lips cut in his infancy in such a way that he always looks as though he is laughing. He carries forever the mark of the world's cruel laughter.

Let us think now about the heroines of Borowczyk's films. They are clearly becoming victims — hurt, perishing, and dying (which could probably also be read as an additional stimulant). There are also a few female "dark characters," like the heroine of one of the parts of *Immoral Tales*, the eponymous seventeenth-century countess Elizabeth Báthory (played by Paloma Picasso), a vampiress on the prowl for the blood of young virgins. Another clearly negative character is the female protagonist of *Lulu* (1980), a film based on Frank Wedekind's two dramas (*Earth Spirit* [1895] and *Pandora's Box* [1902]). Lulu is a sort of perverse Lolita, a scruple-less young person, leading astray the men who fall in love with her. But as the film moves on, we begin to understand that her attitude is in a sense a response to the hypocritical morality of the world she has come to live in, a cynical way of adapting to its mores. She is simply the product of enslavement by men — fulfilling the expectations directed at her of male fantasies. This is the context in which we ought to view her sorry demise (and not as a moralizing punishment for sins). Is it a criticism of still dominant social relations based not only on class but also on sexual inequality?

Another man appears in Lulu's life. However, this one will not be pleased with the usual "tricks" — he is the legendary Jack the Ripper, a character as mythical as another active at the same time (and in the same city) — Sherlock Holmes. In Borowczyk's film, the part of Jack the Ripper was played by the demonic Udo Kier — as though he had "jumped in" from the film discussed previously. He seems to be the embodiment of the Teutonic element of vampiric expression. I have no way of knowing if this is "dead serious" since, as with all of Walerian Borowczyk's films, the artist leaves me uncertain whether he is being absolutely serious, or perhaps just being deadpan, with an ironic wink in the audience's direction. He often seems to be doing a balancing act on the tightrope between solemnity and the absurd, bringing a given mood or situation to its extreme and is therefore almost caricature. It seems reminiscent of the mood in the great works of German expressionist filmmakers — an association intensified perhaps by the physical resemblance between Udo Kier and Conrad Veidt, the unforgettable somnambulist Cesare in the brilliant *The Cabinet of Dr. Caligari* (1920) by Robert Wiene.[3] As Francis Picabia writes about *The Cabinet of Dr. Caligari* in his *Instantaneisme*: "Many an entertaining film originated in America, only a few in France; Germany presented us with The Cabinet of Dr. Caligari as a masterpiece, a film, in my opinion, entirely ridiculous" (Picabia 2002: 85).

> *Laughs exude from all our mouths; our blood flows and we extend ourselves without ever reaching an end; we never hold back our thoughts, our signs, our writing; and we are not afraid of lacking. (Cixous 1997: 349)*

In *The Margin* (1976), based on the novel by André Pieyre de Mandiargues, one embarrassing scene involves oral sex with a prostitute to the soundtrack of Pink Floyd's "Wish You Were Here." The scene is as absurd as it is agonizing. It also brings back the theme, present in a few other films by Borowczyk, of prostitution (the protagonist Joe Dallesandro, an actor of Andy Warhol's Factory, played a prostitute himself in Paul Morrisey's *Flesh* [1968]). But watching *The Margin* we do not get the impression that the director is in any way stigmatizing the life of those women. It is the man who pays for the services of one of them that seems a strange specimen of a weird breed. The story is a tale of an encounter of someone, who, it seems, has it all but nonchalantly throws it away with someone who has nothing and exists on the margins of society yet retains her dreams — naïve dreams of happiness.

> *Now women return from afar, from always: from without, from the Heath where witches are kept alive; from below, from beyond "culture"; from their childhood which men have been trying desperately to make them forget, condemning it to "eternal rest." The little girls and their "ill-mannered" bodies immured, well-preserved, intact unto themselves, in the mirror. Frigidified. But are they ever seething underneath! (Cixous 1997: 348)*

In a similar way as prostitutes — the sad products of culture, beings subjugated to the rules introduced by someone else — Borowczyk seems to look at the existence of those enclosed in a convent. In *Behind Convent Walls* (1977) we see a group of young women, full of life, who have effectively been sentenced by their families to a life in the convent. Subjected to a strict regime, or rather trained like animals, they are deprived of the power to indulge in any kind of intimacy, over which they continually fight with the despotic mother superior — a female spy at the service of church patriarchs.

> *Men have committed the greatest crime against women. Insidiously, violently, they have led them to hate women, to be their own enemies, to mobilize their immense strengths against themselves, to be executants of their virile needs. (Cixous 1997: 349)*

Borowczyk shows the power over another human being as a taming of energy, a blocking of its free flow. The fate of the imprisoned women is symbolized in one of the scenes by butterflies (one of the habitual elements of Borowczyk's work) — this time enclosed in a glass display cabinet. As Joseph Campbell says:

> *The gods are personifications of the energies that inform life — the very energies that are building the trees and moving the animals and whipping up the waves on the ocean. The very energies that are in your body are personified by the gods. ... Now, a deity that is not recognized and revered and allowed to play into our conscious life becomes an idol. ... The energy gets blocked and becomes what we call a devil. The deity goes into reverse and becomes a negative power, a threatening power. (Campbell 1994: 28)*

Borowczyk's film ends in tragedy: the main female protagonist — this part played by the director's wife Ligia Branice — dies. She, just like the heroine of *Goto, Isle of Love* (played by the same actress) chooses death, rejecting a life in which love is impossible. It is love that is the main theme of Borowczyk's films, even when the world presented by the artist is devoid of it and reveals itself only as a yearning. Although *Goto...* is set in a place that brings to mind coarse Soviet Russia, it is not really a film about a totalitarian regime. The "anti-fascism" that this film seems to profess speaks to us in these words: Love is a thing that cannot be bought, taken by force, or imprisoned. Love is a free bird! Love — the monster of all times. And, as the protagonist of *Mother Joan of Angels* by Jerzy

Kawalerowicz (1960) says: "Love is at the bottom of everything that happens in the world."

My favorite Borowczyk film is probably *The Beast* (1975), which opens with quite an unusual scene of horses coupling. The story is quite heavily embroidered, and the toying with convention makes this horror a very funny film. The action takes place in a French chateau of an austere Marquis, the inhabitants of which are being attended to by black servants. At night, when everyone is asleep, strange things begin to happen. The main props that we notice are the Podkowiński painting *Frenzy of Exultations* (1894) and a centrally placed chess table. As Michel Pastoureau says:

> *The game of chess is not a game at all. It is a dream. A dream about the routes of the figures and the structure of the board. A dream about the world order and the destiny of man. A dream, in medieval vein, of everything that hides beyond the seeming reality of beings and things. (Pastoureau 2006: 320)*

In the woods surrounding the palace lurks a black hairy Beast. The heroine dreams a dream of a woman from times past (we are transported back to the eighteenth century) and her encounter with the Beast, which seems like the crown of male dreams. Seeing the woman wandering alone in the woods, the beast exposes its large black penis (but how sensitive and defenseless he is). The woman, paradoxically, (but how conventional) discovers pleasure in being raped. Deceitfully led on, the Beast becomes a victim of a praying mantis disguised as an innocent, who, having performed her maenadic ritual, runs away naked down a path in the woods to tempt and provoke her next victims — other defenseless Beasts, lost in the depths of the woods. The Beast is the fear of man, which he is not able to tame, incapacitate, describe, or classify.

> *Here they are, returning, arriving over and again, because the unconscious is impregnable. They have wandered around in circles, confined to the narrow room in which they've been given a deadly brainwashing. You can incarcerate them, slow them down, get away with the old Apartheid routine, but for a time only. As soon as they begin to speak, at the same time they're taught their name, they can be taught that their territory is black: because you are Africa, you are black. Your continent is dark. Dark is dangerous. You can't see anything in the dark, you're afraid. Don't move, you might fall. Most of all,*

don't go into the forest. And so we have internalized this horror of the dark. ...We the precocious, we the repressed of culture, our lovely mouths gagged with pollen, our wind knocked out of us, we are the labyrinths, the ladders, the trampled spaces, the bevies – we are black and we are beautiful. (Cixous 1997: 349)

But let us go back to *Immoral Tales*, mentioned at the beginning. The first part, as already stated, is called "The Tide" but the sea in French is feminine. André and his young cousin are going on a biking trip (a little bit like the characters in the *Story of the Eye* by Bataille). There is no carelessness here, however, as the trip has been planned up to the minute by the boy, who is taking Julie to the seaside for one reason only — he wants to give her a lecture on the phenomenon of the rising tide!

Jean Douchet, a French critic, the co-creator of the New Wave and a contributor of the *Cahiers du Cinéma,* who took part in the discussion at Zamek Ujazdowski, defined this film as a dialogue between nature and culture. According to him, the film is about pleasure, including visual pleasure, which comes from watching it. Without a doubt, the film is filled with beautiful cinematography of the seaside landscape. And yet, (as I dare to respond to Jean Douchet) we only have male pleasure to deal with here, as André has planned the trip for one strictly defined reason, being a peculiar kind of "dialogue between nature and culture" otherwise known as fellatio. In that fragment of "The Tide" the woman is identified with nature, subordinated to the will of man whose pleasure (in the words of the French critic) she is obliged to accept. She becomes a silent element of nature. There is a very symbolic scene in the movie when André asks Julie about her previous experiences; he then touches her lips with his finger and says "untouched!" The woman is silent, only the man has the power to speak and interpret. "From now on, who, if we say so, can say no to us? We've come back from always" (Cixous 1997: 349).

The words uttered by André on the rock during the tide (throughout its entirety he does not stop lecturing) become grotesque. Just as all his rush, calculation and nervousness become almost pretentious faced with the immovable landscape, the wetness of the sea, and the tide regulated by the moon, which he is trying to grasp with his feeble mind. Having reduced himself to a tiny piece of meat he uses to communicate with the world, he becomes nothing more — a small piece of meat, thrown on a big rock drifting between the sea and the sky. The femininity of nature is all-embracing. If we could stay silent and let it carry us, lead us, then the calls of the seagulls and the rhythmic sound of the returning waves of the amniotic fluids of the planet, vibrating in space, will bring us back to the innocence we constantly dream of. O! Let your grand, fortified, speaking identity be melted in Her! And let Her (as we allow) speak-through-your-self.

> *But look, our seas are what we make of them, full of fish or not, opaque or transparent, red or black, high or smooth, narrow or bankless; and we are ourselves the sea, sand, coral, seaweed, beaches, tides, swimmers, children, waves ... (Cixous 1997: 358)*

Are Walerian Borowczyk's films chauvinist? Or, on the contrary, as postulated on the last day of discussion by the Italian critic Alberto Pezzotta, are they feminist cinema? I found Borowczyk's own words important; they were quoted by Michael Lévy, who took part in the creation of many of the movies I have described here. As the director's assistant, from time to time he would also act a small part, and he told us about a situation that took place in the early 1970s during a presentation of *Immoral Tales* in London. There were voices among the young audience who had just seen the film, accusing Borowczyk of misogyny and the objectification of women. He responded to the attacks, saying he is only an eye, capturing what has been happening from time immemorial. He also asked them if it would not perhaps be better if they directed their anger at the institutions, which covered up the state of affairs.

Perhaps this is where the secret of the unpopularity of this director stems from. He is only the seeing eye, registering things, and what he manages to register is being left without a commentary, leaving room for interpretation. In this way, does he set in stone the dominating clichés? A difficult question. This room for interpretation can make you feel quite uneasy. If this is not the love we want, and not the world we would like to be living in, then do we know for sure what the world we would like to rediscover is like?

> *Wherever history still unfolds as the history of death, she does not tread. Opposition, hierarchizing exchange, the struggle for mastery which can end only in at least one death (one master — one slave, or two nonmasters ≠ two dead) — all that comes from a period in time governed by phallocentric values.*

The fact that this period extends into the present doesn't prevent woman from starting the history of life somewhere else. Elsewhere she gives. She doesn't 'know' what she's giving, she doesn't measure it; she gives, though, neither a counterfeit impression nor something she hasn't got. She gives more, with no assurance that she'll get back even some unexpected profit from what she puts out. She gives that there may be life, thought, transformation. This is an 'economy' that can no longer be put in economic terms. Wherever she loves, all the old concepts of management are left behind. At the end of more or less conscious computation, she finds not her sum but her differences. I am for you what you want me to be at the moment you look at me in a way you've never seen me before: at every instant. When I write, it's everything that we don't know we can be that is written out of me, without exclusions, without stipulation, and everything we will be calls us to the unflagging, intoxicating, unappeasable search for love. In one another we will never be lacking. (Cixous 1997: 361)

Translated by Lula Męcińska

Acknowledgments

The above article is an extended and modified version of a text that had first appeared in Polish in "Obieg" magazine, as well as in English in "Intertekst" online magazine. We wish to thank The Centre for Contemporary Art Ujazdowski Castle and Łaźnia Centre for Contemporary Art for their kind permission to use the text in this book. – Editors

Notes

1. In July 1209 the crusaders surrounded the town of Béziers. They demanded that all the Cathari be given away (around 500 people). The city refused, and after an unsuccessful defense it was conquered. All of the inhabitants were slaughtered — between 7 and 12,000 people, according to sources. When asked how to recognize the Cathari among the citizens, the papal legate Arnaud Amaury, one of the crusaders' leaders, responded with the infamous words "Kill them all! God will know his own." Those words paraphrased and caricatured by Walerian Borowczyk were used in *The Strange Case of Dr. Jekyll and Miss Osbourne*.

2. ATTN! Cannes, do not confuse with Domini canes.
3. Conrad Veidt also played the part of the mutilated man in the Paul Leni adaptation of Victor Hugo's *The Man Who Laughs* (1928), while the last film in his career was *Casablanca* (1942), in which he played the part of a Nazi major.

Bibliography

Breton, A. 1944. *Arcane 17*. New York: Brentano's.
Campbell, J. and Moyers, B. 1991. *The Power of Myth*. New York: Anchor Books.
Campbell, J. 1994. *The Way of Myth*. Boston and London: Shambhala.
Cixous, H. 1997. "The Laugh of the Medusa," trans. K. Cohen and P. Cohen. In R. R. Warhol and D. Price Herndl (eds.), *Feminisms: An Anthology of Literary Theory and Criticism*. New Brunswick: Rutgers University Press.
Haraway, D. 1983. "Cyborg Manifesto". Retrieved 1 March 2015 from https://wayback.archive.org/web/20120214194015/http://www.stanford.edu/dept/HPS/Haraway/CyborgManifesto.html
Hussakowska-Szyszko, M. 1973. "Stosunek do Nadrealizmu w Polskim Dwudziestoleciu Międzywojennym." In *Zeszyty Naukowe Uniwersytetu Jagiellońskiego, Prace z Historii Sztuki*, fasc. 11. Warszawa, Kraków: Wydawnictwo Uniwersytetu Jagiellońskiego.
Pastoureau, M. 2006. *Średniowieczna gra Symboli*, trans. H. Igalson-Tygielska. Warszawa: Oficyna Naukowa.
Picabia, F. 2002. "Manifest Błyskawiczności," trans. Ł. Demby. In A. Gwóźdź (ed.), *Europejskie Manifesty Kina. Antologia,*. Warszawa: Wiedza Powszechna.
Taborska, A. 2007. *Spiskowcy Wyobraźni: Surrealizm*. Gdańsk: Słowo/obraz terytoria.
Wilson, S. 1995. "Feminities/ Mascarades," *Courtault Institute*. Retrieved 1 March 2015 from www.courtauld.ac.uk/people/wilson-sarah/FEMINITIES-MASQUERADES.pdf

Kamila Wielebska is a curator, art historian and writer. Her main field of research is visual culture explored in a broad sociopolitical context, and the history of fashion. She is interested in redefining concepts and revaluating ideas, particularly those concerning the tradition of surrealism. She has worked as an editor-in-chief of *Intertekst* (published by Laznia Centre for Contemporary Art in Gdańsk) and co-edited *Story of Sin: Surrealism in Polish Cinema* (2010, together with Kuba Mikurda). She has been published in a variety of journals, including *ARTMargins*, *Flash Art*, and *Frieze*, as well as exhibition catalogues. Currently she is a freelancer and attends the Programme for Creative Producers at the Wajda School of Film in Warsaw.

CHAPTER 11
Enjoying Excess
A Batraillean Interpretation of *Story of Sin* (1975) by Walerian Borowczyk and Stefan Żeromski

Marta Rabikowska

> There are, in fact, a multitude of beautiful flowers, since the beauty of flowers is even less rare than the beauty of girls ... It is interesting to observe, however, that if one says that flowers are beautiful, it is because they seem to conform to what must be, in other words they represent, as flowers, the human ideal. At least at first glance, and in general: in fact, most flowers are badly developed and are barely distinguishable from foliage; some of them are even unpleasant, if not hideous ... Risen from the stench of the manure pile – even though it seemed for a moment to have escaped it in a flight of angelic and lyrical purity – the flower seems to relapse abruptly into its original squalor: the most ideal is rapidly reduced to a wisp of aerial manure ... It is impossible to exaggerate the tragicomic oppositions indicated in the course of this death-drama, endlessly played out between earth and sky, and it is evident that one can only paraphrase this laughable duel by introducing, not as a sentence, but more precisely as an ink stain, this nauseating banality: love smells like death.
>
> —Georges Bataille *Visions of Excess* (1985)

The opening passage of George Bataille's essay "The Language of Flowers" (1985) is concerned with the universality of human ideals and offers an immediate rebuttal to the legitimacy of any origins of such ideals. Bataille dares us to see through the "nauseating banality" of the tragicomic oppositions of good and evil. Borowczyk's adaptation of *Story of Sin* is from a novel of the same title by the Polish writer Stefan Żeromski (1864–1925). It was published as a serial in the daily press, *Nowa Gazeta*, between 1906 and 1908. Borowczyk reveals an analogous understanding: one that suggests that human ideals do not follow "the verbiage of the old poets, as the faded expression of an angelic ideal, but on the contrary, as a filthy and glaring sacrilege" (Bataille 1985: 12). In fact, there is not one film by Borowczyk in which love does not smell like death. Both Borowczyk and Bataille resist such oppressive rapture between good and evil, as represented in the images of the two sides of the protagonist of *Story of Sin*, Ewa Pobratyńska (Grażyna Długołęcka). The statuesque body of a woman — half sleeping, half daydreaming — is lying on white sheets with her pubic area discreetly veiled — covered with delicate rose petals — from the curious eyes of the audience. The image represents a woman who has not yet experienced the touch of a man, but still succumbs with pure joy to the touch and smell of the corporeal flower of her own body. Capturing Western imagination for millennia, this clichéd, mythical image of seductive innocence encloses its inherent antithesis: the image of a whore, still embellished with her floral accessories — as if the same rose while enduring corruption and exploitation — trying to point to her virginal origins, allegedly intact for the enjoyment of its exploiters.

From a Western, Christian perspective, those two images, put next to each other, symbolize the highest and the lowest point of human morality, and it is precisely this perspective, and the morality stemming from it, which those two images help us to question and subvert. In his films, Borowczyk, like Żeromski in his novels, employs the most hyperbolic imagery to signify the virulent power that moralistic discourses exert upon individuals and society alike. In this chapter, I will try to show that while producing "high and low" elements, Borowczyk and Żeromski create a forceful aesthetic that transgresses such a polarization. To illustrate the materialistic effect of the narration I will draw upon Roland Barthes's analysis of signification in the writings of Ignatius Loyola, Fourier, and de Sade. As Barthes observes in all of those writings, "the image always sweeps on beyond the signified toward the pure materiality of the referent" (Barthes 1977: 62).

In Borowczyk's adaptation of *Story of Sin*, as well as in the original text, it is through excess that the "pure materiality of the referent" is swept onto the signifier projected onto the screen. By applying such an approach, both Borowczyk and Żeromski contest the mythical dichotomy between good and evil. In the argument below, "excess of base matter" (the term derived from Bataille's philosophy) will be regarded as the conceptual point of connection between Borowczyk and Żeromski, along with an interweaving thread in the narrative tapestry of the film and the novel alike, leading to a discussion of both artists' affective approach to signification and objectification. Following

Bataille, I will look at "excess" in *Story of Sin* — both the novel and its film version — as a poetical device, as well as one allowing for the articulation of political views on morality and humanistic values. At the same time, the mere act of "looking at" excess will involve the observation of the articulation of perception per se, as both artists were particularly innovative in expressing ways of perceiving the world whether on the page or on the screen. Furthermore, it will be argued that the act of producing excess and the act of perceiving it conceive each other. Like the two opposite moral standpoints, illustrated in the opening clichéd images, together they make for two sides of the same coin. Although we can never see the coin in its entirety, we know it is there as a whole, as only through its existence are we able to distinguish the meaning of the two images. The coin is "the base matter" — one of many terms that Bataille used to infer base materialism, sacrifice, eroticism, heterogeneity, unproductive expenditure, desire, or "something which lacks a possible proper name" (Noys 1998: 514).

In *Visions of Excess*, Bataille compares base matter to a "big toe," which holds the whole human stature, including its moral values and abstract beliefs (Bataille 1985: 20–23). Although man relies on his big toe to help him stand, he still looks down on his foot with disgust: "he sees it as spit, on the pretext that he has this foot in the mud" (Bataille 1985: 20). Humanity cannot accept being determined by the material, dirty and earthly base, which is perceived as external and animalistic (Bataille 1985: 51). Yet at the same time it is precisely the base itself — which enables all high and heavenly ideals — that humanity needs in order to stand erect with its head turned skyward. Although the impact of base matter is obvious, it is not easy to grasp it, as it can only be recognized through "the traces of the active flux of instability," since "base matter only exists as difference" (Noys 1998: 512).

Bataille believed that only through releasing foul, suppressed desires into the world can we grasp that difference and change the world for the better. This political footing is important for his interpretation of excess and brings a new angle to the interpretation of Borowczyk's film. If all "repressed and taboo affects are necessarily those with the greatest revolutionary potential" (Grindon 2010: 307), Borowczyk's narration might spark a serious revolt. In Borowczyk's *Story of Sin*, it is precisely through exaggeration, excess and reckless expenditure that the radical impact of base matter can be traced and the oppressiveness of morality can be laid bare.

The Appeal of the Novel and the Aim of the Film

From the moment of publication, *Story of Sin* gained a reputation for being a scandalous novel. Disappointed by the range of disreputable themes and the incredibly loose structure of the novel, Żeromski's contemporaries, including his fellow national writers, defined the work as cheap; suitable for "uneducated servants" seeking pleasure in a "sewage-type" of literature.[1] Żeromski's inflated aesthetics were seen as a distraction from the sociopolitical content of his other novels, which gave foundation to the monumental position of the writer in the canon of Polish literature. Żeromski's readers did not value his "historically disjointed" narrative (Dyboski 1926: 556), regarding it as a waste of poetical means, privileging form over content. Żeromski's specific style, widely recognized for its emotional despondency and luscious descriptions of natural phenomena, has acquired its own nominal definition, made from the writer's surname: "Żeromszczyzna." The term signifies a mawkish yet fervent narrative, rich in embellished, clichéd imagery, emotive pathos, or simply kitsch. It is this style per se that had attracted Borowczyk's imagination. When interviewed upon the making of *Story of Sin*, Borowczyk stated with admiration: it was "the first Polish erotic novel, and maybe the only one" (Borowczyk 1976: 14). Diluted to some extent by the social censorship of his era, Żeromski's narrative describes intercourse, rape, prostitution, giving birth, murder, and, for the first time in Polish literature, overt innuendos to female sexual desire.

Borowczyk found rich inspiration in the material, but most of all he appreciated the shape of the narrative; its complexity, its multileveled structure full of digressions, abundant with extraordinary and improbable events, with hyperbolic, bizarre characters, with multiple locations, with a variety of mise en scène, with leaps of time, memory, and imagination (Borowczyk 1975: 14).

Story of Sin is the story of the tumultuous journey of a young woman, Ewa, through space and time. It presents the psychological and sexual transformation of a woman exposed to adverse circumstances and ill powers, which push her from the heavens of purity to the hells of debauchery and murder. Having sacrificed her virginity to an unreliable and already married lover, Łukasz Niepołomski, she never stops desiring him against the social and religious restraints of her times.

While experiencing Łukasz's indifference and apparent betrayal, Ewa experiences extreme mood swings, leading to reckless and volatile actions, which include murdering her baby, winning a fortune in a casino, nursing a dying man, building a relationship with her rapist, murdering a man for his own sake, prostituting herself, recuperating on her rescuer's farm and finding her virtue again before losing it to his sexual appetite, and, finally, sacrificing her life for Łukasz in the name of unconditional love. Filled with unexpected vagaries of melodramatic action and sumptuous scenery, the narrative offers an unstable combination of lyricism and realism, which inspired three film adaptations of the book: first, a silent film in 1911 by Antoni Bednarczyk, the second in 1933 by Henryk Szaro, and the third in 1975 by Borowczyk. From the perspective of Żeromski's readers, however, the novel did not have the same attractiveness to the eyes of the cinema audience, who were more appreciative of the novel's adaptation onto screen. Even today, the interpretation of the novel tends to be reduced to moral didactics. Wacław Borowy (1936), the first and most established critic of Żeromski's writing, while criticizing the novel's stylistic flaws, admits that the only conclusion it offers can be summarized thus: "Evil is eternal and invincible, and beauty and noble passions often become its weapons" (Borowy 1936: 404).[2]

A strong echo of the Western-Christian axiology can be heard in Borowy's statement: although ravished through sin, the ideal of human morality is protected through sacrifice. According to such interpretation, Ewa's histrionic fall and subsequent death brings forward a principal warning, which serves as an ethical weapon offered to the readers. Only through such interpretation can the writer's "real," morally driven intentions be diagnosed and the impiety of his narrative be excused. Otherwise, his ostentatious obsession with sinful desires would undoubtedly be classified as kitsch or pathology.

Contrary to Borowy's moralizing account, Borowczyk adapts the core story of Ewa's moral descent not in order to preach but rather to relish the absurdity of the whole idea of moral struggle. He focuses on the main theme of the clash of moral values in order to create an adventurous version of the Manichean ideology, so solemnly testified by Borowy. Borowczyk admitted in an interview that "cinema should provide entertainment, surprise and attraction" (Borowczyk 1975), and undoubtedly his adaptation of the novel is a fulfillment of this statement. By selecting scenes most relevant to his overarching script, Borowczyk creates a remarkably well-structured story, yet it is not as faithful to the original text as is commonly thought.[3] Including all the episodes from the novel would not have been possible within the length of a realistic feature film, as many of them offer repetitive meanings. Some of them would disturb the "adventure" by conveying vagueness and narrative complication, which Borowczyk wanted to avoid. By omitting many subplots and chapters, Borowczyk constrains the ideological complexity of the text and builds a frame for a romantic drama with a one-dimensional heroine who copes with one-dimensional obstacles and exemplifies the fraud of morality. Being organized around the oppositions of spirit versus flesh, corruption versus virginity, Borowczyk's narrative is built on a few clearly cut symbolic allegories: angelic Ewa, Ewa in love, Ewa the nurse, promiscuous Ewa, Ewa the victim, Ewa the murderess, Ewa the prostitute, and Ewa the savior.

Interestingly, there is no Ewa the philosopher in Borowczyk's film. Yet in the novel Ewa is heavily exposed to literary, religious and philosophical texts, and she reveals deep existentialist sensitivity within Żeromski's intricate third person, indirect speech (Rabikowska 2000). Żeromski puts strong emphasis on the influence of textual excerpts on Ewa's own intellectual and spiritual understanding of her situation, even though such knowledge disturbs the verisimilitude of Ewa's character of a 19-year-old female clerk working in a Russian office in nineteenth-century Warsaw.

According to some of Żeromski's critics, the intellectual and emotional growth of Ewa did not fit her dramatic persona and unnecessarily overloaded the narrative with philosophical quotations, thus distressing the realistic effect of the novel (Hutnikiewicz 1967; Markiewicz 1995). Borowczyk decided to abandon that baggage as well, but he managed to illustrate Ewa's psychological drama through other means. In the novel, Ewa's inner monologues show a woman with a deep capacity for self-reflection, while in the film that capacity is dramatically reduced and supplanted by fast action, as well as realistic allegories (for example, a book standing for Reason), and images of her physical presence (the one significant exception is Ewa's initial confession to a priest, whom she challenges on the mere idea of Christian chastity).

From a feminist and psychoanalytical perspective, this one-dimensional approach to Ewa's character, alongside the reduction of her intellectual competence, might imply an objectifying approach to women in Borowczyk's adaptation. Although I am not analyzing Borowczyk's approach to filming women, I would like to extend the concept of objectification into the semiotic field of signification. In fact, despite her one-dimensional identity, I do not agree that Ewa is objectified in Borowczyk's film any more than other signs in his narrative. As I will show next, objectification of signification is Borowczyk's method of articulating what Żeromski had established in language. Being interested in producing entertainment, Borowczyk stayed faithful to the novel's ethical and aesthetic expression (underappreciated by the writer's contemporaries), and did so by intensifying affect whilst decreasing the impact of ideological contemplation in his characters' development — a decision that bolstered the structure of the story and, not against all odds, abounded it with the very essence of florid "Żeromszczyzna."

Tableau vivant of Affect

Techniques of objectifying signs in Borowczyk's film and Żeromski's novel draw attention to the role of signification rather than moralization. The way signification is objectified in both works highlights bold projections of desire. I use the word "projection" purposefully to debate its psychoanalytical roots and emphasize its materialistic effect. As psychoanalysis has indicated, the denial of desire purifies humanity from shame and disgust. Of course, the effect of suppression and projection with its pathological consequences follows the denial, a problem well described in Freudian studies (see Baumeister 1998 at al.; Boag 2006; Pollock 2006). Where psychoanalysis diagnoses excess as a result of denial or lack, Bataille proposes the expansion of desire through the excess of purposeless energy, but his transgression "does not deny the taboo but transcends and completes it" (Bataille 2006: 63). Being wasted, desire escalates to the extent that it becomes objectified. In other words, by transgressing itself, desire becomes its own object. Barthes explains how this power from "objectifying" crystalizes the essence of the referent in a metaphysical act of transgression, which the critic attributes to sexual and religious passion. The narratives of Loyola's ascetic meditations, like de Sade's sadomasochistic orgies and Fourier's jubilation, "exceed the language that constitutes them" (Barthes 1977: 5). The process of materializing the signified, which Barthes observes in Loyola's *Exercises*, reflects the approach to signification in Borowczyk's film and Żeromski's novel:

> *The most abstract things (which Ignatius calls "invisibles") must find some material movement where they can picture themselves and form a tableau vivant: if the Trinity is to be envisioned, it will be in the form of three Persons in the act of watching men descending into hell; however, the basis, the force of materiality, the immediate total of desire, is of course the human body: a body incessantly mobilised into image by the play of imitation which establishes a*

literal analogy between the corporeality of the exercitant and that of Christ.
(Barthes 1977: 62)

The metaphysical passion, which Loyola feels for Christ, emits from the energy of imitating the "body" of the signified. Produced with a camera or with a writer's pen, signification has the force of materiality transferrable onto the audience (exercitant). Żeromski and Borowczyk both communicate the drama within their poetical tableau vivants, which are inscribed with their passion for the drama to impact the audience. In fact, Roman Dyboski made a remarkable comment that *Story of Sin* "is a cinematograph drama in some of its strong effects" (Dyboski 1926: 555). The materialization of "passion" in Żeromski's language encapsulates the affect of cinema, which Gilles Deleuze identifies as "a correlation between a perception-image and a camera consciousness which transforms it" (Deleuze 2005 [1983]: 76).

Representation is to be perceived by the audience, so it has to incarnate the effect of affect in advance when such effect is produced through the lens of the response of the audience. Borowczyk was acutely aware of the power of that effect when he admitted that he was more interested in the readers of the novel and the viewers of his film than in characters (Borowczyk 1976: 15). Żeromski himself was interested in cinema and its transformative-affective power, and tried to learn about the shooting process when Henryk Szaro was making *Story of Sin* in 1911. When it proved to be a "cinematograph drama" in the eyes — or rather in the hearts — of his readers it was before the novel had been adapted for the screen. There was a reason why Żeromski's nickname was "hearts of hearts" (Borowy 1936: 403): his narrative spoke through materialized emotions to be directly felt by the audience. Like in mystical and orgiastic writings, and like in the dark cinema auditorium, the corporeality of the signifier in Żeromski's language is not just a metaphor of the referent, but the body of the referent (Christ in Loyola).

In the same way, Borowczyk approaches the force of his picture where there is no difference between the plot and the palpable "objects," whether concrete or abstract, emotive or conceptualized. From this perspective, David Thompson's (Thompson 2008: 164) observation that in Borowczyk's *The Beast* "the fantasy eventually overwhelms the real world" cannot be sustained, but it inadvertently supports the concept of the materialistic power of Borowczyk's narrative. Thompson must have fallen under its affect himself when he admitted further: "it is as if Borowczyk saw life and death, creation and destruction, as equal in their power to inspire" (Thompson 2008: 146). Objectifying signs for pleasure contests the dichotomy between fantasy and the real world, even between life and death, and on the metaphysical level signifies transgression. Nevertheless, in Borowczyk's narrative it is an aesthetic act that communicates political value of desire rather than its subconscious drive. The shocking images of enlarged body-related signifiers (like penises, lips, tongues, legs, vaginas, sweat, tears, blood) in Borowczyk's films are the examples that, whilst drawing unsolicited attention to the director's moral stature, express the power coming from the materialization of affect within representation. Such images do not stand for something else; they are not projections of lack, or fetishes of suppressed desires.[4]

The ejaculating horse in *The Beast* is not a metaphor of the life drive, it is an ejaculating horse that "sweeps beyond" its discursive meaning to the physical sensation of the picture, signifying animality, erection, desire, orgasm, and sperm. Such images are there to be looked at, enjoyed, and destroyed. A big gramophone's tube, in extreme close-up, can be interpreted as an all-swallowing vagina or a living muscle of a monster (well-established meanings in Western culture; Noble 2000). Giving a classical waltz a squeaky, rasping tone coming from an old, stuttering record, Borowczyk gives this symbol an extra audio affect.

The "monster" opens in front of our eyes while we are watching Ewa making love to Count Zygmunt Szczerbic (Olgierd Łukaszewicz) and poisoning him at the same time. Nevertheless, we are not invited to observe the sadomasochistic projection of hidden desires, but to enjoy the mere act of sacrilege of base matter. Borowczyk knows exactly what impact such close-ups have on the audience, and thus gives away his sense of irony. That affective enjoyment of sacrilege is emphasized in the narrative by the acts of "looking at," perceiving and peeping through holes and binoculars, all of which do not occur in the novel.

The erotic power of perception is further embodied in the work of the camera, which often sensually encircles the objects, like Ewa's corset on the bed, which, while flashing with eroticism, strikes with obvious crudeness. Żeromski triggers this precise effect when he makes Łukasz look at the bra: "the fact that she was there a moment ago without her bra, only in her shirt, seemed to be obvious to this man, visible to his eyes, captured as if on the film tape" (Żeromski 1956: 33).[5] Intriguingly, Żeromski's expression: "captured as if on the film tape" seems to be indicative of Borowczyk's metatextual irony, saturating the entire film. The director acknowledged it himself:

> *I was trying to tell this story seriously and keep a necessary distance to it, as I was aware that it was impossible to capture it in purely psychological categories. (Borowczyk 1975:16)*

It is very clearly expressed in the scene when Ewa receives a stranger in her hotel room and makes love to him in return for his favors. Maude Goodman's painting *The Heart is Young* (1895), hanging on the wall in the same room, represents a woman playing a small pianola in the company of three young girls and a man, who sits behind the instrument looking leeringly at the woman's body. She looks out of the frame, as if asking the audience for help.

Borowczyk clearly enjoys making connections with his audience in this metatextual way: all of a sudden we realize that we are looking at a painting that in its own fashion "looks" at us, all the while serving as an object of perception of the characters, too. The look is the point of connection between the film and reality, between shame and pleasure. It materializes the trace of that irresistible power of desire that physically underpins the film. Although this painting does not appear in the text (Żeromski mentions a religious painting of Correggio), Borowczyk adds it to the narrative next of many other universal symbols, which he exposes, worships, and destructs. The connecting nerve between their projection and reception, incited in the moment of affect, deprives them of their universal meaning. The act of Ewa's sexual forfeit in the same scene (which in the novel exists only in innuendos) along with an image of her kissing the stranger in the shower as well as her naked body under a wet, transparent gown attract more attention than the painting. However, only through their excessive duplication. The scene destroys its own universalizing dialectics.

The literal and allegorical acts of projection and perception are the narrative elaborations on the power of production and consumption of desire. It can be said that both artists "project off" the traces of base matter to discharge desire. When Borowczyk was making *Story of Sin*, his lead actress Grażyna Długołęcka noticed that "the director tried to correct the writer by bringing forward more sex in each scene than the original text permit" (*The Story of Sin* 2004 [1975]). From the Batailléan point of view, Borowczyk's excess, which Długołęcka saw as a misinterpretation of the classic novel, reinforces the novel's psychosomatic impact in which Żeromski invested so much energy. In the narrative of Żeromski and Borowczyk, whoever allocates morality to desire deludes themselves in the same way as universal discourses can oppress their victims. Borowczyk used to say that there is more pornography in Disney's films than in his overtly sexualized images, as Disney's productions are driven by "repressed desire that you can feel a mile away" (Borowczyk, quoted in Adler 1985: 25).

An early scene in which Ewa and Łukasz meet in the local park after Ewa's confession in the church illustrates one such situation of "sexual overcharge." In the novel, this accidental encounter in a public place is still very innocent and distant. When she meets Łukasz, she is shy and passive, while Łukasz applies a whole repertoire of quotations from the French encyclopedists, such as Rousseau and Diderot, to contest Ewa's Catholic beliefs. In the film, the same scene acquires frivolity, physicality and erotic playfulness: they run across the park, chase each other, accidently touch each other, and jump over shrubs — all the while talking about Church credos and libertine philosophy. In that overzealous, almost feverish, "stalk and hunt" game, Ewa even bumps into a pram with a baby — a dramatic omen of her future act of infanticide. Although this eroticized and dramatized version of their meeting differs from the original description, it also responds to the affective poetics of the text. The dialectically structured conversation, itself an allegory of a classical debate between theology and libertarian philosophy, bears the very eroticism of a sexual game, as accorded with Ewa's inner confusion:

> *She wanted to but she couldn't. In the last minute, when she was ready to do it, she was stopped by a horrifying laughter. If she were asked then, she would answer undeniably, that it was Satan that obscured her soul with his scarlet wings. She felt weightiness and suffocation. And the most ghastly thing – she was experiencing some satisfaction because of those new, unknown commotions in her. (Żeromski 1956: 77)*

When Żeromski reports on a moral battle tearing Ewa's conscience, his words signify the physical and psychological affectation such a battle aggravates. "She was seized by the attacks, deft impulses, and shivers of the awaken conscience ... In the tremor of the body, in fear and prostration she was seeking in the dark, in the depth of her soul – is it everything, is it everything?" (Żeromski 1956: 22).

The semantics of Ewa's inner monologue is constituted from a flaring religious passion, but the syntax transgresses that meaning to erupt with an erotic force. Żeromski's words have a physical energy, which arouses the reader. A vibration of the physiologically determined nouns and verbs escalate through the jolting syntax preposterously arrayed with the rhythm of repetitions, assonances, and allegories, which together prompt the pulse of physical arousal. In Borowczyk's film, desire yields such vibration on different levels of the narrative. Borowczyk's interviewer, Susan Adler, made a revealing comment in a footnote when explaining the meaning of desire in Borowczyk's editing: "Borowczyk has used the word *montage* in its correct meaning of film editing and assembly but also in the sense of mounting as in sexual intercourse" (Adler 1985: 25).

In *Story of Sin* this observation refers to the mounting rhythm of the allegorically clashing imagery (angel and whore), the restlessness of the camera, the tempo of the editing, and sensual framing. Within the tableau vivant frame, each scene makes a "pulse" followed by another "pulse." This rhythm, like the Deleuzian "vector," creates a dynamic screen situation. As Felicity Colman explains:

> this moment is not constituted through binary structures (say the difference between the calm air and the storm). Rather, the screen-vector is created through differences that are self-affecting in their constant variation and movement. (Colman 2011:128)

The temporal movement of the edit and the spatial movement of the plot overlap and intensify dizziness. Borowczyk's narrative breathes fast, as if it was one aroused body. The spasmodic speed of Ewa's journey through spaces, moods, various men's arms and countries is synchronized with anxious movements of her own body. Ewa rarely rests — only before or after sex. She trembles and shivers through emotions, she walks in circles, runs up and down the stairs, shoots through rooms, gets on the train, jumps out of the train, embarks the boat, sails, and departs again. The shaky camera accompanies her every move, bringing different parts of her spasmodic body to the fore, while refocusing abruptly on material objects or panoramic views of the landscape. The film has the same erotic tempo and convulsion that Żeromski captures in his "burning and palpitating" style and illogical structure (Borowy 1936: 416).

The Lacanian jouissance comes to mind: the totalizing, almost painful ecstasy, which triggers a metaphysical moment, yet one that goes beyond the human-made version of good and evil. It is the moment of a total connection with the signifier — ecstasy of affect — that transgresses the experience of consciousness. It is that moment that makes the "żeromszczyzna" and "borowszczyzna" a threat to the dominant discourses of morality.

A statement from Spinoza's *Ethics* explains this postulation further: "Knowledge of good and evil is nothing but an affect of joy or sorrow in so far as we are conscious of it" (Spinoza 2001 [1677]: 170). The film's body is a source of affect, of joy, and sorrow, from which our own understanding of good and evil transpires beyond the universal ethics. Politically speaking, excess destroys the promise of liberated spaces and offers a more radical disorienting freedom that inscribes instability onto all discourses (Noys 1998: 503). The resulting knowledge cannot be compared to the traditional intellectual critique derived from the consciousness of cogito (like, for example, in psychoanalysis, Hegelian idealism, or Marxist materialism).

Realistic images and emotive symbols, which mark Ewa's drama in the film, are the allegories of the dialectics within which she is trapped. Interpreting those allegories from a Bataillean perspective stresses the role of signification in Borowczyk's film and enables a discussion of his representation that takes us away from the analysis of the subconscious and brings us closer to the analysis of the politics of desire. To achieve the affective understanding of the difference between good and evil both Żeromski and Borowczyk materialize affect on the level of representation. In both works the strategy of turning the realistic and, in fact, banal plot into an excess of poetical imagery, with the objectification of the experience of affect (coming from experiencing the word on the page and the image on the screen), highlights the poignancy and the ridiculousness of the allegory of good and evil with which humanity is fed. If we consider that the overarching meaning of *Story of Sin* lies in the contestation of the dichotomy between the human ideal and base matter, the signification of their perpetual coexistence, occurring everywhere like "a stain of ink," becomes key to both the film and the novel's full understanding. The viewer and the reader are encouraged to see *Story of Sin* not as a moral warning directed against evil, but as a moral statement denying the closure of any universal discourse.

Notes

1. Władysław. Reymont, the pillar of the nineteenth century literary critique and a Nobel Prize Winner, considered the style of *Story of Sin* as deprived of either logic or idea, while Eliza Orzeszkowa, the most established female voice of that era, accused the writer of erotomania (Eile 1965). Borowy concedes: "The novel is not easy to

appreciate. Its plot lacks too much in consistency and psychological conviction. Its sometimes strained style is not quite adapted to the painful realism of its subject matter" (Borowy 1936: 405).
2. Borowy writes: "A still earlier work by Żeromski, the novel called *Story of a Sin* (1906), seems to have been influenced by the general disenchantment of the day … The principal characters are not particularly connected, either, with the crowded events of the time. Their sins are not to be explained by social conditions: they seem to derive from the general order of the world. The hero, a scholar with a subtle mind, who quotes Plato and Shakespeare in his conversation, turns thief; and – what is even stranger, perhaps – after having written a series of love-letters which are among the best of their kind forgets and neglects the woman he loved. She – a pure and good-hearted girl when we make her acquaintance in the beginning of the book – becomes a murderess and a courtesan. Her influence is destructive for all around her: an old philanthropist, for instance, because he desires her, forsakes and undoes a lifetime of noble work. But it echoes faithfully the poet's mood of that time: the mood which was rightly called Manichean. For, indeed, it was the only conclusion of the book: that Evil is eternal and invincible, and that beauty and noble passions became its weapons" (Borowy 1936: 404–405).
3. A few significant episodes are completely excluded from the film, like a profound conversation between Ewa and her lover's wife, Róża Niepołomska; an ambiguous affair between Ewa and Count Szczerbic, whom she will murder; the dramatic coastline walk of Ewa contemplating suicide; a spiritually saturated encounter between Ewa and an old Polish poet, Jasniach; or the friendship between Ewa and Marta, a pure daughter of the utopist Bodzanta, who rescued Ewa from her gutter existence as a prostitute. Some less meaningful episodes are absent too, such as a parodical chapter with Barnawska, a pawnbroker auntie of Ewa, who provides loans to her family, or a sexually saturated scene of an implied orgy with some unknown chums, which Ewa relishes after she murders Szczerbic.
4. It must be said that he does it through the camera of one of the best Polish cinematographers, Zygmunt Samosiuk, who gave Borowczyk's film a very unique, sensual character.
5. All citations from *Story of Sin* are my own translation.

Bibliography

Adler, S. 1985. "Enticement to Voyeurism." *Cinema Papers* 50, February–March.
Barthes, R. 1977. *Sade, Fourier, Loyola*, trans. R. Miller. London: Jonathan Cape.
Bataille, G. 1985. *Visions of Excess*. Selected Writing, 1927–1939, trans. A. Stoekl. Minneapolis: University of Minnesota Press.

———. 2006. *Eroticism*, trans. M. Dalwood. London, New York: Marion Boyars.
Baumeister, R., et al. 1998. "Freudian Defense Mechanism and Empirical Findings in Modern Social Psychology: Reaction Formation, Projection, Displacement, Undoing, Isolation, Sublimation, and Denial." *Journal of Personality* 66(6).
Boag, S. 2006. "Freudian Repression, the Common View and Pathological Science." *Review of General Psychology* 10(1).
Borowczyk, W. 1976. "Interview with Andrzej Markowski," trans. M. Rabikowska. *Kino* 4.
Borowy, W. 1936. "Żeromski." *The Slavonic and East European Review* 14(41).
Colman, F. 2011. *Deleuze & Cinema: The Film Concepts*. Oxford and New York: Berg.
Deleuze, G. 2005 [1983]. *Cinema 1*, trans. H. Tomlinson and B. Habberjam. London: Continuum.
Dyboski, R. 1926. "Żeromski and Reymont." *The Slavic Review* 4(12).
Eile, S. 1965. *Legenda Żeromskiego*. Krakow: Wydawnictwo Literackie.
Grindon, G. 2010. "Alchemist of the Revolution: The Alchemist Materialism of George Bataille." *Third Text* 24(3).
Hutnikiewicz, A. 1967. *Stefan Żeromski*. Warszawa: Wydawnictwo Litrackie.
Markiewicz, H. 1995. *O Prusie i Żeromskim*. Krakow: Wydawnictwo Literackie.
Noble, M. 2000. *The Masochistic Pleasures of Sentimental Literature*. Princeton: Princeton University Press.
Noys, B. 1998. "George Bataille's Base Materialism." *Cultural Values* 2(4).
Pollock, G. (ed.). 2006. *Psychoanalysis and the Image*. Oxford: Blackwell.
Rabikowska, M. 2000. "Intertextuality in Żeromski's Novel: The Case of Story of Sin," Ph.D. dissertation. Poland: University of Silesia.
Spinoza, B. 2001 [1677]. *Ethics*, trans. W. H. White. London: Penguin.
Story of Sin. 2004 [1975]. DVD. London: Nouveaux Pictures.
Thompson, D. 2008. "Pleasures of Flesh: Walerian Borowczyk." In M. Atkinson (ed.), *Exile Cinema: Filmmakers at Work Beyond Hollywood*. New York: New York University.
Żeromski, S. 1956. *Dzieje Grzechu*, vol.1 and 2. Warszawa: Czytelnik.

Marta Rabikowska (MLitt Glasgow; Ph.D. Silesia, Poland) is Principal Lecturer in Creative Industries at the University of Hertfordshire. Having originally studied European modernist literature, she went on to develop expertise in visual cultures and media before becoming a filmmaker. Her research incorporates practice-based methods, including ethnography and experimental documentary filmmaking. She has co-directed and co-produced (with Matthew Hawkins) a number of award-winning films, such as *Belonging, Consumption and Place* (First Jury Prize at the Film Festival of the Association of Consumer Research in Milan in 2007) and *Migration, Health and Place* (funded by the Leverhulme Trust in 2010). She has published widely on the politics of culture and creativity, visual methods and everyday post-communism, and is the editor of the book *The Everyday of Memory: Between Communism and Postcommunism* (Peter Lang 2013). She has also been engaged in community activism in London, mainly as Director of the Short Film Festival, Edge of the City. She is a recipient of research grants from the AHRC, British Academy, and the Leverhulme Trust, among others.

CHAPTER 12

The Beach, the Bubble, and the Boudoir
The Meeting Spaces of Walerian Borowczyk and André Pieyre de Mandiargues

Jonathan Owen

The eleven minute film *A Private Collection* (1973) offhandedly inaugurates Walerian Borowczyk's fateful "erotic turn" — a spirited embrace of the "permissive" era's representational taboo-busting for which Borowczyk, more than any of his transgressive art house bedfellows, would see his career and reputation seriously damaged. Sure enough, then, *A Private Collection* opens with a close-up of sexual penetration, administered at high speed, in regular, frantic thrusts. But if this description suggests a tendency toward the hyper-explicit and crudely literal from the outset, we should note that the copulating figures depicted here are not only shown in black silhouette, but are also mechanical automata: subsequent shots reveal the figures as part of a ribald wind-up contraption: two toy pillars and a pediment inscribed with the word "University," framing the couple's "extra-curricular" activity. Savagely frank yet witty, direct yet enigmatic, these images are an apt opening for a study of vintage erotic mechanisms, scandalous *joujous* and onanistic fancies whose tone of antiquarian eccentricity and crankily perverse cultivation jars somewhat against the self-conscious contemporaneity and polemical urgency of sexual revolution, 1970s style.

The high voice and tapered hands that guide us through this cabinet of libidinal curiosities — like, supposedly, the collection itself[1] — belong to the distinguished French novelist, poet and essayist André Pieyre de Mandiargues. A friend of Borowczyk's, Mandiargues had himself long charted erotic territory in his writing, and his earliest published work, such as the 1946 volume of stories *Le Musée Noir*, already displayed a trademark blend of eroticism, cruelty, and baroque fantasy. It was in the 1960s and 1970s, though, that Mandiargues would contribute — beyond his own books — to that vogue for erotically fixated material that he had diagnosed (and applauded) in his 1969 essay "Un Puissant Moteur de la

Literature." Films adapted from Mandiargues' work include Jack Cardiff's modish *The Girl on a Motorcycle* (1968, adapted from the 1963 novel *La Motocyclette*) and Jacqueline Audry and Renzo Cerrato's 1969 *Le Lys de Mer* (from the 1956 novel of the same name, translated as *The Girl Beneath the Lion*), while, more indirectly, Mandiargues proudly detected in Pier Paolo Pasolini's notorious *Salò* (1975) the traces of his long pseudonymous neo-Gothic novel *L'Anglais Décrit dans le Château Fermé* (1953, translated as *Portrait of an Englishman in His Chateau*), which like Pasolini's film offers a modernized spin on de Sade's theater of sexual atrocity (Mandiargues 1979: 11).

Amidst these adaptations and ascribed influences, Mandiargues' most important cinematic relationship by far is with Borowczyk. Besides Mandiargues' unique, curatorial collaboration on *A Private Collection*, Borowczyk would adapt four of the Frenchman's works: the short stories "La Marée" and "Le Sang de L'Agneau,"[2] which respectively form sections of the portmanteau films *Immoral Tales* (1974) and *Heroines of Evil* (1979), and the novels *La Marge* (1967, translated as *The Margin*) and *Tout Disparaîtra* (1987), adapted as *The Margin* (1976) and *Love Rites* (1988) respectively.[3] These films represent not only the most sustained but also the most sympathetic cinematic engagement with Mandiargues' work. Clearly receptive to this rare attunement of sensibilities, Mandiargues lavished public praise on Borowczyk, most notably in the preface he contributed to a collection of texts by and about the filmmaker, *Borowczyk: Cinéaste Onirique* (Mandiargues, quoted in Borowczyk 1981: 7–8). The affinities between the artists, which amount as much to a similar worldview and common cosmology as to a shared poetics, were, I would suggest, largely evident even before Borowczyk began adapting Mandiargues's work for cinema.

This chapter will first offer an overview of Borowczyk and Mandiargues' most significant shared characteristics, before analyzing their relationship in a more textually specific way through a study of three films, *Immoral Tales*, *The Margin*, and *Love Rites* (space constraints prevent discussion of the episode from *Heroines of Evil*, a worthwhile and patchily inspired Borowczyk entry but a much less artful one than *Immoral Tales*, its portmanteau sibling). Many of the relevant qualities abound in compact yet vivid form in *A Private Collection* — that obscene dollhouse microcosm provided by Mandiargues' supposed *"logis particulier"* — and I shall refer frequently to this pivotal short throughout the following summary.

To some extent Borowczyk and Mandiargues' affinities can be subsumed under a common sympathy for surrealism. Both artists tempered their constitutive individualism to proclaim a loose fidelity to this movement, and Mandiargues had even belonged to the second, postwar incarnation of André Breton's surrealist group, if in an "amphibious," half-involved manner (Mandiargues and Mallet 1975: 139). There is a surrealist tenor, for instance, to both artists' sensitivity toward material reality, pitched between fetishistic delectation and scientific inquiry. The viewing implements that proliferate throughout Borowczyk's work — A Private Collection typically abounds in peepholes and projectors, alongside an omnipresent toy policeman clutching a telescope — are not only appendages of voyeurism but also instruments with which to probe the world's textures and penetrate its secrets. Likewise, when Mandiargues' guide produces from his collection a framed set of tabulated stones, only to reveal pornographic accounts where we expect to read explanatory captions, the voiceover's reference to "*une collection scientifique*" is an ironic joke that also helps recall the extensive enumerations of natural phenomena in Mandiargues' prose as well as, say, the eponymous structure of Borowczyk's short *Grandma's Encyclopedia* (1963) — both cases suggesting a furtive epistemological drive (Owen 2014: 225–26).

Both artists display an intense fascination with objects, even if, unlike Borowczyk, Mandiargues has as much taste for the natural as for the handmade object. To grasp how the aforementioned Jack Cardiff adaptation of *La Motocyclette* fails to capture Mandiargues' sensibility, one need only imagine a Borowczyk version. Borowczyk would have fastidiously and lovingly transposed all the detail that Cardiff's "psychedelically" tinged but generally conventional film disregards; he would have approximated the book's long descriptions of vehicles, the paraphernalia of road travel, the leather outfit worn by the female protagonist, and the antiquarian volumes collected by her lover. Both Borowczyk and Mandiargues invest objects with an implicit, often threatening agency of their own. It is unsurprising that, in *A Private Collection,* Borowczyk should have made an "erotic" film literally devoid of erotic activity among animate beings, and if elsewhere his human characters use objects for their own gratification, it is seldom clear that they are not being obscurely manipulated in turn. The role of objects here, as of other non-human agents, can be seen to visualize the determining power of external forces, whether natural or social.

The erotic component of both oeuvres is more complex than reputation or a superficial first glance might suggest. Both artists emphasize sexuality as a shocking and scandalous power, a transgression of socially imposed limits — and yet their understanding of transgression can be aligned with Georges Bataille's precise conception of the erotic, which stands distinct from straightforward liberationist perspectives.[4] For Bataille, eroticism (unlike mere animal sexuality) is at once prohibited and produced by the codes of civilization. Transgressive acts of eroticism gain potency from their own interdiction, and ultimately reinforce the taboos without which transgression is impossible (Bataille 1987: 36; Bond 1982: 14–15). Mandiargues and Borowczyk themselves offer a dense imbrication of transgression and taboo, license and prohibition, revelation and concealment. As in the opening of *A Private Collection*, where the sex act is both forthrightly displayed and obscured, erotic content is often viewed obliquely in their work, through layers of obfuscation, as though the awareness of social condemnation, the impediments of censorship, were integral to the erotic experience. Despite his association with highly graphic imagery, Borowczyk is arguably as notable for what he does not show.

Borowczyk and Mandiargues follow Bataille further in his identification of transgression and sacred experience. In language akin to Bataille, Mandiargues argues for the power of eroticism to "push literature ... towards a certain absolute ... a certain beyond" (Mandiargues 1971: 323). In Borowczyk, admittedly, the garbing of sex in religious ceremony strikes a stronger note of sardonic provocation than in Mandiargues, who lacked the fervid anticlericalism rife among his surrealist companions. With both artists, however, the erotic mimics the sacred in its lack of expansiveness, its charged containment in bounded, often forbidding spaces — note how, already, the mechanical copulation at the beginning of *A Private Collection* is framed within the toy building. Such containment approximates the erotic not only to the sacred but also to the ludic: as propounded by anthropologist Roger Caillois, a close colleague of Bataille, the game is characterized by hermetic isolation from everyday life, its enclosure in a separate space and time (Caillois 2001: 66). Borowczyk and Mandiargues' depiction of the erotic is colored by a concern for play, games, and contests, though sometimes in darker shades than the bawdy playthings of *A Private Collection*.

As if the properties enumerated here were not conspicuous enough in his work, Borowczyk's association with an explicitly surrealist-affiliated writer has the virtue of foregrounding the surrealist character of his own output, and of signaling its persistence into the most critically maligned and misunderstood phase of his career. In fact "La Marée" ("The Tide"), the first Mandiargues work that Borowczyk adapted, has a particularly high surrealist pedigree, having been written, at the request of Breton, for the catalog of a 1959 surrealist exhibition

(Mandiargues and Mallet 1975: 80). The basis for the first section of *Immoral Tales*, "The Tide" takes place in a locale privileged in Mandiargues' writing: the rocky Norman coast that Mandiargues has described as a foundational, even sexually formative feature of his youth (Mandiargues was delighted that Borowczyk had instinctively grasped the story's personal significance in calling its unnamed protagonist "André") (Mandiargues and Mallet 1975: 82).[5] Among the four sections of *Immoral Tales*, this is the only one that substantially unfolds in an exterior, natural setting. Indeed this story fuses sexual initiation and a union with nature: it depicts an act of inter-cousin fellatio whose climax is regulated by the male cousin to coincide with the incoming of the tide.

The story's erotic content can be linked to Mandiargues' notion, already cited, of "a certain beyond," of the ludic or transgressive space beyond normal reality. Synchronized with the interval between the departure and arrival of the tide, the cousins' erotic relation "is inscribed in a temporal beat, between the ebb and flow, in an intermediary time where desire pours forth" (Castant 2001: 217). In this sense the erotic activity measures out a temporal gap, "between the ebb and flow;" it acquires the status of a transcendent exception, a hiatus in the natural world's mechanics. And yet this erotic encounter is also dominated by nature: the cousin's wristwatch and timetable of tidal movements secure the subjection of sex to natural phenomena, emphasized as much in their mechanical predictability as their pre-cultural anarchy. Borowczyk's film version foregrounds the regulated, ritualized aspects of the story. This emphasis is achieved not only by the cool neutrality of Borowczyk's approach to his characters — a departure from Mandiargues' gravely rapturous tone — but also by the integration of the story into a film full of overtly ceremonial and hieratic eroticism, organized around Catholic iconography and spiritual and aristocratic power: subsequent episodes deal with a devout act of masturbation, the "bloody countess" Erszebet Bathory, and an incestuous session between Pope Alexander VI and his daughter Lucrezia Borgia. As with the religious practices from which these other episodes draw their erotic incitements and appendages, their props and poses, nature in this first section acts as a regulatory principle that grants order and meaning to the erotic. Mediated by the imperious male cousin, nature is implicitly revealed as a master of human endeavor, a determinant preceding religious and social systems.

Borowczyk endows the coastal setting with imposing presence, his gift for texture provoking a tangible sense of wet and cold. The insistent sound of lapping waves — even heard, non-diegetically, over the story's opening caption — aids images of mossy, rock-laden ground and of the cousins cast against and dwarfed by the cliff walls; the whole effect being to suggest the engulfing omnipresence of the natural world. Borowczyk hereby achieves the sense of human dissolution into nature described by Mandiargues, a communion literalized in quintessential Borowczyk fashion, when the female cousin reaches beyond her human liaison to grasp and fondle a stone. In heightening the presence of the environment, Borowczyk also emphasizes the natural enclosure of this space — a match for the confined interior settings in the film's other sections. It is as though Borowczyk has made the natural world resemble the hermetic haunts of the erotic that his cinema favors. At this strictly visual and aural level, then, Borowczyk reiterates the ambiguity we have noted: this environmental enclosure at once presents an eroticism consigned to its separate, exceptional space, sealed off in its distinction from everyday reality, and reinforces the idea of nature's pervasive, inescapable domination (Richardson 2006: 111).

If the "The Tide" section, like *Immoral Tales* generally, shows Borowczyk both at the height of his formal powers and at his most attuned to Mandiargues' ideas, I consider his subsequent Mandiargues adaptation, *The Margin*, one of his least satisfying films. Mandiargues' novel is the story of Sigismond, who visits Barcelona on a commercial assignment, only to receive there a letter relating the deaths of his wife and child. Sigismond surmises the letter's content but delays reading it fully, suspending the moment of explicit revelation. The time prior to reading the letter is treated as a "bubble" of permitted license, as Sigismond indulges in Barcelona's lurid nightlife. This bubble is yet another variant of the erotic enclosure, an enclave of transgression bound by time as much as space.

As an adaptation, Borowczyk's film is marked by compromise and dubious deviations. He relocated the film's setting to Paris, unable to shoot in Barcelona due to the book's aggressive criticism of General Franco. The role of the young Spanish prostitute who sporadically accompanies Sigismond in his bubble is changed and expanded to accommodate the Dutch *Emmanuelle* (1974) star Sylvia Kristel, and a sinister but underdeveloped pimp character is added (a villain to replace the pustulant specter of Franco in the novel?). More generally, Borowczyk's extreme opacity with regard to his characters is at its most pronounced here, aided by a characteristically impassive Joe Dallesandro as Sigismond. This contrasts with Mandiargues' sustained focalization of the novel through the perceptions, thoughts, memories and fantasies of its protagonist. Borowczyk's externalized approach is not illegitimate per se, but without such illumination of inner life as Mandiargues provides, it is difficult to know how to take the Sigismond of Borowczyk's film. The bare details of the narrative, preserved from the novel, make possible several readings of his behavior. Are we to take the most obvious approach and see Sigismond's relationship with Kristel's prostitute as a relatively standard and unremarkable study of erotic obsession, a reading enabled by the prostitute's expanded role? Or are we to pursue more interesting but less grounded interpretations of this relationship as a possibly traumatized response to the letter Sigismond receives, part of the "margin" of transgression shocked into existence by a glimmer of terrible revelation? Is Borowczyk's film more conventional than Mandiargues' novel, or more "modernistically" obscure?

Similar uncertainties arise with regard to the role of objects in the film. While Borowczyk retains some of the objects and their bizarre usages featured in the novel — such as an egg rolled over the prostitute's body during sex-play — the film generally abandons the complex network of objects established by Mandiargues, and recalls the celebrated metaphoric shifts of Bataille's novel *Histoire de l'oeil* (1928) in both its richness and its emphasis on spherical objects like eggs and testicles (all relating back to the immaterial sphere that is Sigismond's "bubble"). Borowczyk renders the film's objects at once more enigmatic and more easily reducible to idiosyncratic erotic props. In view of the central, near-animistic role of objects in Borowczyk's films, it is surprising that he should have neglected the possibilities offered by this novel to explore the power of objects: particularly marginalized, as it were, is Sigismond's glass tower (changed here, not so surprisingly, to the voyeuristic implement of the telescope), which is placed, guardian-like, over the resealed letter and exercises a near-magical authority.

But the film does have many virtues, notably concerning the construction of spaces and environments. The opposition Borowczyk creates between the country residence where Sigismond lives with his family and the seedy night world of 1970s Paris — an alternation of boundless, hazily shot pastoralism with cramped, shabbily elegant urban grime — adds a level of meaningful textural variation arguably lacking in Mandiargues' novel. Borowczyk's Paris, whose inhabitants seem to be clad predominantly in black, is a sinister as well as a licentious space, a match for the deathly foreboding offered by Mandiargues' Barcelona (Thompson 2008: 166). The typically oppressive sense of environment combined with the lack of explicit character motivation might even be seen to reinforce that message of determinism that pervades Borowczyk's work with perhaps greater insistence than in Mandiargues' fiction.

If *The Margin* departs, sometimes unwisely, from its fictional source, then *Love Rites* — Borowczyk's final feature and an adaptation of Mandiargues' last novel — is in turn very faithful to the original, and offers a distillation of many of the key themes and tropes shared by both artists. In fact, we virtually return full circle to the opening image of *A Private Collection*, as cited at the beginning of this chapter: this film's scenes of barely visible copulation, shot through the veils and clutter of a dimly lit boudoir, recall the silhouetted automata of that first foray into the erotic. While *Love Rites* is hardly Borowczyk's most distinguished film, its shrouded, even coy eroticism — which is further strained through the high-cultural allusions and verbal grandiloquence that Borowczyk preserves from the novel and supports with inserted paintings, photographs and texts — gives the lie to the notion of Borowczyk's career as simply trailing off into the evermore flagrantly pornographic. That visual veiling is also apt for a film that presents a story of masquerade and concealed intent: indolent, self-regarding Hugo picks up Myriam, a young woman who has ostentatiously attracted his attention on the Paris metro, and is drawn into an erotic liaison that will turn grisly, quite literally at Myriam's hands.

Like Borowczyk's celebrated 1964 animation *Angels' Games*, *Love Rites* traverses a series of confined spaces, charting the development of Hugo and Myriam's affair: the platforms of the metro, a church, and finally the boudoir supposedly belonging to the fearful, never-seen madam Sarah Sand, where most of the film unfolds. All these spaces are stages for theatrical recitation and play-acted identity, while the church setting merely underlines the "sacred" solemnity present throughout. The boudoir is a quintessential Mandiargues and Borowczyk setting: it is a space of scientific as well as theatrical exhibition, a museum housing its "particular collection" of choice flora and fauna (such as a butterfly seen nestling above Myriam's pudendum). It is here that the erotic turns violent, as Myriam dons a set of claws to lacerate Hugo's skin before verbally abusing him and expelling him from the boudoir. The sex-baited trap recurs throughout Mandiargues' work — compare the story "Le Passage Pomeraye" (1946), where a man pursues an erotic invitation only to be transformed surgically into a half-reptilian monster — and here makes for a comeuppance to the male erotic subject, the sexual flâneur of surrealism.

In another departure from the surrealist and Batailleen traditions both artists otherwise evoke, the closeted arena of Myriam's boudoir, while preserving that ludic character, sacred ambience and sense of distinction from the everyday that Borowczyk and Mandiargues generally invest in their erotic spaces, is hardly detached from the real world or lacking in the "fatal consequence" from which, according to Caillois, the game is "sheltered" (Caillois 2001: 66). Not only is Hugo genuinely physically hurt by Myriam's game, but his subsequent arrest for the murder of a girl who commits suicide in front of him can be read as enacting the effective sentence of condemnation that Myriam metes out for his poor performance of the game — just as in Borowczyk's first live-action feature *Goto, Isle of Love* (1968), the losers of the combats staged between prisoners meet their execution. For Myriam herself, the sado-erotic game can be considered a means of violently working through traumas — traumas that are personal (Myriam was, on her own testimony, repeatedly raped by her brothers as an adolescent) and even, implicitly, historical-political (references are made to Myriam's Jewish ethnicity and to the Holocaust, with Myriam joking that she is sufficiently Jewish "to qualify for the ovens").

In the aforementioned essay "Un Puissant Moteur de la Literature," Mandiargues, far from considering erotic content artistically detrimental, recommends its use as a means of revitalizing literary facilities, even counseling that every celebrated writer write an erotic book. Borowczyk's post 1973 career may not constitute a cinematic revitalization — flawed if interesting films like *The Margin* suggest otherwise — but it does show strong continuity with his earlier, more acclaimed work in merit and implication: its decor is no less ornate, and its interiors no less ominously constricting, for the copulating bodies within. Mandiargues' ultimate significance for Borowczyk is that he helped the filmmaker translate his barbed sensibility into the language of surrealist erotica. No less than Mandiargues' voluptuous yet fearful prose, Borowczyk's erotic cinema is as likely to claw as to caress.

Notes

1. While Mandiargues' voiceover commentary presents the collection as his own, it has since been revealed that many of these "antique" objects not only belonged to Borowczyk but had been made by him as well.
2. "Le Sang de L'Agneau" had already been "unofficially" adapted by the Japanese filmmaker Shūji Terayama as a sequence in *Throw Away Your Books, Rally in the Streets* (*Sho o Suteyo Machi e Deyō* [1971]). Terayama's use of Mandiargues, prior to Borowczyk's own adaptations, is interesting given that Terayama — whose own work

bursts with surrealism, eroticism and provocation — is something of a fellow traveler to Borowczyk and was known to be admired by him (Bird 2010: 79). Both filmmakers contributed to the erotic portmanteau film *Private Collections* (1979).
3. Also worthy of mention is Borowczyk's short *Venus on the Half-Shell* (1975), which features drawings and commentary by Mandiargues' wife, the artist Bona Tibertelli de Pisis.
4. Borowczyk's files at the Cinémathèque française confirm that at some point — probably in the early 1980s — the filmmaker was considering adapting Bataille's story "Le Mort."
5. *A Private Collection* was also originally intended to be part of *Immoral Tales*, thus suggesting how far Mandiargues presents a guiding force over Borowczyk's first sustained erotic feature.

Bibliography

Bataille, G. 1987. *Eroticism*, trans. M. Dalwood. London and New York: Marion Boyars.
Bird, D. 2010. "Devils' Games: Surrealism in Polish Émigré Cinema." In K. Mikurda and K. Wielebska (eds.), *A Story of Sin: Surrealism in Polish Cinema*. Warszawa and Krakow: Era Nowe Horyzonty and Korporacja Ha!art.
Bond, D. J. 1982. *The Fiction of André Pieyre de Mandiargues*. Syracuse: Syracuse University Press.
Caillois, R. 2001. *Man, Play and Games*. Urbana: University of Illinois Press.
Castant, A. 2001. "Erotique des arts Visuels chez Mandiargues." In F. Aubral and M. Makarius (eds.), *Erotique, esthétique*. Paris: L'Harmattan.
Mandiargues, A. P. D. 1971. *Troisième Belvédère*. Paris: Gallimard.
———. 1975. *La Désordre de la Mémoire: Entretiens avec Francine Mallet*. Paris: Gallimard.
———. 1979. *L'Anglais Décrit dans le Château Fermé*. Paris: Gallimard.
———. 1981. "Préface." In W. Borowczyk, *Borowczyk: Cinéaste Onirique*. Paris: Collection La Vue/B. Diffusion.
Owen, J. 2014. "An Island near the Left Bank: Walerian Borowczyk as a French Left Bank Filmmaker." In E. Mazierska and M. Goddard (eds.), *Polish Cinema in a Transnational Context*. Rochester: University of Rochester Press.
Richardson, M. 2006. *Surrealism and Cinema*. Oxford: Berg.
Thompson, D. 2008. "Pleasures of the Flesh: Walerian Borowczyk." In M. Atkinson (ed.), *Exile Cinema: Filmmakers at Work beyond Hollywood*. New York: SUNY Press.

Jonathan Owen completed his Ph.D. on Czech cinema, at the University of Manchester. He has worked as an Associate Research Fellow at the University of Exeter and a Teaching Fellow at the University of St Andrews. He is author of the monograph *Avant-Garde to New Wave: Czechoslovak Cinema, Surrealism and the Sixties* (Berghahn, 2011) and has published numerous book chapters as well as articles for journals, including *Framework* and *Canadian Slavonic Papers*. His research interests are European cinema, avant-gardes, cult and exploitation cinema, and international co-productions.

CHAPTER 13
Sex and the Sacred
The Obstacles to Desire Becoming its Objects

Jakub Majmurek

The notion of religious cinema is probably the last one that comes to mind when we think about Walerian Borowczyk and his movies. It seems "obvious" that Borowczyk would be dubbed anything but religious. However superficially correct that may be, that intuition misses the vital role that religious imagery plays in Borowczyk's oeuvre. However libertine the explicit meaning of his movies are, there is a desire to orbit constantly around a religious field, or — to be more specific — around symbols, images and rituals associated with the Roman Catholic Church.

In all of Borowczyk's movies, every time the Church does appear, we can easily identify a fascination the filmmaker felt toward Catholicism's visual heritage, from religious paintings of the high Middle Ages to nineteenth-century canonicals. The sacred is always objectified as a relic, a holy painting, etc., which proves how strongly his imagination was shaped by a Roman Catholic outlook. In Roman Catholicism, quite contrary to the reformed Churches, God and the sacred do not speak through words or through the law. The Catholic God is not "the God of the Book," but the God objectified in different sets of sacred objects, relics, holy locations, etc.

In Borowczyk's movies the sacred rarely interacts with desire in the form of prohibiting law, the letter of the word of God, or cutting living flesh and mutilating its carnal desires. In Borowczyk's world the sacred and the sexual encounter each other on the surface of different objects, because desire itself also often takes objectual forms. In all his movies, the camera (no matter who happens to be a director of photography on a particular project) is "erotically" zooming in on the objects, looking at them desirously for much longer that is necessary for storytelling.

How do the sacred and the sexual (or perhaps "the desired" might be more appropriate words here) interact with each other in Borowczyk's oeuvre? Or to put this question differently: how does the Catholic field structure the desire expressing itself in the director's visions? In the following chapter I'll try to show that in Borowczyk's movies we can see three patterns of such interaction. In the first one, the Catholic field is acting as an agent of prohibition — as an obstacle to free articulation of desire. Contrary to what intuition might tell us, it is the rarest pattern in Borowczyk's oeuvre. In the second one, the institution of the Church is hiding the excesses of desire, which hidden "behind convent walls," only externally repressed, are bursting with perverse energy. Finally, in the last one, Borowczyk depicts how religious objects, seemingly the obstacles for desire, are themselves sexualized. In other words, in Borowczyk's works, we can see how in the field shaped by Catholic imagery the repression of sexuality and the Church's repressive measures are themselves sexualized (Žižek 2000: 257).

Behind the Walls of the Prohibition

Of all Borowczyk's movies, *The Story of Sin* (1975) is the one embedded most strongly in the idea of the sacred as an obstacle for desire. The movie opens with a scene of confession, filmed in a single, static shot. The camera is positioned opposite to a confessional; in the middle of the screen we can see the priest, and on the left a woman — Ewa, played by Grażyna Długołęcka — kneels at the confessional. We can guess that she's just finished her confession. The priest, played by Zbigniew Zapasiewicz, begins to lecture Ewa about the significance of sexual purity, the value of her virginal virtue, and the necessity to struggle with sinful, carnal desires. While instructing her, he's looking straight at us — the audience, giving the impression that he's actually talking to us. At the end of confession, the priest closes the upper doors of the confessional, his face now hidden behind it. As the voice of the moral teaching of the Church and of the law ruling sexual conduct, he's now hidden, separated, and faceless.

In the movie we see Ewa fall in love with a tenant hiring a room in her parents' apartment, one Łukasz Niepołomski (Jerzy Zelnik) — a free-thinking scholar trying to get from the Catholic Church an annulment of a marriage in which he is not happy. Her parents, afraid what calamities an affair with a married man could bring to their respectable family, force Niepołomski to leave the town. Ewa is unable to deal with the forced separation from her beloved man. She abandons her parental home, finds Niepołomski, and becomes his common-law wife. The man, however, abandons her, as he has to travel to Rome (he isn't able to get an annulment of his marriage in Poland). His departure, together with an unwanted pregnancy, results in Ewa's nervous breakdown. It is the first step on her path toward moral downfall: she becomes a sex worker, gets involved in criminal activity, etc.

The law of the Church makes it impossible for Ewa and Łukasz to form a happy conjugal union. The story of their "sin" is literally ignited by the law, uttered by the priest in the first scene. The law is not only purely prohibitive — in a certain, perverse way it's also productive. It produces all the transgressions and moral violations that Ewa is committing on her "path of sin." While on the explicit level the law prohibits access to the object of desire (in this case to the conjugal union with Łukasz), on a less explicit level it posits the subject as the object of desire, subjected to its automatism. Sin is therefore nothing but a name for that subjection to the automatism of desire unleashed by the prohibitive law. As Alain Badiou puts it in his analysis of St. Paul:

> *What is sin exactly? It is not desire as such, for if it were one would not understand its link to the law and death.* Sin is the life of desire as autonomy, as automatism. *The law is required in order to unleash the automatic life of desire, the automatism of repetition. For only the law fixes the object of desire, binding desire to it regardless of the subject's 'will.' It is this objectual automatism of desire, inconceivable without the law, that assigns the subject to the carnal path of death. …The life of desire fixed and unleashed by the law is that which, de-centered from the subject, accomplishes itself as unconscious automatism, with respect to which the involuntary subject is capable only of inventing death.* (Badiou 2003: 72)

"Objectual automatism of desire, inconceivable without the law, that assigns the subject to the carnal path of death" seems like an apt description of Ewa's fate. Her desire assumes objectual form in two ways. First, in the sense of automatic desire animating her actions in her scheme of repetition and compulsion, and second in the way desire is often mediated through the objects. The love affair between Ewa and Łukasz starts with the exchange of love letters. Borowczyk depicts them not as a mere transparent medium, carrying the love discourse, but looks at them closely in their material dimension. Borowczyk seems to be as interested in the letters' content as he is in their shape, color, type of handwriting, and the contrast between the blackness of the ink and blank sheet of paper. Even more often than in his other feature films, Borowczyk fills the movie with close-ups of different objects. They don't have any narrative function whatsoever, and the eye of the camera is contemplating them in an apparently erotic manner, like they are embodying the cursed desire shaping the existence of Ewa and Łukasz.

In *Behind Convent Walls* (1977) we seem to look at the sacred as something that separates subject from the object of its desires. The titular walls signify the demarcation line between secular and religious life. They demarcate the space of what Peter Sloterdijk calls the "ethical secession" (Sloterdijk 2013: 222), the space of separation from the violence of reality and its earthly games (games of desire included). But the walls of the convent not only fail to separate carnal urges from the holy place of the convent, but also change the sacred into a stage of desire. It often happens in the movies of Borowczyk: the apparently repressed Catholic world, under its grim, ascetic (and hypocritical) surface, is bursting with rainbows of desire and all its possible manifestations.

The Acherontic Current of Roman Catholicism

In the aspect I have just discussed, Borowczyk follows in the footsteps of authors of the gothic novel. For them — English gentlemen of the second half of the eighteenth century — Roman Catholicism was something strange and exotic. It was both more sophisticated (in terms of richness of ritual, liturgy, and visual culture surrounding the religion) and more primitive (in terms of totemic idolatry, the pagan cult of saints, etc.) than the Church of England they knew. For gothic novel authors, the Catholic world had become the stage on which they could present all their fears and desires, which were impossible to articulate in the England of William Pitt and Pitt the younger.

In Borowczyk's movies the Church — on the surface a sacred institution — reveals its underground, acherontic current of desire bursting beneath the facade. In the first novella comprising the portmanteau movie *Heroines of Evil* (1979), it's the papal court itself that becomes the stage for desire. The movie is set in the 1520s; we see the papal court from the point of view of Rafael Santi, working as a papal artist. In the first shots we see a series of close-ups of erotic paintings from the times of ancient Rome. They depict couples engaged in sexual activity and — one can argue on a more symbolic level — the Roman god Eros still present underneath the surface of Catholic Rome.

The next shot presents a site of ancient ruins on the outskirts of Rome. Among the ruins we see a young couple having intercourse. Rafael himself is looking at them through a telescope; the woman he's observing will become his lover. Their passionate (and, as it turns out, fatal for Rafael) relationship will take place at his living quarters at the papal court. The court vibrates with desire. Its tastes are undoubtedly secular and sensual; it is the site of sexual and romantic intrigue and naked bodies of both sexes. Rafael is commissioned to paint *The Three Graces*, three young, naked girls symbolizing the erotic vitality of nature. In two scenes we visit what looks like an ancient gymnasium. It's full of young, almost naked men — their bodies appear to have been shaped by a strict athletic regime and definitely not an ascetic one.

If in the first novella of *Heroines of Evil* the Roman Catholic Church seems to work as a screen to hide pagan, erotic content, in "Lucrezia Borgia," the final novella of Borowczyk's *Immoral Tales*, it works rather like an amplifier of erotic perversion. The novella is actually one scene depicting the notorious Borgia family. Rodrigo Borgia, who in the years between 1492 and 1503 wore a papal tiara as Alexander VI, seems like an ideal hero for Borowczyk: immoral libertine *avant la lettre*, celebrating his radical freedom in a stream of love affairs, orgies, conspiracies, and murders. The scene looks like a celebration of the Borgia family. At the beginning the Borgias are depicted in the tradition of religious painting, especially the paintings that portray groups of saints, priests, and laymen a so-called *sacra conversazione*. In Borowczyk's work (un)sacred conversation of the Borgias turns into a regular orgy in which Lucrezia Borgia — notorious for being promiscuous and a poisoner — is having intercourse with her father and one of her brothers. Here, the Church becomes the space in which sexual desire — suppressed by its rules — can be staged in all its anarchic, perverse forms.

The Erotic Core of the Religious Sublime

In *Behind Convent Walls* something else is going on: it shows how the objects of religion, sacred relics embodying apparently puritan and Catholic doctrine, are becoming the objects of sexual fixation. We see a nun marking her body with stigmata using rose thorns — her action is presented as implicitly sexual in its nature. The other nun is masturbating using a wooden crucifix.

In the second novella of *Immoral Tales*, "Thérèse the Philosopher," Borowczyk depicts the same process. In the very first scenes of the novella, Thérèse — a young teenage girl living in France at the end of the nineteenth century — is strolling through a space filled with Catholic canonicals: liturgical robes, pastorals, crosses, etc. The space is sparsely lit and Thérèse is behaving like she is sleepwalking — somehow the whole situation has a dreamlike quality and is filled with eroticism. The girl's dress is a bit too childish for her age; she looks like an overgrown Alice in some kind of Catholic wonderland, where canonicals seem to work like some strange machines of desire, simultaneously gathering it like capacitors and radiating it all around them. In the other scene, Thérèse, locked in her room by her mother, gets erotically aroused from reading a novel — a religious publication — illustrated with very graphic engravings.

The Dialectical Work of Profanation

In most of the cases I have presented here, the protagonists of Borowczyk's narratives are women. Their relation to the objects of their desire very often assumes a form we may be tempted to call masochistic. There's some truth in that intuition, but it fails to describe the situation wholly.

A psychoanalytic approach marks the difference between sadistic and masochistic modes of experiencing desire in their relation to the law. A sadistic subject sees the law as a barrier standing between him (or her) and the object of his desires; all he wants is to destroy that barrier in order to be able to enjoy fully his desired object. A masochist on the other hand perceives the law as something that, while separating the subject from the fulfillment of their desires, seems to absorb the jouissance promised by that object. Submitting to the law is, then, a chance to gain access to that jouissance.

In Borowczyk's movies it is the objects, not the law, which seem to capture the jouissance; very often the same objects that are apparently standing between the characters and their desire. In the narrative of his movies Borowczyk shows how barriers for desire are becoming its object and not just the cause of desire. But does Borowczyk simply ask his audience to submit to the desired objects...? Is this the ethical, prescriptive content of his oeuvre? Not really. What he's proposing is rather the ethic of profanation. By profanation, I mean — following Agamben's formulation — "to profane means ... to return the object [which was once sacred] to the free use of men" (Agamben 2007: 73).

We can argue that religious and desired objects have one thing in common. They're separated from all the other, ordinary objects — elevated beyond them. The same elevation and sublimation in the work of desire and in religious acts takes place in the poetic. "Making a thing poetically sublime" is the parallel process to "making a thing desired," or "making a thing sacred." In *Blanche* (1971), Borowczyk depicts the deadly consequences of the ethics of submission to poetic, religious or amorous sublimation. In the movie we have three parallel processes of sublimation: sublimation of Blanche into an unattainable object of desire; religious sublimation turning the ordinary object into the sacred, and political sublimation transforming the body of the king into the embodiment of sovereign power. The fate of the characters following these processes of sublimation ends in carnage. On the other hand, in all his movies, Borowczyk proves that, for him, a life where there are no sublimated objects would be unbearable. Between the path of deadly submission to the sublime and a world where there's nothing elevated beyond common use, Borowczyk's cinema maps a difficult, infinite road of dialectical profanation, which — like all good dialectic — is able to preserve the sublime in the act of profanation by sublating it.

Bibliography

Agamben, G. 2007. *Profanations*, trans. J. Fort. New York: Zone Books.
Badiou, A. 2003. *Saint Paul: The Foundation of Universalism*, trans. R. Brassier. Stanford: Stanford University Press.
Sloterdijk, P. 2013. *You Must Change Your Life: On Antropotechnics*, trans. W. Hoban. Cambridge: Polity.
Žižek, S. 2000. *The Ticklish Subject: The Absent Centre of Political Ontology*. London: Verso.

Jakub Majmurek is a film and art critic, political columnist, and philosopher. He is the co-author of many book concerning movies (*Story of Sin: Surrealism in Polish Cinema* [2010]) and social and political philosophy (*L'Idée du Communisme II* [2011]). He writes mainly for *Dziennik Opinii*, a liberal online journal of opinion.

CHAPTER 14

Reflecting on *The Strange Case of Dr. Jekyll and Miss Osbourne* (1981)

Budd Wilkins

The Strange Case of Dr. Jekyll and Mr. Hyde, Robert Louis Stevenson's classic novella about the enduring struggle that rages within the human heart between its beneficent and bestial tendencies, seems upon reflection like an ideal metaphor for the 1970s: a decade brimming over with battles for liberation on global as well as personal fronts; a decade that took serious the counterculture mantra "the personal *is* political." So it's perhaps unsurprising that, by the early 1980s, more than a handful of film adaptations had tinkered with the story's basic building blocks with an eye toward emphasizing its ongoing relevance to the zeitgeist. To take only two of the most radical examples: Hammer Films' *Dr. Jekyll and Sister Hyde* (1971) sees Jekyll swapping sexes as well as personalities; *Dr. Black, Mr. Hyde* (1976) recasts the story as a Blaxploitation potboiler. And Walerian Borowczyk's incendiary *The Strange Case of Dr. Jekyll and Miss Osbourne* (1981) stands as the capstone to this trend.

The film's triumvirate of lead actors constitutes something of an unholy trinity of seasoned pros drawn from various strata of international cult cinema. The participation of Udo Kier in the title role instantly aligns Borowczyk's subversive handling of the material with Paul Morrissey's equally revisionist, Warholian diptych *Flesh for Frankenstein* (1973) and *Blood for Dracula* (1974). In the latter film, Kier's vampire count is a pathetic, even risible, figure. Kier's scrawny frame and pop-eyed physiognomy imbue his Dracula with some of the trapped-animal desperation of Peter Lorre's child-murderer in Fritz Lang's *M* (1932). Borowczyk, on the other hand, plays up Kier's ambiguous sexual allure — his aura of semidetached availability registers somewhere between angel and devil. Morrissey amps up his films' gag factor (when it comes to camp humor as well as gross-out gore), whereas Borowczyk casts a woozy, dreamlike spell amid the (mostly off-screen) bloodshed, an achievement that's aided considerably by Bernard Parmegiani's atonal electronic score. What's more, Borowczyk uses an entirely different actor for his Mr. Hyde (Gerard Zalcberg), rather than attempt a metamorphosis via makeup and montage.

Borowczyk's casting of the other leads likewise displays his penchant for playing to type while at the same time slyly subverting it. In films as diverse as Stanley Kubrick's *A Clockwork Orange* (1971) and Roger Corman's *The Masque of the Red Death* (1964), Patrick Magee specialized in characters whose aura of institutional authority was invariably tinged with a touch of madness. Magee's bellicose General suffers sexual humiliation at the hands of his treacherous (and just as lecherous) daughter. Howard Vernon was for several decades an axiom in the films of Jesus "Jess" Franco, the astonishingly prolific Spanish filmmaker, who, at the time of his death in early 2013, had helmed almost 200 films. In many of them, Vernon played some variation on the mad doctor archetype he established in Franco's *The Awful Dr. Orlof* (1962). Borowczyk flips the script here by casting Vernon as Dr. Lanyon, the staunch materialist and ideological antagonist of Jekyll's vaguely Nietzschean "transcendental medicine."

Borowczyk streamlines the novella's convoluted multiple-narrator storyline into a haunting, dreamlike chamber play — a strategy that suggests Strindberg as much as Stevenson. Aside from a shadowy prelude in which an ill-seen assailant chases and attacks a young girl (as well as a handful of cutaways to the scene of the crime), the majority of the film takes place within the walls of Jekyll's tony townhouse. Borowczyk also tidies up the original's indeterminate timeline, concentrating events over the course of a dinner party in honor of Dr. Jekyll's engagement to Miss Fanny Osbourne. In a move that anticipates Cronenberg's approach to filming *Naked Lunch* (1991), Borowczyk folds in elements of the author's biography, so that Stevenson's wife emerges as a central character in the film, one whose recruitment into Mr. Hyde's murderous spree constitutes Borowczyk's most audacious alteration of the material. The literary-historical fact that Fanny Osbourne read Stevenson's initial draft of the story and immediately consigned its unsettling pages to the flames of the handiest hearth suggests that Borowczyk's version was conceived as a mischievous variation on Freud's famous "return of the repressed."

And Borowczyk's film is nothing if not awash in Freudian imagery: from the broken cane left behind at the scene of the first attack (a droll correlative for Hyde's sexual frustration) to the poison-tipped arrows Hyde uses, like some venomous Eros, to dispatch several of his victims. (Not to mention the comically exaggerated prosthetic phallus that skewers victims of both sexes.) In one of the most remarkable scenes, Fanny spies on Henry in his laboratory while he methodically fills a bathtub with the ruddy tincture that will change him back into Mr. Hyde; the camera lingering in close-up on Fanny as her expression slowly changes from abject horror to one of rapt fascination. Her face is repeatedly framed between two slightly opened doors that constitute a narrow and decidedly vaginal slit, the perfect complement for the uterine waters of the tub Jekyll ecstatically thrashes around in. Bodies of water, of course, have often been used to represent the fluid and amorphous nature of the unconscious, and Borowczyk draws attention to the element's disruptive nature by cutting several times to shots of the room viewed topsy turvy in the blood-red fluid. Borowczyk stages the transformation — with Jekyll immersing himself and Hyde emerging in his place — in one unbroken shot, a bravura bit of direction by anyone's estimation.

The central importance of this sequence can be deduced from the inordinate amount of screen time it occupies (five minutes out of an 87 minute film). As if that weren't indication enough, there's a parallel scene near the end in which Fanny joins Jekyll for a splash in the tub's transformative waters. Jekyll's alchemical elixir seems to stand for some sort of collective unconscious, a primordial reservoir of atavistic instincts Henry and Fanny can access. Borowczyk's eccentric iconography surely paved the way for another meditation on the unruly potentialities of the unconscious: Brian De Palma's latter-day masterwork *Femme Fatale* (2000). Nor is this the only sort of idiosyncratic iconography to be found in Borowczyk's film. The objet d'art that comprises Fanny's dowry is none other than Vermeer's *Woman in Blue Reading a Letter*. Explicit reference is made to the notion — really more of an art-historical hypothesis — that the woman in the portrait is in an advanced state of pregnancy: "Seven months," Fanny's mother approvingly suggests. The painting's presence in Jekyll's household is intended as a sort of wish fulfillment. Mrs. Osbourne expects that reality should soon conform to the one depicted in the painting.

The film's attitude to such ideas of "sympathetic magic" is decidedly more ambivalent. Fanny and Henry's initial attempt at furtive lovemaking fails when Henry suffers "performance anxiety" under the disapproving gaze of his father's portrait. And it isn't exactly a coincidence that the film ends with these images tossed onto a bonfire of repressive Victorian vanities, a conflagration that decimates patrimony and matrimony in one fell swoop. In another of Borowczyk's ironic parallels, the film climaxes with an act of lovemaking that blurs together hitherto opposed boundaries: Fanny and Henry writhe on the floor of his carriage, Jekyll and Hyde alternating appearances until they are entirely interchangeable; hungry kisses become bloody love bites; sex shades into vampirism. Ultimately, consummation proves a palindrome for being consumed. The couple's cannibalistic love rites reach fever pitch, Parmegiani's pulsating score culminates in a shivery crescendo, and it seems like sound and image are about to come apart entirely. It's a moment of apocalyptic amour fou worthy of Borowczyk's surrealist predecessors. (One thinks in particular of the antinomian couple in Luis Buñuel's similarly scathing *L'Age d'Or*.) And then abruptly, as though to shatter the spell, the end titles come up — one last, brazen act of coitus interruptus.

Budd Wilkins is an internationally published film critic and film historian. He contributes to *Slant Magazine, Little White Lies, Video Watchdog, Film International, Movie Mezzanine, Not Coming To A Theater Near You,* and *Acidemic Journal of Film and Media.*

CHAPTER 15

The Perils of Emmanuelle
A Conversation between Odie Henderson, Simon Abrams, and Michał Oleszczyk

Made in 1987, Emmanuelle 5 is, without question, the most unloved film of Walerian Borowczyk's career; so much so that even Borowczyk himself did not identify with the final product, which was largely shaped by other people's hands (see Kuba Mikurda's chapter "Boro: Escape Artist" for a detailed account of its making). Furthermore, the film exists in two different versions, neither of which has found many admirers over the years. What follows is a discussion between Simon Abrams, Odie Henderson, and Michał Oleszczyk — all taking the Love Express, as it were, to the very heart of commercialized darkness that, for Borowczyk at least, Emmanuelle 5 proved to be.

Michał Oleszczyk: Gentlemen, here is a movie that's a real borderline case: a failure by most accounts, but an interesting and revealing one. In most accounts of Walerian Borowczyk's career, *Emmanuelle 5* is seen as a nadir of sorts; the final downfall of an artist who made the pact with the smut money men with *Immoral Tales* (1974) and *The Beast* (1975) and then found himself on a downward spiral. I thought it would be a good idea to discuss the film anew, with you two focusing on the American cut of the film and me providing some comments on the European one. They're both quite different and revelatory.

Simon Abrams: Let me start by saying that I see the American cut as a huge missed opportunity. In theory, this should be the most liberated film Borowczyk ever made, but due to changes introduced by Howard R. Cohen's rewrites and footage directed by Steve Barnett, it feels like it's the most limited.

Odie Henderson: I agree with you in that this version gives an impression that Borowczyk had largely abandoned his art. There are little shots that have some supposed artiness to them, but these things just come out of nowhere, and they reinforce the overall feeling that the director just stopped trying at some point.

MO: In fact, that impression is still there when you watch the European cut, but it's infinitely less pronounced. Lots of stuff had been cut for the American market, and even more had been added.

SA: Allegedly, the stuff he was most involved in making was the film within the film, "Love Express," but overall it's very clear that the American version is torn between his impulse to be really erotic and the producer's impulse to introduce as much goofiness as possible. In this version, the film really does feel like two different movies. Most things happening in Benglagistan have an absurdist, *Heavy Metal* magazine, Euro-trash kind of style.

MO: That's the stuff that was most heavily tampered with in the American cut, but the European version is by no means free of the Euro-trash feel.

OH: That's in keeping with the rest of the "Emmanuelle" series, which is the very definition of Euro-trash. This film is the first one that Sylvia Kristel wasn't in. They started with the whole out-of-focus, Vaseline-on-the-camera aesthetic, and as the time went by, the films became more and more like snobbier versions of Roger Corman movies, including lots of trashy elements, which sort of dominate here.

MO: That's because the American version was actually reshaped and distributed by Corman, who allowed the exploitation elements in the second half of the film. In fact, in an interview he gave to Kuba Mikurda, Corman says he merely rented his studio to Alain Siritzky, the producer of the European version, and it was him who also produced the American cut.

OH: The shot I originally wanted to point to as the opening image for our discussion was the one where Emmanuelle escapes the island and picks up a machine gun ...

MO: That's exactly the stuff introduced in the American cut, absent from the European one.

OH: That's also the moment when the film really goes insane. It turns out that she's truly all-purpose: she literally does everything, but mostly seduces nerdy guys who wouldn't stand a chance with her in real life. All the guys here are really goofy-looking; there's not a man in the film who looks like he'd actually be capable of commanding anyone who looks like this chick.

SA: But that's the whole hypocritical philosophy of the "Emmanuelle" series, at least how I see it: as long as the guy looks like a nerd, he's actually a real man — it's all the guys with a "real man" look that are actually scum. The hypocrisy is in this film, too: the guy who she ends up falling in love with tells her he doesn't watch her films, since they are smut — and yet he winds up sleeping with her!

OH: Exactly. And the guy with the most virile look, Prince Rajid (Yaseen Khan), turns out to be the most corrupt, so again it's the sensitive guy who turns out to be the real and reliable man. It harkens back to the first *Emmanuelle,* in which the men who were abusive toward the main character were always ritzy, aristocratic types. But coming back to Borowczyk's installment, it's definitely very schizophrenic — at least in the American cut.

MO: The schizophrenia is also there in the European cut, but it's not as extreme.

SA: It's very frustrating, because there's a lot of fascinating stuff on the fringes of this movie. For example, there are bits and pieces of interesting statements on orientalism and exoticism in pornography.

OH: The issues of race are all over this movie: it's a staple of porn to have a blonde woman go to an exotic island filled with brown-skinned people. This is exactly what happens here when Emmanuelle goes to Benglagistan and is the only blonde in the entire area. It's not a coincidence that this aspect has been truncated in the American cut.

MO: Exactly. The European cut has plenty of interracial sex, starting in the dance studio, and continuing onto the island. The actual location was the French island Reunion, east of Madagascar, with a large Creole population. Borowczyk included lots of images of interracial couples (including lesbian ones), all of which were cut from the American version!

OH: But there are also signature Borowczyk touches to be found here: that image of Emmanuelle making an origami dick out of a napkin has to be one of the strangest things I have seen in a movie for a while.

MO: The extended "Love Express" sequence in the other cut even has an erotic gadget (the fellatio slot machine) designed by Borowczyk and included in *A Private Collection* (1973).

SA: There's also a trace of an idea here that's not fully developed. The movie acknowledges that Emmanuelle is a social climber and an independent woman, but at the same time she needs rescuing. She gets rescued by the guy she's falling in love with, Charles D. Foster, played by Crofton Hardester …

OH: … and then she gets rescued by Eddy (Dana Burg Westburg), the photographer she meets in the American version only.

SA: She is also literally handed a parachute by a man in the end. Also, the big finish is provided by the card she gets from Charles D. Foster, saying that he loves her. It's almost like the film holds on to some very archaic notion of chivalry and white-knightism, all the while blaming the ugly aspects of it on the corruption of modern life. Still, I don't really believe this sentiment; I don't think Borowczyk believes it, either.

OH: No, and you see it in the way he frames his shots. Of course, the film is supposed to be titillating and erotic, but most of the naked women in the film are really badly framed. It's almost like the director was saying: "OK, I know the genre obligates me to present this content, so I will present it in the most lackadaisical manner available."

MO: In his defense, one has to say that the European cut, while not fully satisfying in this respect, has many more interesting erotic shots, also ones located in the harem. But overall, I would say that much of the "big" sex is shot in quite a generic way.

SA: He also aims some cheap shots at film business, especially in the Cannes sequence, where you see the pornographers avidly defending their work as respectable erotica.

OH: Exactly. The film is a parody of sincere European, soft-core sexploitation films. It's like a sexploitation film by someone whose heart isn't in it.

SA: It is basically a gesture of disdain toward the genre, as if Borowczyk was saying: "See, I'm taking the check for my job, but just watch what I'm going to do with it!"

MO: I fully agree with this, and it is also present in the European cut, even though it plays a touch differently. First of all, the entire Cannes sequence is intercut with long stretches of the extended version of "Love Express," so the entire segment takes up almost one third of *Emmanuelle 5*. Second of all, Emmanuelle herself seems less confident in those scenes in the European cut; she's bullied by journalists in a more harassing way. Last but not least, in the European cut you can see more posters of movies that played in Cannes that year, which makes Borowczyk's attack more poignant and specific: we see Sylvester Stallone as *Cobra* (1986) and, rather interestingly, the poster for Alain Cavalier's *Therese* (1986), a story of the Catholic saint, in many ways Emmanuelle's opposite number.

OH: At the same time, you can clearly sense there's a critique going on here of the way porn photographers are treating the women they takes pictures of. It's especially apparent in the harem scenes that they are not really treated as women, but as subjects to be exploited.

SA: The paradox at the center of this film is that it says an independent woman's task in the modern, sexually liberated world is to stand up against being turned into an object by bullying male filmmakers — exactly like the ones behind *Emmanuelle 5*!

OH: The American cut is incongruous in that there are obviously two pieces here: the part in which Charles D. Foster is supposed to have a sort of stabilizing effect on Emmanuelle, and then there's the supposedly vile exploitative aspect of her being in Benglagistan. At the end, the balance is shifted toward the Benglagistan scenes, which are pure exploitation and have been added by Siritzky for the U.S. market. Still, even allowing for those alterations, it's somehow surprising just how tame the film is in placing the big sex scenes in the dramatic structure: sometimes you feel as if one is just about to happen (like when Emmanuelle has her little moment with the woman accused of not being a virgin), but it doesn't. It reminded me of lots of soft-core erotica I saw as a teenager, where you really had to look fast, or you'd miss the naked flesh. It's almost as if the movie is doing just enough to qualify as sexploitation, but doesn't really go all the way in fear of being called that.

SA: There's something really coy at the heart of the American cut, which is best exemplified by the scene in the harem, when you can see naked butts emerging from that little partition and all the women are giggling. Again: it's that strategy of teasing, of showing just so much, but not an inch more.

OH: When the photographer shows up in the harem, the women are all over him, and yet he's not there to have sex with them: he only takes their pictures.

MO: While in the European version, the introduction to the harem is an extended, very sexualized passage.

SA: I wonder about the adventurer guy, whom I'm tempted to see as slightly autobiographical. He's an Indiana Jones type of guy, an adventurer and a jack of all trades. It's not unlikely that Borowczyk saw himself as someone like that, especially since his resourcefulness on the film set is notorious: he would do everything himself, from making the props to painting the walls.

OH: That whole thing made me wonder a little bit, since the guy who directed the first *Emmanuelle*, Just Jaeckin, did a movie in 1984 called *The Perils of Gwendoline in the Land of the Yik Yak*, which featured Tawny Kitaen on an island filled with more topless women than I have ever seen in my life. It also had this Indiana Jones-y type of character, played by Brent Huff, who is basically useless — he's trying to save her, but she has to do everything on her own. It came out before *Emmanuelle 5*, and I think the American cut of it is a nod toward that kind of film, with a machine-gun wielding heroine whom the genre requires to need a man, even though he proves totally ineffective.

MO: Borowczyk actually wanted to make this kind of film from the mid 1970s onwards; at the time of working on *Emmanuelle 5*, he had finished a script of "The Iron Temple" based on the Harry Dickson ("American Sherlock Holmes") book series.

SA: My biggest problem is that, no matter which version you watch, *Emmanuelle 5* is very frustrating in how it treats its main character — it basically tries to have it both ways, but is halfhearted about each of them. We see her in her Paris dance studio, where she's presented as an independent woman: owning her own business, proud of her body, leading a group of people, etc. At the same time she's being turned into sex object, and then we get the critique of that, since Borowczyk doesn't want to invest himself in the material. It makes for a very strange viewing experience and I think it makes this film a failure.

OH: The nude pictures of Monique Gabrielle we see in the film are actual Penthouse pictures of her — this was the first time they had cast an American as Emmanuelle, after which they immediately back to casting European women. One difference between American and European women in porn is that American women are usually presented as more puritanical, and I wonder to what extent the director is trying to play this angle here (especially since he played it so blatantly in *The Beast* with the character of Lucy).

MO: That angle is mostly played by the producer of the American version, which indeed is much more puritanical.

OH: Still, it's interesting to imagine how one could read the director's intent based solely on the American version. In that take, the relative restraint of the film looks like Borowczyk is mocking the puritanical nature of American sexuality: (1) by having an American Emmanuelle, (2) by shooting it in English, and (3) by including so many potentially sexual situations that go nowhere. There are plenty of moments like this, where you feel the film is backing up — as in the scene with the guy positioned at crotch level of Emmanuelle during a casual conversation, which seems to be almost accidental. It's abandoned very quickly, whereas in typical porn it would have been used to lead into a sex scene. That restraint is abandoned once violence kicks in in the second half.

MO: It never kicks in in the European cut — that stuff was all added.

OH: Right. It's funny, because the scenes with the machine guns look like some cheap Hanna-Barbera animation in *The Flintstones*: the same guys get shot about six times. The camera lingers on people being killed much more than it does on sexual situations. The latter are framed in a typical Cinemax, soft-core fashion, where what you are seeing is never quite enough: one boob, one butt cheek, one leg.

MO: Interesting how violence seemed more acceptable to American producers than, for example, the interracial sex footage.

SA: I agree with your idea of it almost being an auto-critique of the genre, especially based on other Borowczyk films I saw. He's definitely trying to bring his own approach here, which is relatively dryer and more humorous than usual erotic fare. This movie has such a weird tone, though, because every time actual self-critique pops up, something so goofy happens it throws you off base.

MO: That is true for both versions, but it has to be said that the goofiness quota is drastically lower in the European one.

OH: When we discuss the alterations made for the American market, we also need to remember that this movie was made in 1987 and it has a very 1980s feel to it. In general, I'd say that 1970s movies were more serious in their approach to sexual material — it's in the 1980s that so much goofiness was introduced in all kinds of exploitation pictures, like *Dead Heat* (1988) and others. There was this profound fear throughout the decade that if you approached exploitation subjects, you needed to throw in as much goofy bullshit as possible, otherwise your viewers would zone out and disengage. Every time things started to get a little bit serious, something dopey had to happen.

SA: To diffuse the tension.

OH: Yeah.

SA: Which is why I feel the American version ends up being so limp, because there's no investment of personality or raising of the stakes. *The Beast*, which I think is his best film, has an intentionally sleepy first half, until the titular beast shows up and all you can say is: what the fuck?

OH: Exactly. *The Beast* feels like an episode of *Upstairs, Downstairs* for about an hour, and then there's the beast segment and it feels almost like an afterthought:

"Oh, right, you came to see this, so here it is." Even more so: "Now that I only have half an hour left, I'm going to give you everything under the sun, and more." And that really works. The American cut of *Emmanuelle 5* is the opposite case, which only goes to show that this is not really the movie he wanted to make: his own stuff is simply thrown into it. I also need to say, as a native of the great state of New Jersey, that Charles D. Foster is, of all things, a doorknob salesmen from NJ, which did not escape me. He's a millionaire with a Spruce Goose-like plane on the side of his bed. Emmanuelle is playing with it just like Bette Davis used to play with her cigarettes. When I saw this, I hoped for a really trashy ending, in which his Spruce Goose takes off for him just like Howard Hughes' one never did — they are flying it thanks to her love and then crash into a mountain and die together in flames.

SA: See, but that would be good! I want to see this movie!

OH: That would be a great, European fuck-you type of ending; sadly, the movie doesn't go all the way, at least not in the American cut. What's still very European in both versions, though, is that most of the women's breasts are real. That's a very European approach to the female body; some of the naked women in this film would have never made it into American porn in the 1980s. As for the American lead, Monique Gabrielle's body type is sort of middle-of-the-road, but she's very different from Sylvia Kristel, the original Emmanuelle. Kristel's thing was to create the sense of being a European mystery woman: she would give you something of her body, but you would never know who she was. In *Emmanuelle 5*, it's more like: "All this woman is, is her body, there's nothing more." Possibly until she grabs a machine gun and proves to be a better shot than Sarah Palin.

SA: She could probably shoot at Russia from that Island!

OH: Ha, ha!

MO: I think we solved the mystery of the American cut: the machine gun-wielding Emmanuelle is the Rambo-Emmanuelle for the Reagan era of cold war warriors.

SA: Mostly, I'm just disappointed with how condescending the film ultimately is, no matter which version you watch. I think it's the crowning of the process you can see Borowczyk going through in the 1980s of basically falling out of step with what happens in world cinema — even in exploitation cinema. I see *The Strange Case of Dr. Jekyll and Miss Osbourne,* for example, as an attempt at making his own *Blood for Dracula*-type of thing, but it's burdened by all his little flourishes, which he includes almost compulsively. *Emmanuelle 5* is really a commentary by him on how lowly he found screen erotica in the 1980s. Still, I'd much rather see him engage in a project fully his own than to see him in this mode, which bears traces of resentment. It's as if he's criticizing movies of his time by making one.

OH: But that's the famous Truffaut/Godard/French New Wave's maxim: the best way to criticize a movie is to make another movie. In the case of the American cut of *Emmanuelle 5,* though, the film ultimately becomes simply the thing it was supposed to criticize. Borowczyk says: "I'm going to make a critique of this type of film," but the film is taken away from him and it is no longer a critique — it becomes the thing itself. The result of watching the American version is paradoxical: it doesn't merely tease you sexually by not showing enough of what you came to see — it also teases you cinematically by making a promise of being something it fails to become.

SA: And that teasing becomes unbearable, since it doubles the plot's schizophrenia about Emmanuelle's body, which is both accessible to us and denied by the film's "serious" and "moral" approach to porn.

MO: It's funny how much of that applies to the European cut, too, even though it's so different. There's no violence, no exploitation, no stupid scenes like Emmanuelle removing her coat and flashing her torso at restaurant guests — and yet you can still feel that Borowczyk is out of his element, simply because he is required to follow a formula, not invent one like he usually did.

OH: The effect is that of a hired prostitute reading her client passages from Tolstoy. On the other hand, this film may be more calculated than we are giving it credit for. Considering his other films and considering the year this came out, that's a real possibility. Here we are, watching a Borowczyk film and waiting for "the beast" to show up, so to speak — and it doesn't! That coitus interruptus dynamic is also present in *The Beast,* every time the servant is having sex with the heiress — they keep being interrupted by people.

SA: When sex is interrupted in *The Beast*, you can see the woman rub on a bed post, and somehow that in itself is explicit enough for me — the film remains intriguing, where here it just falls flat. There's definitely not enough rubbing in *Emmanuelle 5*, at least in its American incarnation.

OH: Ha! I think the American cut would have been much different, had it been prepared even five years prior to 1987. It was at the beginning of the 1980s — with adolescent movies like Bob Clark's *Porky's* (1982) that sex on the screen had lost its darker edge and became mostly goofy and devoid of repercussions.

MO: That tendency probably made the American distributor so keen on taking the edge off this film.

OH: It's funny, since there are many movies produced by Corman in the 1970s that have that exotic female-colony aspect, like Jack Hill's *The Big Doll House* (1971) and *The Big Bird Cage* (1972), but they are much darker than this Americanized version of the film. Even if there is silliness about the sex in them, there are also repercussions and consequences.

SA: With movies like *The Big Bird Cage*, the director's strategy is: "Here is my cake, I'm going to eat it, it will be delicious, it will be awesome." The American cut of *Emmanuelle 5* is all about eating the cake and keeping it, too. It's important to remember that Borowczyk was hired for this thing because of his reputation for making "classy" erotica — the producers wanted his name on this picture, because it gave it a sort of Euro-trash pedigree. He seemed to fit that bill, and they were clearly hoping for him to bring the entire series up a notch. But they miscalculated and actively prevented him from putting his mark on the material.

OH: Because in a series like that there's a pattern and you simply have to fill that pattern to make a generic film. I'd give Borowczyk credit: he did try to color outside the lines — he didn't just follow them.

MO: That's certainly true.

OH: By the time the movie was being shot, he was probably too tired of all the fighting.

MO: He famously left the set and later claimed he only took part in the editing of the European version.

SA: You can definitely see his energy in the film-within-the-film, which almost made me wish the entire framing structure wasn't there, so that Borowczyk could plunge into that footage and expand it. "Love Express" sounds like "Oriental Express" and Banglagistan is definitely an oriental extreme of sorts, complete with a dictator and his harem.

OH: There are two strands within the Emmanuelle series: the high-brow eroticism and the low-brow exploitation, and it seems like the American cut of *Emmanuelle 5* is the freaky experiment that tries to have them both, to marry them off to each other.

SA: But they are not interested in each other and they part ways.

MO: One of them originated more or less in Borowczyk's head; the other in the heads of producers behind the American version.

OH: They're like oil and water. They just don't mix.

Odie Henderson has spent almost 30 years working in Information Technology, but his true love is writing about movies. His work has appeared at *RogerEbert.com*, *Slant Magazine's House Next Door*, *Big Media Vandalism*, *Movie Mezzanine*, *Vulture.com*, and *Salon.com*. In 2013, he programmed the "Black American Cinema" sidebar at the Off Plus Camera Film Festival in Krakow, Poland. Based in the NYC area, he loves noir, musicals, and good trash.

Simon Abrams is a native New Yorker, and regular contributor to the *Village Voice*, *RogerEbert.com*, *Vulture*, and *Esquire*. He once booped Gaspar Noé's nose.

Michał Oleszczyk, Ph.D. is a film critic, script consultant, and translator based in Warsaw. He teaches film studies in the "Artes Liberales" Department at the University of Warsaw, as well as script development at Warsaw Film School. He is a regular contributor to *RogerEbert.com, Slant Magazine,* and numerous

Polish media outlets. His work has also appeared in *Cineaste, Sight & Sound*, and *IndieWire*. He published the first Polish book on the work of Terence Davies, and has co-authored (with Kuba Mikurda) three books on the work of Guy Maddin, Brothers Quay, and Terry Gilliam. His Polish translation of J. Hoberman and Jonathan Rosebaum's *Midnight Movies* was published in 2011.

CHAPTER 16
Revisiting *Love Rites* (1988)

Kevin Lee

The lasting image of Walerian Borowczyk's last feature film, *Love Rites* (1988), is that of a butterfly perched atop a vagina, and as such it pithily embodies how his work is often characterized: the artful presentation of a pussy. It's the money shot; the moment we spend over an hour waiting expectantly to reach, tailing Hugo (Mathieu Carrière), a well-to-do Parisian Everyman, as he in turn patiently accompanies Myriam (Marina Pierro), a dark-haired stranger who seems uncommonly receptive to his amorous overtones. He first spies her on the subway, introduced in the film's voice-over narration with literary flair: the Metro is the Parisian equivalent to the *Bocca della Verità*, that Italian marble face whose gaping mouth is believed to test one's honesty upon the insertion of one's hand. But long before Hugo has had a chance to insert any of himself into the body he desires, he unknowingly inserts his whole being into the Metro's tunnel of destiny, a subterranean orifice that beckons him further and deeper into his all-consuming lust, even as he surfaces to the ground arm in arm with his newfound consort.

Borowczyk implicates the viewer (and perhaps himself) in Hugo's tunnel vision by having the camera frequently dote on the gap between Myriam's ever so slightly parted knees as she sits on the subway. These shots are nowhere near Hugo's point of view; like many other shots in the film, they suggest an unseen voyeur peering at an erotic encounter occurring in public, sometimes with discretion, sometimes not. The voyeuristic current is manifested outright by the comic appearance of an Asian shutterbug, who harbors no compunction over snapping photos point blank as the couple swap tongues on the street.

This fraught relationship between looking and touching brings us back to the pubic-perched butterfly, itself a physical manifestation of a butterfly tattoo etched above Myriam's genitalia. The image is a synesthetic triumph, conveying specific and rarefied sensations of delicacy and lightness that lift the moment above mere pornography. Paradoxically, it's an experience of touch that can only be had by looking; it is an image more rarefied than the more mundane shots of Hugo's hand caressing Myriam's thigh that are played ad nauseum throughout their time together — endless compulsive touches devoid of feeling.

The depth of feeling in the pubic butterfly tattoo is compounded by the story behind its inscription, rendered as it was by a sex maniac, who tortured the hapless Myriam while in bondage. It's a story that, in Hugo's words, postpones the quenching of his lust while paradoxically intensifying it. The same can be said for much of the dialogue of this extraordinarily garrulous film. From scene to scene, Myriam and Hugo indulge in a smorgasbord of personal recollections and philosophical musings, their verbal intercourse a veritable precursor to those celebrated Linklater-Hawke-Delpy gabfests (except here Hawke and Delpy eventually turn into Michael Douglas and Sharon Stone in full S&M mode). As Hugo learns too late, all that conversational foreplay was his bid at salvation: every moment spent listening to Myriam's myriad thoughts and memories is a chance to see the butterfly in her, rather than the cunt. Likewise, Borowczyk's cinematic swan song is a defiant embrace of idle conversation and symbolic imagery — weigh stations on a journey of Eros more fulfilling than its climax. Otherwise, our baser filmic impulses might amount to a mere collective groping in the dark.

Kevin Lee is a filmmaker, critic and producer of nearly two hundred video essays exploring film and media. He is Founding Editor and Chief Video Essayist at *Fandor Keyframe* and founding partner of dGenerate Films, a distribution company for independent Chinese cinema. He was supervising producer at Roger Ebert Presents At the Movies, and has written for *The New York Times, Sight & Sound, Slate,* and *Indiewire*. He is pursuing an MFA in Film Video New Media and Animation and an MA in Visual and Critical Studies at the School of the Art Institute of Chicago.

C. Still from *Immoral Tales* (1974), copyright by Argos Films

D. Still from *The Beast* (1975), copyright by Argos Films

Walerian Borowczyk Filmography

SHORT FILMS

1946. *Sierpień (August)*
1949. *Głowa (The Head)*
1950. *Tłum (The Crowd)*
1955. *Żywe fotografie (Living Photographs)*
1955. *Jesień (Autumn)*
1955. *Atelier Fernanda Legera (The Atelier of Fernand Leger)*
1957. *Dni Oświaty (Education Days,* with Jan Lenica)
1957. *Strip-Tease,* with Jan Lenica
1957. *Był sobie raz (Once Upon a Time,* with Jan Lenica)
1957. *Nagrodzone uczucia (Rewarded Feelings,* with Jan Lenica)
1958. *Dom (House,* with Jan Lenica)
1958. *Szkoła (School)*
1958. *Sztandar młodych (Banner of Youth,* with Jan Lenica)
1959. *Les Astronautes (Astronauts,* in collaboration with Chris Marker)
1959. *Terra incognita*
1959. *Le Magicien (The Magician)*
1959. *La Tète (The Head)*
1959 *La Foule (The Crowd)*
1959. *Les Stroboscopes: Magasins du XIX Siecle (Stroboscopes: 19th Century Stores)*
1960. *L'Écriture (Writing)*
1961. *La Boîte à Musique (The Music Box)*
1961. *Solitude*
1961. *Les Bibliothèques (Libraries)*

1961. Les Écoles (Schools)
1962. Le Concert de M. et Mme. Kabal (The Concert of Mr. and Mrs. Kabal)
1962. La Fille Sage (A Well-Behaved Girl)
1963. L'Encyclopédie de grand-maman en 13 volumes (Grandma's Encyclopedia)
1963. Renaissance
1963. Holy Smoke
1963. Gancia
1964. Les Jeux des Anges (Angels' Games)
1964. Le Musée (The Museum)
1965. Le Dictionnaire de Joachim (Joachim's Dictionary)
1966. Rosalie
1966. Le Petit Poucet (Tom Thumb)
1967. Dyptique (Diptych)
1967. Gavotte
1969. Le Phonographe (The Phonograph)
1972. La Bête de Gévaudan (The Beast of Gévaudan)
1973. Une Collection Particulière (A Private Collection)
1975. Escargot de Vénus (Venus on the Half-Shell)
1976. Brief von Paris (Letter from Paris)
1977. L'Amour "monstre" de Tous les Temps (The Greatest Love of All Time)
1979. L'Armoire (Wardrobe, a segment of *Collections Privées / Private Collections*)
1979. Jouet Joyeux (Happy Toy)
1981. Hyper-Auto-Erotic
1981. Hayaahi
1984. Scherzo Infernal
1990. "Almanach des Adresses des Demoiselles de Paris" (Almanac of Addresses of the Young Ladies of Paris, episode of *Série rose*)
1990. "Un Traitement Merité" (A Justified Treatment, episode of *Série rose*)
1991. "L'experte Halima" (The Expert Halima, episode of *Série rose*)
1991. "Le Lotus D'Or" (Golden Lotus, episode of *Série rose*)

FULL-LENGTH FEATURE FILMS

1967. Théâtre de Monsieur et Madame Kabal (Theatre of Mr. and Mrs. Kabal)
1968. Goto, L'Île D'Amour (Goto, Isle of Love)

1971. *Blanche*
1974. *Contes Immoraux* (*Immoral Tales*)
1975. *Dzieje Grzechu* (*The Story of Sin*)
1975. *La Bête* (*The Beast*)
1976. *La Marge* (*The Margin*)
1977. *Interno di un Convento* (*Behind Convent Walls*)
1979. *Les Héroïnes du Mal* (*Heroines of Evil*)
1980. *Lulu*
1981. *Docteur Jekyll et les Femmes* (*The Strange Case of Dr. Jekyll and Miss Osbourne*)
1983. *L'Art d'Aimer* (*The Art of Love*)
1987. *Emmanuelle 5*
1988. *Cérémonie D'Amour* (*Love Rites*)

COLLABORATIONS

1958. *Sztuka Ulicy* (*Street Art*, dir. Konstanty Gordon, co-writer with Szymon Bojko)
1958. *Stadion* (*Stadium*, dir. Stanisław Jędryka, 1958, artistic director)
1972. *Au Bout des Fusils* (*Gunpoint*, dir. Peter Graham, co-editor, cameraman)

Index

9 1/2 Weeks (1986) 6

Abrams, Simon 10
absurd 85, 94
Adler, Susan 143
affect 138, 139, 140, 141, 142, 143
Alexander VI 152, 163
Alexandra, Charlotte 90
All That Jazz (1979) 6
allegory 67, 137, 141, 142, 143, 144
Alphaville (1965) 96, 97, 101
ambimodern 103, 107
anarchy 122, 152
Anatomy of the Devil (1992) 3, 38, 39, 40, 41, 52, 109
Anderson, Wes 7
Andréani, Jean-Pierre 89
Andrei Rublev (1966) 100
Angels' Games (1964) 3, 8, 14, 20, 34, 43, 51, 61, 65, 67, 68, 69, 73, 75, 155
Anglais Décrit dans le Château Fermé, L' (1953) 105
animal, animality 91, 111, 116, 134
animation 2, 4, 17, 20, 21, 25, 34, 54, 55, 56, 57, 58, 59, 60, 61, 62, 65, 81, 93, 94, 95, 98
Annecy 43, 105
Antonisz, Julian 59, 60
Arc, Joan of 85
Ariès, Philippe 115
Aristocratic 112, 114, 115
Astronauts (1959) 1, 4, 18, 19, 35, 61
Audry, Jacqueline 149
August (1946) 100
Austerity 84
automata 51–52
Autumn (1954) 16, 104
Awful Dr. Orlof, The (1962) 167

Barcelona 31, 153
Baroque 95, 100
Barthes, Roland 133, 138, 139
base (matter) 133, 134

Bataille, Georges 9, 34, 69, 70, 113, 132, 138, 141, 150, 154
Bathory, Erszebet 52, 71, 74, 75, 152
beast 9, 26, 112, 114, 115
Beast, The (1975) 3, 7, 29, 30, 34, 38, 39, 43, 44, 57, 58, 90, 91, 95, 99, 111–116, 127, 139, 140, 170, 176, 177, 179
beauty 80, 132, 136
Beauty and the Beast 111
Beauty and the Beast (1946) 9, 114
Beauty and the Beast (1991) 58
Bednarczyk, Antoni 136
Behind Convent Walls (1977) 33, 34, 37, 94, 95, 99, 126, 160, 162, 163
Bellamy, Florence 90
Belson, Jordan 50
Benayoun, Robert 104, 105
Benedetti, Pierre 91, 111
Berinizi, Jacopo 90
Berinizi, Lorenzo 90
bestiality 111, 116
Big Bird Cage, The (1972) 180
Big Doll House, The (1971) 180
Bird, Daniel 21, 43, 44, 97, 105, 114
Black Cat, The (1934) 91
Blanche (1971) 3, 5, 22, 25, 27, 37, 44, 48, 52, 95, 104, 165
Blood for Dracula (1974) 166, 179
Bohdziewicz, Antoni 21, 24
Borgia, Lucrezia 152
Borowczyk, Ligia – see Branice, Ligia
Borowszczyzna 143
Borowy, Wacław 136
Boucher, François 98
Branice, Ligia 9, 15, 17, 18, 19, 20, 21, 22, 25, 33, 41, 43, 44, 85, 86, 89
Brasseur, Pierre 89
Bresson, Robert 6, 18, 25
Breton, André 20, 21, 49, 105, 121, 150
Broadhurst, Lucy 111, 112, 114, 115
Buñuel, Luis 2, 4, 5, 31, 69, 84, 92, 104, 113, 169

Cardiff, Jack 149, 150
Carels, Edwin 9
Carrière, Mathieu 183
catastrophism 105
Catholic Church 10, 142, 159, 160, 161, 162, 163
Cavalier, Alain 174
Cerrato, Renzo 149
Chomón, Segundo de 107
Christ 26, 139
Christianity 85, 133, 136
cinema of attractions 107, 108
cinematograph 108
Clark, Bob 180
Clockwork Orange, A (1971) 167
Cobra (1986) 174
Cocteau, Jean 9, 114
Cohen, Howard R. 170
Cohl, Émile 42, 107
collages 3, 95
Colman, Felicity 143
Colour of Pomegranates, The (1968) 101
community 83
composition 93, 94, 95
Concert or Mr. and Mrs. Kabal, The (1962) 51
conscience 83, 142
convulsive 80
copulation 111
Corman, Roger 36, 167, 171
Cornell, Joseph 104
Correggio, Antonio Allegri da 141
Cracow 14, 43, 94
Criminal Life of Archibaldo de la Cruz (1955) 5
Croce, Fernando F. 9
Cronenberg, David 167
curiosity 104
Cylindre Sauterelle (Cylinder Grasshopper) 105, 109

Dallesandro, Joe 31, 97, 153
Danvers, Lise 90
Darke, Chris 96
Davis, Bette 178
Dauman, Anatole 18, 19, 22, 26, 30, 31, 38
Dauman, Florence 44
De Palma, Brian 168

Dead Heat (1988) 177
death 93, 112, 113, 116, 139
Deleuze, Gilles 95, 115, 143
della Francesca, Pierro 101
Delpy, Julie 184
Derrida, Jacques 9, 114, 115
Desboeuf, Philippe 90
desire 82, 134, 138, 140, 152
destruction 139
Diary of a Chambermaid (1967) 5
Diderot, Denis 142
Diptych (1967) 5
Discovery of Animal Magnetism, The (1779) 113
Disney, Walt 13, 21, 25, 35, 58, 142
Długołęcka, Grażyna 29, 43, 133, 141
documentation 104
Douglas, Michael 184
Dr. Black, Mr. Hyde (1976) 166
Dr. Jekyll and Sister Hyde (1971) 166
Duccio, di Buoninsegna 101
Duchamp, Marcel 105
Dyboski, Roman 139
dystopia 97

ecstasy 143
Effi Briest 85
Eisenstein, Sergei 4, 22, 27, 61
Emmanuelle (film series) 27, 31, 32, 36, 40, 153
Emmanuelle 5 (1987) 6, 10, 35, 36, 56, 170–181
Ernst, Max 49, 94
"EROS" 105
d'Estaing, Giscard Valery 28
ethics 137
Ethics (1677) 145
excess 105, 133, 134
Exposition Internationale du Surréalisme 105
Eyes Without a Face (1959) 89

fantasy 30, 58, 98, 139, 140
Fassbinder, Rainer Werner 28, 85
fatalism 77, 78, 79
fate 79
Fellini, Federico 2, 27
feminism 137

Femme Fatale (2000) 168
fetishism 5, 104
flatness 95, 99
Flesh for Frankenstein (1973) 166
flowers 132
Fontane, Theodor 85
Fosse, Bob 6
Fourier, Charles 133, 138
Franco, Francisco 153
Franco, Jesus 167
Franju, Georges 89
Freud, Sigmund 30, 138
futurism, futuristic 96

Gabrielle, Monique 35, 178
Galdós, Benito Pérez 84
Gilliam, Terry 25, 48, 55
Giotto, di Bondone 101
Giżycki, Marcin 8
God 79, 80, 85, 115
Godard, Jean-Luc 95, 179
Goddard, Michael 94
good, and evil 83, 133, 136, 145, 146
Goodman, Maude 141
Goto, Isle of Love (1968) 3, 22, 23, 24, 48, 51, 56, 57, 62, 89–90, 94, 95, 99, 122, 126, 156
Grandma's Encyclopedia (1963) 3, 20, 150
graphic arts and design 93, 94, 105
Greatest Love of All Time, The (1977) 51
Gunning, Tom 61, 107

hallucinogenic 113
Händel, Georg Friedrich 89
Hardester, Crofton 173
Hawke, Ethan 184
Heartfield, John 94
Hegel, Georg Wilhelm Friedrich 145
Henderson, Odie 10
Heroines of Evil (1979) 33, 57, 109, 162, 163
Herzog, Werner 92
Hill, Jack 180
Hirsch, Hy 8, 48, 50–51
Histoire de l'oeil (*The Story of Eye*, 1928) 154
horror 114
House (1958) 3, 18, 49, 69, 94

Huff, Brent 175
Hugo (2011) 52
humanism, humanity 132, 133, 134, 145, 146, 150
Hummel, Lisbeth 91, 111
Hussein, Saddam 115
hypnotic 113

icon painting 94
iconography 108
idealism 145
illogical 143
Immoral Tales (1974) 6, 8, 25, 26, 27, 28, 29, 30, 31, 34, 37, 39, 40, 41, 42, 56, 57, 62, 64, 65, 70, 72, 73, 90, 98, 104, 105, 118, 123, 124, 128, 129, 149, 163, 164, 170
immorality 109
inanimate 98
industrialization 107, 108
intercourse 112
intimacy 109, 114
irony 140

Jackiewicz, Aleksander 16, 23, 24
Jacquet-Droz, Henri Louis 52
Jacquet-Droz, Jacquet 52
Jaeckin, Just 175
Jetée, La (1962) 19, 95
Jewish 156
Jędryka, Stanisław 18, 25
Joachim's Dictionary (1965) 3, 20, 61
Jordan, Larry 50
jouissance 143
Juliette, Miss 82, 84
Justine, Miss 82, 84

Karina, Anna 85
Khan, Yassen 172
Kier, Udo 33, 92, 166
King, Zalman 6
Kitaen, Tawny 175
kitsch 136
Kristel, Sylvia 31, 32, 153, 154, 171, 178
Kubrick, Stanley 167
Kuc, Kamila 8, 77
Kunstkamera 8, 49, 51
Kurz, Iwona 8

L'Anglais Décrit dans le Château Fermé 149
La Grande Crécelle (The Big Rattle) 105
La Motocyclette (1963) 149, 150
labyrinth 93, 95
Lacan, Jacques 143
L'Âge d'or (1930) 5, 92, 169
Lancelot du lac (1974) 6, 25
Land Without Bread (1933) 5
Lane, Sirpa 91, 112
Lang, Fritz 166
Le Figaro 78
Le Lys de Mer (The Girl Beneath the Lion,
    1969) 149
Le Passage Pomeraye (1946) 155
Lee, Kevin B. 10
Leibnitz, Gottfried Wilhelm 95
Lenica, Jan 3, 16, 17, 18, 19, 20, 24, 43, 94, 105
Leviticus 113
Linklater, Richard 184
lithography 94
Lorre, Peter 166
loss 114
Love Rites (1988) 7, 10, 36, 37, 109, 149, 155,
    183–184
Loyola, Ignatius 133, 138, 139
Luchini, Fabrice 6, 70, 90
Lyne, Adrian 6

M (1931) 166
Machine célibataire (bachelor machine)
    106, 109
Mademoiselle O'Murphy (1751) 98
Magee, Patrick 92, 167
magic lantern 103, 108
Maison Tellier 86
Majmurek, Jakub 10
Makavejev, Dušan 4
Mandiargues, André Paul Édouard Pieyre
    de 10, 104, 105, 108, 149, 153
Marais, Jean 114
Marée, La (The Tide, 1974) 31, 70, 118, 128,
    151, 152
Marey, Étienne-Jules 3
Margin, The (1976) 31, 32, 97, 125, 149
Marker, Chris 18, 19, 22, 95
Marquise of O, The (1976) 6
marriage 15, 114

Marx, Karl 145
Masque of the Red Death (1964) 167
masturbation 32, 41, 42, 113, 164
Mathurin 111, 112, 114, 116
Maupassant, Guy de 8, 9, 77, 79, 80, 85, 86
Méliès, Georges 4, 13, 17, 35, 42, 52, 60, 61,
    107, 108
memory 135
Mesmer, Franz 113, 114
metamorphosis 116
Meter, Russ 4
Mikurda, Kuba 8, 171
mise en abyme 104
modernism 107
montage 4, 143
morality, moral 82, 83, 85, 86, 133, 134, 136,
    138, 144
Morion, Pierre 109
Morrissey, Paul 166
Mother (1926) 4
motherhood, mother(s) 38, 78, 86
murder 135, 137
mutoscope 108

Naked Lunch (1991) 167
Nancy, Jean-Luc 116
Ndalianis, Angela 95
Niepołomska, Róża 145
Niepołomski, Łukasz 135
novel 135, 140, 144
Nowa Gazeta 132

objectification 133, 137, 140
objects 56, 57, 60, 94, 99, 104, 105, 139, 159,
    160, 161, 163, 164, 165
Oleszczyk, Michał 10
Olgierd Łukaszewicz 140
Once Upon a Time (1959) 49
orgy 82
Orzeszkowa, Eliza 145
Oshima, Nagisa 4, 40
Othello 111, 114
Owen, Jonathan 10

painting 93, 94, 99
Paisan (1946) 5
Palin, Sarah 178

Parajanov, Sergei 100
Paris 16, 19, 20, 22, 31, 32, 35, 37, 44, 154
Parmegiani, Bernard 92, 169
Pasolini, Pier Paolo 4, 149
passion 139
pastiche 114
pathology 136
Perils of Gwendoline in the Land of the Yik-Yak, The (1984) 175
Perrault, Charles 91
personal 109
perspective 96, 99, 100
perversion 104
phenakistiscope 108
Phonograph (1969) 105
photographs 3, 95
physical 142
Piano Tuner of Earthquakes, The (2005) 52
Picasso, Paloma 71, 90, 124
Pièce détachée femelle 105
Pierro, Alessio 44
Pierro, Marina 33, 36, 37, 44, 92, 183
Pisis, Bona Tibertelli de 157
Plato 145
pleasure 141
Pobratyńska, Ewa 133
Podkowiński, Władysław 3
Poe, Edgar Allan 91
Polański, Roman 7, 18, 36, 67
Popović, Ljuba 51
Porky's (1982) 25, 28, 29, 34, 36, 37, 40, 65, 70, 73, 180
pornography 2, 82, 86, 103, 104, 108, 114, 150
Portrait of an Englishman in His Chateau (1953) 149
Potter, Cherry 34
printing 93
privacy 109
Private Collection, A (1973) 5, 26, 30, 35, 39, 49, 52, 56, 57, 60, 99, 100, 104–110, 122, 148–156, 173
prostitute 137
Prudent, Rosalie 77–86
psychoanalysis 137, 138
psychological 142
Pudovkin, Vsevolod 4
punishment 109

Quattrocento 101
Quay Brothers 7, 48, 52

Rabikowska, Marta 9
Ray, Man 49
realism 77, 78, 137
religion 142
Renaissance (1963) 3, 20, 49–50, 65, 69, 105
representation 145
repressed 134
revolutionary 17, 134
Rewarded Feelings (1957) 3
Reymont, Władysław 145
Robert-Houdin, Jean Eugène 52
Robinson, Jeremy Mark 44, 64, 95
Rochefoucauld, François de la 90
Rococo 101
Rohmer, Eric 5, 6, 90
Romilda 112
Roots (Raíces, 1955) 94
Rosalie (1966) 3, 8, 16, 20, 51, 77–86
Rossellini, Roberto 5, 6
Rousseau, Jean-Jacques 142
Różewicz, Stanisław 8, 21, 28
Różewicz, Tadeusz 15, 66
Rubin, Barbara 4

Sade, Donatien-Alphonse-François de 37, 39, 82, 133, 138, 149
Saint-Jean, Guy 89
Salò, or the 120 Days of Sodom (1975) 28, 149
Samosiuk, Zygmunt 145
Sang de L'Agneau, Le (1988) 109
Sarde, Alain 36, 37
Scherzo Infernal (1984) 34, 62, 100
School (1958) 3, 52, 94, 95, 104
sci-fi 96
Scorsese, Martin 52
Selznick, Brian 52
Série Rose (1989–91) 6, 37, 38, 39
sex, sexual 27, 28, 38, 40, 58, 69, 70, 72, 73, 135, 150, 159, 160, 163, 164
Shakespeare, William 9, 111, 145
Sigismond 153, 154
signifier 143
Singer, Ben 107
Siritzky, Alain 171, 174

Smith, Harry 50
Snazell, James 9
society 133
solitude 84
sovereign 114, 115
Spinoza, Baruch 145
Stallone, Sylvester 174
Stevenson, Robert Louis 91, 166–167
Stone, Sharon 184
Story of a Sin (1906) 7, 9–10, 51, 135, 145
Story of Sin (1975) 10, 52, 132–145
Strange Case of Dr. Jekyll and Mrs. Osbourne, The (1981) 10, 33, 37, 44, 57, 91–92, 123, 166–169, 179
subconscious 140
suicide 98
suppression 138
surrealism, surrealist 5, 16, 20, 21, 27, 49–50, 55, 58, 69, 71, 94, 118, 120, 121, 149, 150, 151, 156
surveillance 109
Švankmajer, Jan 7
Szaro, Henryk 136
Szczerbic, Zygmunt 140

taboo 134, 148, 151
Taking of Power by Louis XIV, The (1966) 5
Tarkovsky, Andrei 100
Thaumatrope 108
The Girl on a Motorcycle (1968) 149
The Heart is Young (1895) 141
The Hour of Our Death (1981) 115
Theatre of Mr. and Mrs. Kabal (1967) 4, 20, 21, 24, 51, 61, 62
Therese (1986) 174
Thompson, David 30, 139
Tolstoy, Leo 80, 85, 86, 179
Tomaszewski, Henryk 13, 25, 26, 28, 29, 30, 32, 43, 94
Tourne-disque de haute précision 106

Tout Disparaîtra (1987) 36, 149
Tovoli, Luciano 33, 95
transgression, transgressive 111, 113, 140, 142, 150, 152
Trial, The (1962) 95
Trip to the Moon, A (1902) 52
Tristana (1970) 84
Truffaut, François 20, 179

Ulmer, Edward G. 91
Un Chien Andalou (1929) 5, 104
Un Puissant Moteur de la Literature (1969) 148, 149, 156
Upstairs, Downstairs (1971) 177

vanity 82
Venus on the Half-Shell (1975) 157
Vermeer, Johannes 99, 168
Very, Noël 22, 92
victim 137
virgin 133
Visions of Excess (1985) 132, 134
voyeurism 104

Wajda, Andrzej 8, 15, 17, 66
Warhol, Andy 4, 31, 125
Warnell, Philip 9
Welles, Orson 95
Westburg, Dana Burg 173
whore 133
Wild Orchid (1989) 6
Wilkins, Budd 10
Woynarowski, Jakub 8

Zalcberg, Gérard 92, 167
Zola, Émile 86
Zoophilia 39, 111
Żeromski, Stefan 7, 9, 10, 26, 133, 134, 138, 139, 141
Żeromszczyzna 135, 138, 143

www.ingramcontent.com/pod-product-compliance
Lightning Source LLC
Chambersburg PA
CBHW072154100526
44589CB00015B/2218